TE ⬙ W9-ATN-806
TRAVEL ✦ SMART®

A GUIDE THAT GUIDES   v
WHY VISIT TEXAS?   1
PLANNING YOUR TRIP   7
Climate 7• When to Go 8 • How Much Will It Cost? 9 • Transportation
10 • Special Events 11 • Camping, Lodging, and Dining 12 • Recommended
Reading 13

❶ HOUSTON   15
❷ GALVESTON   31
❸ CRADLE OF TEXAS   45
❹ AUSTIN   57
❺ HILL COUNTRY   73
   ✪ Scenic Route: Hill Country Back Roads   87
❻ NEW BRAUNFELS   89
   ✪ Scenic Route: River Road   102
❼ SAN ANTONIO   103
   ✪ Scenic Route: Hill Country Loop   119
❽ CORPUS CHRISTI BAY AREA   121
❾ RIO GRANDE VALLEY AND SOUTH TEXAS   135
❿ WEST TEXAS/BIG BEND   147
   ✪ Scenic Route: Davis Mountains   160
⓫ EL PASO   161
⓬ PANHANDLE/HIGH PLAINS   173
   ✪ Scenic Route: High Plains Perspective   186
⓭ DALLAS   187
⓮ FORT WORTH   203
⓯ ARLINGTON/MID-CITIES   219
⓰ EAST TEXAS PINEY WOODS   231
APPENDIX   243
Planning Map 244 • Mileage Chart 246 • Special Interest Tours 247 •
Calendar of Events 254 • Resources 257
INDEX   259
MAP INDEX   262

BIG BEND NATIONAL PARK (SOUTH RIM)

© John Elk III

TEXAS

TRAVEL ✦ SMART®

Second Edition

Mary Lu Abbott

John Muir Publications
Santa Fe, New Mexico

Acknowledgments
With thanks to all the visitors bureaus and all the individuals in the tourism business in Texas for their assistance in gathering and checking information.

John Muir Publications, P.O. Box 613, Santa Fe, New Mexico 87504

Printed in the United States of America.
Second edition. First printing August 1999.

ISSN 1094-8821
ISBN 1-56261-449-5

Editors: Marybeth Griffin, Nancy Gillan
Graphics Editor: Heather Pool
Production: Marie J. T. Vigil
Design: Marie J. T. Vigil
Cover Design: Janine Lehmann, Marie J. T. Vigil
Typesetter: Melissa Tandysh
Map Style Development: American Custom Maps—Jemez Springs, NM
Map Illustration: Kathleen Sparkes—White Hart Design
Printer: Publishers Press
Front Cover Photos: *small*—© John Elk III (Dallas skyline)
                    large—© John Elk III (Palo Duro Canyon State Park)
Back Cover Photo: © Leo de Wys, Inc./Steve Vidler (Cadillac Ranch in Amarillo)

Distributed to the book trade by
Publishers Group West
Berkeley, California

TEXAS TRAVEL·SMART: A GUIDE THAT GUIDES

Most guidebooks are basically directories, providing information but very little help in making choices—you have to guess how to make the most of your time and money. *Texas Travel·Smart* is different: By highlighting the very best of the state and offering various planning features, it acts like a personal tour guide rather than a directory.

TAKE THE STRESS OUT OF TRAVEL

Sometimes traveling causes more stress than it relieves. Sorting through information, figuring out the best routes, determining what to see and where to eat and stay, scheduling each day in order to get the most out of your time— all of this can make a vacation seem daunting rather than fun. Relax. We've done a lot of the legwork for you. This book will help you plan a trip that suits *you*—whatever your time frame, budget, and interests.

SEE THE BEST OF TEXAS

Author Mary Lu Abbott has lived in Texas for more than 30 years. She has hand-picked every listing in this book and gives you an insider's perspective on what makes each one worthwhile. So while you will find many of the big tourist attractions listed here, you'll also find lots of smaller, lesser known treasures, such as the dramatic Palo Duro Canyon located just outside Amarillo in the Panhandle/High Plains area; or the fascinating nocturnal flight of bats at Austin's Town Lake that occurs each evening at dusk from March through October. And each sight is described so you'll know what's most— and sometimes least—interesting about it.

In selecting the restaurants and accommodations for this book, Abbott sought out unusual spots with local flavor. While in some areas of the state hotel and motel chains are unavoidable, wherever possible the author directs you to one-of-a-kind places. We also know that you want a range of dining options: One day you may crave the latest in New American cuisine by nationally acclaimed chefs, while the next day you may be just as happy (as would your wallet) with a hamburger and fries or the local Tex-Mex enchiladas and tacos. Most of the restaurants and accommodations listed here are moderately priced, but the author also includes budget and splurge options, depending on the destination.

CREATE THE TRIP YOU WANT

We all have different travel styles. Some people like spontaneous weekend jaunts, while others plan longer, more leisurely trips. You may want to cover as much ground as possible, no matter how much time you have. Or maybe you prefer to focus your trip on one part of the state or on some special interest, such as history, nature, or art. We've taken these differences into account in our selection of destinations and sights.

Though the individual chapters stand on their own, they are organized in a geographically logical sequence so that you could conceivably fly into Houston's George Bush Intercontinental Airport, drive chapter by chapter to each destination in the book, and end up close to where you started. Of course, you don't have to follow that sequence, but it's there if you want a complete picture of the state.

Each destination chapter offers ways of prioritizing when time is limited: In the Perfect Day section, the author suggests what to do if you have only one day to spend in the area. Also, every Sightseeing Highlight is rated, from one to four stars: ★★★★—or "must see"—sights first, followed by ★★★ sights, then ★★ sights, and finally ★—or "see if you have spare time"—sights. At the end of each sight listing is a time recommendation in parentheses. User-friendly maps help you locate the sights, restaurants, and lodging of your choice.

And if you're in it for the ride, so to speak, you'll want to check out the Scenic Routes at the end of several chapters. These take you over the back roads, into the mountains, through the canyons, and across the plains of Texas.

In addition to these special features, the appendix has other useful travel tools:

- The Planning Map and Mileage Chart help you determine your own route and calculate travel time.
- The Special Interest Tours section shows you how to design your trip around any of six favorite interests.
- The Calendar of Events provides an at-a-glance view of when and where major events occur throughout the state.
- The Resources section tells you where to go for more information about national and state parks, individual cities and counties, local bed-and-breakfasts, and more.

HAPPY TRAVELS

With this book in hand, you have many reliable recommendations and travel tools at your fingertips. Use it to make the most of your trip. And have a great time!

WHY VISIT TEXAS?

From cities with cappuccino bars to ranches where cowboys still ride the range, the real Texas has many faces—and many pleasures and treasures for visitors.

For those who can't decide whether to take an urban vacation, head to the mountains, or languish on the beach, Texas offers the opportunity to sample it all. Cultural arts, fine food, and good wine afford sophisticated fun in the state's metropolitan areas, which include three of the nation's 10 largest cities—Houston (number 4), San Antonio (number 8) and Dallas (number 9). Big Bend National Park and the Davis Mountains in West Texas combine a Wild West ambiance with scenic high-desert terrain and dramatic mountains topping 8,000 feet. Beach lovers have a number of choices. They can slip away to Galveston Island, a romantic Victorian escape with a feel of New Orleans and the Caribbean. They can go farther south to long stretches of less-developed beachfront. Or they can visit the tip of the state, where there's plenty of resort action at South Padre Island.

A distinctive foreign flair adds zest to San Antonio. The border cities of El Paso, Laredo, and Brownsville allow easy day trips into Mexico and give visitors a two-nation vacation.

Texas ranks first among states in the number of roads, and, indeed, the best way to see the real Texas is to explore it by car. You'll find most folks friendly. In fact, the name of the state comes from the Indian word *tejas*, which means—you guessed it—friendly.

HISTORY AND CULTURES

Few states can boast the colorful history that has shaped Texas, from prehistoric Indians, to Spanish conquistadors seeking cities of gold, to legendary frontiersmen such as Davy Crockett. As long as 12,000 years ago, Native Americans called this land home. Some Indians settled by natural springs in the central part of Texas, while others lived in the eastern Piney Woods and some roamed the High Plains.

The Spanish began exploring the Southwest in 1519. In about 1681 they established the first mission in what is now Texas at Ysleta, outside El Paso, and continued their forays into the territory from Mexico, which belonged to Spain at the time. A few years later, the French explorer La Salle, seeking the mouth of the Mississippi River, wandered onto the Texas coast and in 1685 staked a short-lived claim to the territory for France. By the early 1700s, the Spanish had a firm hold on the territory, building missions in the area now called San Antonio and establishing well-traveled trade routes from Mexico across southeast Texas toward Florida. The early Spanish *vaqueros* indelibly stamped a legacy of ranching on Texas, bringing horses and livestock and introducing roundups, branding, and other skills that later became associated with the American cowboy.

While some Anglos had pushed into the territory by the early 1800s, it wasn't until the 1820s that recognized settlements began. As Spain opened the area to those who accepted its rule, a Missouri frontier businessman named Moses Austin received permission to bring 300 Anglo families to settle in Texas. He died before organizing the journey, and the Texas territory changed hands, becoming part of Mexico when it won its independence from Spain. But the Mexicans were eager for development, and Moses Austin's son, Stephen F. Austin, brought in the first group of settlers, thereby earning the title "the Father of Texas."

By the 1830s, some 2,000 Anglo, European, and Mexican families lived in southeast Texas, but there was growing unrest with the Mexican government, particularly after it halted immigration from the United States into the area. In 1835, the first shots of the Texas Revolution rang out in a little town called Gonzales, not far from San Antonio. The scrappy Texans declared their independence in 1836, then immediately suffered a history-making defeat after a 13-day siege at the Alamo in San Antonio. Greatly outnumbered, the band of about 180 men fought to their deaths. Two weeks later, a massacre of 300 Texas prisoners of war by the Mexican army at Goliad led to the rallying cries, "Remember the Alamo, remember Goliad," as General Sam Houston surprised and defeated the Mexican forces at San Jacinto, outside Houston, to win independence on April 21, 1836.

Texas had the distinction of being an independent country until 1845, when it joined the United States. It seceded from the Union in 1861 to become part of the Confederacy and in 1870 rejoined the United States. Thus, Texas lays the unique claim to a history under flags of six different nations—Spain, France, Mexico, Republic of Texas, the Confederacy, and the United States.

Texas today retains a pride in its multicultural heritage, starting with strong Indian, Spanish, and Mexican backgrounds. Some of the early Spanish missions, including the famed Alamo, still stand, most of them in the San Antonio and El Paso areas. Much of the architecture, both new and old, bears Spanish and Mexican influences, particularly across South and West Texas. Texans celebrate such popular Mexican holidays as Cinco de Mayo and Diez y Seis de Septiembre and have adapted the south-of-the-border beat into their music scene. Throughout South Texas and particularly along the border with Mexico, Spanish is widely spoken, as commonly as English in some places.

Less visibly evident, Indian cultures nonetheless are preserved in museums, parks, and other sites across the state, as well as at two active Indian communities. At the Alabama-Coushatta Indian Reservation north of Houston and at Ysleta del Sur Pueblo, a Tigua Indian community near El Paso, descendants of some early tribes share their heritage with visitors.

From cities to small towns, cowboys are still alive and well in the state, and you don't have to go to a ranch to see them. Many men even in sophisticated Fort Worth, Dallas, and Houston don't walk out the door without wearing their cowboy hats and boots, which they consider everyday dress. Livestock shows and rodeos are among the major events in Houston and other cities. In both the Panhandle and West Texas, real cowboys still rope and brand cattle; and Bandera, in the Hill Country outside San Antonio, is ringed with guest ranches where city slickers can play like cowboys on vacation.

Other cultures have put their stamp on the state. During the 1840s, Texas attracted large numbers of German settlers, who scouted around the central and southern parts of the state and started a number of communities, including the towns of Fredericksburg and New Braunfels. Immigrants also came to Texas from Czechoslovakia, Poland, the Alsace, and other European areas. Well into the twentieth century, German was still spoken in central Texas schools and German-language newspapers were still published. Today, many towns proudly preserve and parade their German roots, attracting visitors with their German restaurants, beer gardens, bakeries, oompah music, and historic sites.

In more recent years, Texas coastal cities and towns have received an influx of Asians, who have started shrimping operations, restaurants, markets, and other businesses. There are large communities of Asians in Houston, Corpus Christi, and smaller fishing towns on the Gulf Coast.

THE ARTS

From resident ballet companies to world-renowned museums and innovative architecture, the performing and visual arts in the state are outstanding. Houston and the Dallas–Fort Worth Metroplex have a bounty of acclaimed live theater, symphonies, ballet, and opera.

Art aficionados can cast their eyes on outstanding collections from African primitive to the latest modern works at such renowned repositories as the Kimbell Art Museum, Amon Carter Museum, the Sid Richardson Collection of Western Art in Fort Worth, the McNay Art Museum in San Antonio, the Kress Collection at the El Paso Museum of Art, and the Menil Collection in Houston, to name only a few. The Fort Worth Museum of Science and History, the Houston Museum of Natural Science, and the Witte Museum in San Antonio have wide-ranging exhibits that entertain both children and adults.

Architecturally, the skylines of Houston and Dallas bear the signature work of such accomplished designers as I. M. Pei and Philip Johnson, and some museum buildings themselves are works of art.

From the big cities to the small towns, festivals celebrate the local arts year-round. Across the state, visitors will find community theater, often performed in beautifully restored turn-of-the-century opera houses.

CUISINE

With its multicultural heritage, Texas has a rich background of foods, ranging from simple, calorie-packed home cookin' to complex, tantalizing Asian-Southwestern cuisines. Both Houston and Dallas have literally thousands of restaurants. Visitors will find everything from kid-friendly neighborhood cafés to elegant fine dining with impeccable service, innovative dishes, and award-winning wines, including many from Texas itself. Outstanding young chefs used both Houston and Dallas as the proving ground for cutting-edge Southwestern cuisine in the 1980s and today have fine-tuned their dishes, often adding touches from Asian cooking.

There's no shortage of steaks, barbecue, and Tex-Mex dishes such as enchiladas and fajitas—foods held dear by Texans for years. In recent years, "cowboy (or ranch) cuisine" has popped up, spawning new restaurants that serve chicken-fried steak, pork chops, and mashed potatoes—with updated seasonings.

Across the state, but particularly in Houston and other coastal cities, Asian immigrants have brought Far Eastern cuisine to Texas. New Thai and Korean restaurants have earned national attention. Tending to like their food fiery, Texans quickly took to these spicy newcomers.

FLORA AND FAUNA

The ecological diversity of Texas surprises many visitors, who come expecting little more than cactuses and tumbleweeds.

Forests of pine trees so dominate the eastern half of the state that the region is called the Piney Woods. Magnolia, dogwood, live oak, and pin oak trees are interspersed on the terrain, and deciduous trees add a speck of color in the fall. Timber country gives way to tree-dotted plains in the central part of the state and to the scrubby growth of mesquite and huisache trees nearer the coastal areas. The Gulf Coast takes on a tropical air with palm trees, oleanders, and bougainvillea in the southern regions and groves of oranges and grapefruit spreading across the Rio Grande Valley.

From the Hill Country westward, small cedars mix with cactus, tall yucca, and desert plants of varying kinds, which add vivid reds, yellows, and oranges to the scene in springtime. Oil wells are the "skyscrapers" on the flat plains around Midland-Odessa, and wheat fields stretch for miles across the Panhandle, which also has ranch lands with scrubby growth—and tumbleweeds rolling across the highways.

Numerous types of wildlife—from bobcats, raccoons, squirrels, and wild turkeys to deer, foxes, alligators, Canada geese, and whooping cranes—are found in the state. Indeed, Texas really has roadrunners, which you're most likely to see skittering across roads in the Big Bend–West Texas area. And, yes, you'll see armadillos—most frequently as roadkill.

THE LAY OF THE LAND

From a coastline that arcs around the Gulf of Mexico for more than 600 miles to mountains that top 8,000 feet, from moss-draped swamps in the east to the Chihuahua Desert in the west, Texas takes in a lot of different terrain.

The state has 3,700 rivers and streams, the most notable being the Rio Grande, which forms the border with Mexico. It flows for hundreds of miles, from the western tip of the state by El Paso to the Gulf of Mexico beyond Brownsville. Scores of lakes also dot the state, most of them in the eastern half.

From rolling, forested land in the east, the terrain gives way to grassy prairies in the midsection, a subtropical coast, and an area of steep hills, canyons, and spring-fed rivers known as the Hill Country in the central-west region. From the prairies and the Hill Country, the land rises to the High Plains, with the altitude changing from about 1,000 feet on the rolling plains to 4,000 feet in the Panhandle. In the midst of the plains lies the spectacular Palo Duro Canyon, an 800-foot chasm with red-hued rock formations similar to those in the Grand Canyon.

OUTDOOR ACTIVITIES

Both land- and water-based activities abound across the state. Fishing lures visitors to lakes in all areas, particularly in East Texas, where waters consistently yield trophy catches, most notably varying species of bass. Along the Gulf Coast, saltwater-fish enthusiasts cast their lines from beaches, boats, and piers and try their luck for tarpon and other game fish on deep-sea excursions.

Birders flock to the state for its premier viewing, from the Piney Woods down along the Gulf Coast, into the Rio Grande Valley, and out to West Texas. Both the coast and the valley offer excellent opportunities for new sightings. On continental flyways and adjacent to Mexican habitats, the valley has more than 370 species of birds.

Hikers will find all types of long and short trails, through deserts, canyons, and woods, along streams, and in urban parks. Austin in particular has an extensive hiking and biking trail along its in-town lakefront. Bikers often do longer excursions in the Austin, Highland Lakes, New Braunfels, and Fredericksburg areas.

Rivers run gentle and wild, offering canoeing, tubing (floating in an inner tube), and some exciting white-water rafting. The Hill Country and Big Bend National Park are popular with river runners. Windsurfers congregate along the central coast, where Corpus Christi Bay and the barrier islands to the south offer good winds.

Golfers won't want for designer courses, with a number offered in both urban and country resort settings. The Dallas–Fort Worth Metroplex and the Houston, San Antonio, and Austin areas have the widest selection of courses.

PLANNING YOUR TRIP

Before you set out on your trip, you'll need to do some planning. Use this chapter in conjunction with the tools in the appendix to answer some basic questions. First, when are you going? You may already have specific dates in mind; if not, various factors will probably influence your timing. Either way, you'll want to know about local events, the weather, and other seasonal considerations. This chapter discusses all of that, while the Calendar of Events in the appendix provides a month-by-month view of major area events.

How much should you expect to spend on your trip? This chapter addresses various regional factors you'll want to consider in estimating your travel expenses. How will you get around? Check out the section on local transportation. If you decide to travel by car, the Planning Map and Mileage Chart in the appendix can help you figure out exact routes and driving times, while the Special Interest Tours section provides several focused itineraries. This chapter concludes with some reading recommendations, both fiction and nonfiction, to give you various perspectives on the state. If you want specific information about individual cities or counties, use the Resources section in the appendix.

CLIMATE

Stretching nearly 900 miles from north to south and about the same from east to west, Texas encompasses every kind of terrain, from swamps to desert, from

8,000-foot mountains to the Gulf of Mexico coast. And the weather is as varied as the geography. In one day, part of the state may have a blizzard with drifting snow while another area may bask in sunny, 80-degree weather. One region may be flooded from torrential rains while another may suffer from a long drought.

Texans say, "If you don't like the weather, hang around 10 minutes and it'll change." Indeed, what Texans call a "blue norther" can blow in and drop temperatures from a balmy 75 degrees to 40 degrees in a matter of minutes. One common denominator, though, is sunshine, which prevails throughout the year across the state. Long stretches of dreary weather are unusual.

Although cold weather usually edges into the Panhandle by early November, winter for most of the state lasts only from late December through February, and often not that long. Cold winds and even some snowstorms occasionally hit the northern and western half of Texas. Hard freezes can (but rarely do) push down to the southern tip of the state.

Spring comes early, with beautiful but often fickle weather and severe thunderstorms. Summer starts in May and by August can be sizzling hot. In the west, low humidity and strong breezes temper the heat, while the south often gets steamy and sweltering as high humidity combines with temperatures in the 90s or 100s. By late September, fall arrives with traditionally sunny warm days and cool evenings.

For summer visits, pack shorts and other cool clothing—and plenty of sunscreen—though it's always wise to have a windbreaker, lightweight sweater, and long pants for cool snaps. In all other seasons, bring a variety of clothes that you can layer. Overall, dress is casual, even for dining in many areas, though a jacket or coat and tie are advisable for men in the best restaurants in the larger cities.

WHEN TO GO

Overall, spring, early summer, and fall are the ideal times to visit the state. From late March through mid-June and from mid-September through mid-November, days are usually warm but not too hot and evenings are pleasant. These months also have a bountiful crop of festivals to celebrate the culture, heritage, food, and music of Texas.

From mid-March through April, the central and southern sections are splashed with color as bluebonnets, reddish-orange Indian paintbrush, and a rainbow of other brightly colored wildflowers blanket fields and grassy sides of highways. In Big Bend and other areas of the west, the desert seems to throb with life as masses of white blossoms shoot up from yucca plants, and cactuses sprout brilliant red, yellow, and purple flowers. In East Texas, forests are sprinkled with delicate white dogwood blooms. The entire state greens up at this time of year, with the eastern half looking particularly lush.

To many Texans, fall is the best of all seasons. The summer heat fades and the morning air grows crisp. The weather usually remains more stable and temperatures more consistent than in spring, though cold snaps can occur in October.

Tourist season for most of the state starts in March and continues into November. Summer is a popular time to come to Texas, but visitors should be prepared for hot days and a bathwater-warm Gulf. At coastal resort towns, prices are highest in summer, less in spring and fall, and lowest in winter. For many inland destinations, prices may vary little over the year, though winter is off-season for most of the state. The coast is warm enough in winter to draw several hundred thousand snowbirds from the Midwest and Canada.

A caveat: Thunderstorms are common in Texas, particularly in spring, and can be severe, producing heavy rains that cause flooding. In the west, the dry, rocky riverbeds can fill with raging water after a rainstorm. At low points, some highways have water markers, which look like vertical rulers stretching six or so feet high. Some scenic highways have low-water crossings, where you can drive through a normally gentle stream. But these crossings and low points can become dangerous after heavy rains.

When you're traveling anywhere in the state—cities or remote areas—never drive into fast-flowing water, even if it seems shallow. Water can rise quickly, suddenly flood a car, and sweep it downstream. Park on high ground and wait for the water to recede.

HOW MUCH WILL IT COST?

With its wide diversity of attractions—from cosmopolitan cities to remote wilderness areas—Texas can accommodate varying travel budgets. Those who want to shop until they drop, dine at world-class restaurants, and be pampered in luxury accommodations can fulfill their wishes here, while frugal travelers also will find plenty of activities and sights that won't burn holes in their pockets.

The cities, of course, are more expensive, but New Yorkers are always pleased that fine dining costs half or less in Houston than it does in the Big Apple. In the Lone Star State, $30 and above per person for a meal (excluding alcoholic beverages) is considered very expensive, and with that price come elegant decor, impeccable service, and cutting-edge cuisine prepared by renowned chefs in nationally acclaimed restaurants.

Lodging runs the gamut from $200 or more a night for resorts with amenities to campsites for around $10 a night. For economical accommodations in beautiful settings, bargain-hunters should head to state and national parks, many of which have campsites.

Entertainment can be as simple and inexpensive as a take-your-own-picnic day at the beach or a float down a cool, spring-fed river in an inner tube. Many museums are free or have minimal admission fees, but you may pay extra for special exhibits. For the ultimate in family fun, there are large entertainment parks in Houston, San Antonio, and the Dallas–Fort Worth Metroplex where admission for a family of two adults and two young children costs more than $100 for a day.

For city visits, budget $75 to $150 (or more) a night for lodging and $35 to $50 per person a day for food (more for upscale dining), though you can find chain accommodations and food options for less. Entertainment costs will depend on your interests, but if you sample theater, museums, and nightlife, and visit several attractions, count on spending $50 or more each per day.

Outside urban areas, lodging is more likely to run $40 to $85 a night (less for camping and some chain motels) and food $15 to $30 per person. Entertainment costs could be $15 or so each—less if you're at the beach or hiking in the mountains or forests.

TRANSPORTATION

The state's two major air gateways are Dallas–Fort Worth International Airport, one of the largest and busiest in the world and home base for American Airlines, and Houston's George Bush Intercontinental Airport, home to Continental Airlines. San Antonio, Austin, and El Paso also have large airports. All major airlines serve these cities.

Additionally, Southwest Airlines, the nation's leading low-cost carrier, is based at Love Field, close to downtown Dallas, and has an excellent network of frequent flights throughout the state.

Amtrak currently serves the state with two routes: the Sunset Limited, crossing the lower half from El Paso through San Antonio and Houston, and the Texas Eagle, coming from the north through Dallas to San Antonio.

A car—or wheels of your choice—is necessary, even when staying in cities, unless you're just flying in and out quickly for business. While urban areas are timidly developing mass transit, the service is limited and sightseeing attractions are often scattered. Besides, to capture the true spirit of Texas and see some of the natural beauty of the state, vacationers should venture beyond the urban attractions and ride the range. All major car-rental firms serve Texas.

Texas has an excellent system of highways, from multilane highways to two-lane farm and ranch roads. Seven major interstates run through Texas.

I-10 crosses the southern tier through Houston, San Antonio, and El Paso. I-20 comes through Dallas, Fort Worth, Midland-Odessa, and out to far West Texas where it connects with I-10; I-30 comes in from Texarkana through Dallas and Fort Worth where it joins I-20. I-40 goes through Amarillo in the Panhandle. I-35 is the major north-south freeway, splitting into east and west legs through Dallas and Fort Worth and rejoining to go through Austin and San Antonio and down to Laredo at the Mexican border. I-45 connects Galveston, Houston, and Dallas, and I-37 connects Corpus Christi and San Antonio. While some interstates afford sweeping views, visitors should exit onto state roads for the most scenic drives. Even ranch and farm-to-market roads are usually paved, though they don't have shoulders.

A couple more caveats: Always carry drinking water in the car and watch your gasoline gauge. Stretches of 50 or more miles between service stations are not uncommon, particularly in West Texas, where the distance between services may be even greater. Watch your speedometer, particularly when passing through small towns where speed limits can drop quickly and local police enforce them. Also, state troopers often sit on major highways with their radar guns to catch speeders. The speed limit on open highways normally is 70 MPH, though traffic on the interstates often moves faster.

SPECIAL EVENTS

Proud of their foods and wines, arts and music, rivers and lakes, multicultural heritage, and futuristic cities, Texans take every opportunity to celebrate, and they welcome visitors to join in the fun. While there are events nearly every week of the year, the majority occur in spring and fall. The Cotton Bowl in Dallas and livestock shows and rodeos in Fort Worth, Houston, and San Antonio kick off the year's major events. Galveston dresses up for one of the biggest Mardi Gras festivals in the country just before Lent. Spring break crowds hit Texas' Gulf Coast in March and April, and Austin celebrates spring with several music festivals. The State Fair in Dallas in the fall is one of the country's largest such fairs, and the chili cook-offs in Terlingua in late fall have gained worldwide attention for their zaniness. Among other events: Houston International Festival, Main Street Fort Worth Arts Festival, Round Top Antiques Fair, and Fiesta San Antonio in April; Kerrville Folk Festival in May; Wurstfest in New Braunfels in October/November; holiday pageants in San Antonio and Dickens on the Strand in Galveston in December.

And in Texas, Thanksgiving comes in April. El Paso now claims the first Thanksgiving occurred on the banks of the Rio Grande in 1598 and celebrates each spring—without pumpkins or football.

CAMPING, LODGING, AND DINING

From rustic cabins and dude ranches to frilly bed-and-breakfasts and luxurious resorts, Texas has accommodations to suit all styles. While familiar chain motels and hotels have properties across the state, there's also a great selection of lodgings with local flavor and history. Historic Accommodations of Texas, 210/997-3980, issues a brochure listing dozens of bed-and-breakfasts, country inns, hotels, and guest houses where you will get a sense of the state's legends and lore.

Camping enthusiasts will find a wide selection of state parks and national parks and forests with campsites in the woods, by lakes, in good birding areas, on the beach, in cities, and in the desert mountains. Campsites run less than $10 a night; full-hookup spaces normally cost $10 to $20. Some parks also have lodges and cabins, which are inexpensive and so popular they often book up for the entire year soon after January 1. For reservations at most state parks, call 512/389-8900 Monday through Friday 9 to 6 Central Time.

Most Texas parks charge a per-person admission fee. If you plan to visit several parks, you'll save money by buying a $50 Gold Texas Conservation Passport, which allows access to parks and wildlife management areas for the member and all passengers in the car. The passport can be purchased at state parks.

The Hill Country, the area west of Austin and San Antonio, has numerous dude ranches, or guest ranches as they're now called. Proud of its cattle-drive, ranching, and rodeo heritage, the small town of Bandera proclaims itself "The Cowboy Capital of the World." Here, city slickers can put on jeans and hats and ride the range with real cowboys.

Several cities and towns are known for their bed-and-breakfasts. Galveston, a major seaport at the turn of the century, has splendid Victorian homes. Jefferson, in East Texas, boasts antebellum and turn-of-the-century lodgings. Fredericksburg, located in the Hill Country, has a number of bed-and-breakfasts, many of which reflect the town's German heritage. For help in locating bed-and-breakfasts, see the Resources section at the end of this book.

Once a staunch meat-and-potatoes destination, Texas today offers a rich smorgasbord of dining—from longtime Texas favorites to the trendiest new cuisines. Most visitors—even fat-content watchers—fancy eating a big, juicy steak when they're in Texas. Indeed, as cuts of beef have gotten leaner—and healthy eaters have decided it's all right to splurge now and then—steak houses have become a hot trend in dining out. In cities, visitors will find new eateries now challenging long-established Texas steak restaurants.

No visit to Texas would be complete without sampling barbecue, the unofficial state dish. Texans have strong opinions about barbecue—how to cook it and where to eat it—and they don't show much respect for how barbecue is cooked in other states. While every Texan seems to have a secret recipe, usually the ribs, brisket, and chicken are marinated, slow-roasted, and served with sauce on the side. Don't be surprised if the best barbecue comes from a hole-in-the-wall café with butcher paper on the tables.

While Texas is renowned for its chili cook-offs, particularly at Terlingua, chili isn't found on all menus. Traditionally, Texans eat it more in the fall and winter. Wherever you decide to sample some, ask how hot (with seasoning) it is before ordering. If a Texan says it's hot, you'd better believe it'll be fiery.

There's no shortage of great chefs and interesting cuisines across the state. Asian influences are strong in the cities, with Vietnamese, Korean, Japanese, Indian, and varying cuisines of China readily available. Greek, Lebanese, Persian, Polish, German, and South American restaurants also flourish in the cities.

While dining at the best urban restaurants will cost $15–$30 or more per person, the majority of restaurants offer excellent food—and usually hefty portions—within the range of $7 to $15 per person. In smaller towns, you'll find the tab runs even less.

RECOMMENDED READING

If you've delved into some of Larry McMurtry's books or seen popular movies based on his works such as *Hud*, *The Last Picture Show*, and *Lonesome Dove*, you've gotten a taste of Texas. This Pulitzer Prize–winning author has written numerous novels set in Texas and the Southwest. *Hud* was based on McMurtry's *Horseman, Pass By*, which was first published by Harper & Row in 1961 and then again by Penguin Books in 1984. McMurtry's trilogy about two Texas Rangers began with *Lonesome Dove* (Simon & Schuster, 1985), which won the Pulitzer, and continued with *Streets of Laredo* (Simon & Schuster, 1993) and *Dead Man's Walk* (Simon & Schuster, 1995).

Two well-respected Texas journalists have books that will make you laugh while providing insights into the quirkiness of the state and its residents. *Molly Ivins Can't Say That, Can She?* (Random House, 1991) is a collection of essays and articles written by an irreverent columnist who pokes fun at politicians. Longtime travel editor and prize-winning writer Jerry Flemmons shares his love of the state in *Jerry Flemmons' Texas Siftings* (Texas Christian Press, 1995).

For a quick, fun read—and a good souvenir to buy in Texas and share with friends—pick up *Don't Squat with Yer Spurs On! A Cowboy's Guide to Life* (Peregrine Smith Book, 1992). It's a collection by Texas Bix Bender of funny sayings and life lessons, such as the title itself.

The late novelist James Michener made the state the subject of one of his epics. Mixing fact and fiction, *Texas* (Random House, 1985) chronicles 450 years of life, love, and strife, starting with the Spanish exploration of the area.

Leon C. Metz's *Roadside History of Texas* (Mountain Press Publishing Company, 1994) provides interesting history with colorful background about numerous towns.

Backroads of Texas (Gulf Publishing Company, 1993) by Ed Syers and Larry Hodge takes travelers on 15,000 miles of sightseeing and shares detailed information along the route. A good companion book is *Texas Bed & Breakfast*, 4th edition (Gulf Publishing Company, 1997) by Gail Drago, Marjie Mugno Acheson, and Lyn Dunsavage, which describes dozens of lodgings and is organized by region.

Texas Monthly, a slick regional magazine, covers current topics and is a good source of updated information about restaurants and entertainment in the state. Also, look at local newspapers on Thursday, Friday, and Sunday for updated listings of restaurants, nightclubs, museums, festivals and special events, exhibits, and activities.

1
HOUSTON

An international business center, energy capital, and home to the second-busiest U.S. port, nine colleges and universities, and the largest medical center in the world, Houston pulsates with renewed vigor as the twenty-first century unfolds. A renaissance is changing the face of downtown, adding everything from a new performing arts center to a garden promenade along the bayou and a 42,000-seat baseball stadium.

Founded in 1836, Houston today is the state's largest city and the nation's fourth-largest, with 1.7 million residents and a metropolitan area of 4.3 million people. Located 50 miles from the Gulf of Mexico, the city sprawls across the flat coastal plains laced with bayous, its magnolias and azaleas, pin oaks and pines creating a greener environment than most visitors expect of Texas.

Restaurants with top-of-the-line cuisine, an eclectic collection of fine museums, a thriving theater district, innovative architecture, and superb shopping put a mark of sophistication on the city. For all its worldliness, though, Houston remains a fun-loving place without pretense. Catch an opera performance one night; scoot your boots across a country-western dance floor the next evening. Dine on delicacies prepared by world-renowned chefs or peel your own shrimp at a funky outdoor café. The Bayou City suits many styles.

Less than an hour's drive away, Galveston frequently pairs with Houston, augmenting its urban attractions with a romantic island escape.

HOUSTON

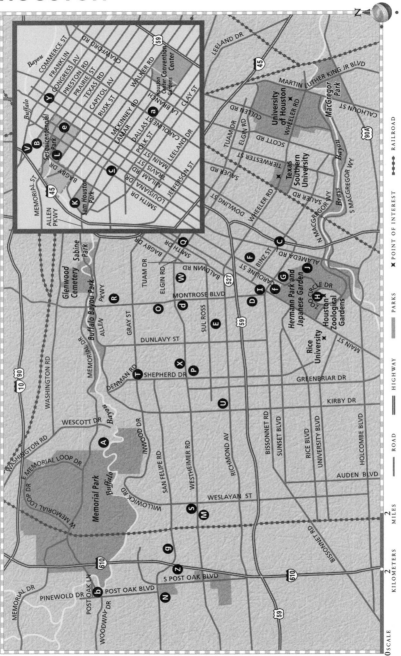

A PERFECT DAY IN HOUSTON

Pick and choose attractions to match your interests. Shoppers should head straight to Mecca—the Galleria, which has 300 shops and restaurants on three levels stretching several blocks. Rest and toast your purchases during dinner at nearby Café Annie. The museum and fine arts–minded should see the Bayou Bend Collection of decorative arts (reservations needed), the eclectic Menil Collection, and the Museum of Fine Arts. Take in a ballet, opera, symphony, or theater performance downtown in the evening. Families might combine the Museum of Natural Science with a baseball, football, or basketball game, Six Flags AstroWorld, or a visit to the Space Center.

ORIENTATION

For visitors, most attractions are congregated in three major areas: downtown, with its theater/entertainment district, restaurants and parks; the Galleria-Uptown with shopping and restaurants; and the Museum District, with 11 museums of wide-ranging interest and the adjacent world-renowned Texas Medical Center. The three generally form a triangle, each within about 15 minutes of the others, and each has multiple choices in lodging. Within the Greater Houston area, the Astrodome/Six Flags AstroWorld complex is another 10 to 15 minutes beyond the Museum District, and Space Center

SIGHTS
- **A** Bayou Bend Collection and Gardens
- **B** Buffalo Bayou Trail
- **C** Children's Museum
- **D** Contemporary Arts Museum
- **E** De Menil Museums
- **F** Holocaust Museum Houston
- **G** Houston Museum of Natural Science
- **H** Houston Zoo
- **I** Museum of Fine Arts
- **J** Museum of Health & Medical Science
- **K** Sam Houston Historical Park
- **L** Theater District (shaded area)

FOOD
- **M** Anthony's
- **N** Café Annie
- **O** Cafe Noche
- **P** Churrascos
- **Q** Damian's Cucina Italiana
- **R** Golden Room
- **S** Grotto
- **T** Hunan River Garden
- **U** Khyber North Indian Grill
- **V** Kim Son
- **W** Ruggles Grill
- **X** Sabine
- **Y** Tasca Kitchen and Wine Bar

LODGING
- **Z** Doubletree Post Oak
- **a** Four Seasons Hotel-Houston Center
- **b** Houstonian Hotel, Club & Spa
- **c** Hyatt Regency Houston
- **d** La Colombe d'Or
- **e** Lancaster
- **f** Park Plaza Warwick
- **g** St. Regis Houston

Houston is about 45 minutes from downtown, between the city and Galveston. Interstate 10 bisects the city east-to-west, and Interstate 45 runs north to Dallas and southeast to Galveston. Interstate 610 forms an inner loop of the city and Beltway 8 (Sam Houston Parkway), a toll road in some areas, makes an outer loop.

The Houston metropolitan area requires 10-digit dialing—use the area code along with the phone number. Area codes are 713, 281, and the newest, 832.

Downtown, visitors can use a free trolley or walk between sights, on ground level or via an extensive underground tunnel system accessed free through numerous buildings and sights. It's possible to walk between some sights in the Galleria-Uptown area and between some museums, or to take cabs within or between the districts, but it's best to have a car for seeing Houston and enjoying its restaurants, which are located throughout the city.

DOWNTOWN SIGHTSEEING HIGHLIGHTS

★★★★ CIVIC CENTER/THEATER DISTRICT
From a distance or close-up, downtown Houston is striking, a relatively new city with most of its temples to commerce built since the 1960s. The tallest building west of the Mississippi, the Texas Commerce Tower, rises 75 stories in a "neighborhood" of award-winning skyscrapers of 60 or more stories, many of them complemented with major outdoor sculptures by such names as Miró. Open plazas with trees, tiered fountains, and a promenade along the bayou augment the steel-and-glass towers.

A walking tour of the lower end of downtown provides a visual feast and a sense of the vibrancy of the city. Start at **Tranquility Park**, Smith and Walker Streets, where a 32-level fountain flows for two blocks and rocket-like towers commemorate the Apollo space flights. Head northward from Walker Street through the skyscraper canyons, concentrating on the area between Smith and Travis Streets up to **Market Square**, Travis and Preston Streets, the commercial center in the nineteenth century. Head to **Buffalo Bayou**, a couple of blocks north or west, and explore the waterfront trail of Sesquicentennial Park. If time allows, go into the underground tunnel, a meandering six-mile walkway that links 55 downtown buildings and three hotels and includes scores of shops and restaurants frequented by thousands of Houston businesspeople on weekdays.

New home of the Astros, the 42,000-seat **Ballpark at Union Station**, with a retractable roof, is scheduled to open in the spring of 2000 on the east side of lower downtown, and a new $75 million performing arts center is being built across from Tranquility Park on the west side.

With resident companies in opera, theater, symphony, and ballet, and as the site of many visiting performances, Houston boasts a lively performing arts scene, with 10,000 theater seats, second only to New York City. Most venues are located in the lower end of downtown, known as the **Theater District**. A number of the buildings are eye-catchers themselves, notably **Wortham Theater Center**, 500 Texas Avenue, 713/853-8000, with a soaring lobby and arched window overlooking its entry plaza, downtown, and Sesquicentennial Park. It's home to the **Houston Grand Opera** and the **Houston Ballet**, 800/828-ARTS (locally 713/227-ARTS), and **Da Camera Society**'s chamber music presentations, 713/524-5050. The fortress-like **Alley Theatre**, 615 Texas Avenue, 800/259-ALLE, has live productions on two stages—and great views of the city at night from its balconies. **Jones Hall for the Performing Arts**, 615 Louisiana, 800/828-ARTS, hosts the **Houston Symphony** as well as other musical programs. Plan ahead to see a performance or check for last-minute tickets upon arrival.

Details: *Between McKinney Ave. on the south, Preston Ave. on the north, Travis St. on the east, and Smith St. on the west. (1 hour)*

★★★ SAM HOUSTON HISTORICAL PARK
1100 Bagby St., 713/655-1912, efle@heritagesociety.org, www.heritagesociety.org

Houston's past sits in the shadow of its downtown skyscrapers in this tree-shaded park with a collection of eight historic buildings dating to the 1820s. The outdoor museum has a frontier cabin, six homes, a church, and three galleries, including an old general store, where the Heritage Society displays historic exhibits. A tearoom serves lunch.

Details: *Mon–Sat 10–4, Sun 1–4, guided tours on the hour until one hour before closing. Galleries free; guided tours $6 adults, $4 seniors and ages 13–17, $2 ages 6–12. (1–1½ hours)*

MUSEUM DISTRICT SIGHTSEEING HIGHLIGHTS

Generally southwest of downtown, the museum district stretches from the University of St. Thomas area by U.S. 59 southward to the Hermann Park area and encompasses a number of galleries as well as museums. Bayou Bend, considered part of the district, is in a residential area west of downtown.

★★★★ **BAYOU BEND COLLECTION AND GARDENS**
I Westcott St. (off Memorial Dr.), 713/639-7750, hirsch@mfah.org, www.mfah.org
A part of the Museum of Fine Arts, the River Oaks home of the late philanthropist Ima Hogg is regarded as one of the country's premier collections of decorative arts, chronicling the evolution of style from the colonial period to the nineteenth century. Furniture, paintings, and other decorative pieces are displayed in 28 rooms. The surrounding 14 wooded acres with formal gardens are particularly pretty in spring.

Details: Tue–Sat 10–4:45, Sun 1–5; 90-minute guided tours of home offered weekdays and Sat; self-guided audio tours available. Home and garden: $10 adults, $8.50 seniors and students, $5 ages 10–18 (under 10 not accepted on guided tour but may do self-guided tour with adult for $1.50); free the third Sun Sep–May. Garden only: $3. Reservations necessary for guided home tour. (2–2¹/₂ hours)

★★★★ **CHILDREN'S MUSEUM OF HOUSTON**
1500 Binz St., 713/522-1138, rapih@sam.neosoft.com, www.cmhou.org
Youngsters will love this bright, colorful museum with a wide array of hands-on fun. Children can paint, act in the KID-TV Studio, learn about archeology, and explore other cultures at a Mexican village and Chinese market. There's also an outdoor playground.

Details: Tue–Sat 9–5, Sun noon–5. $5 adults, $4 seniors, $3 after 3 except Sun, under 2 free. Parking $2. (1–2 hours)

★★★★ **DE MENIL MUSEUMS**
www.menil.org
Located near the University of St. Thomas, slightly north of the other museums, are the world-acclaimed **Menil Collection**, **Rothko Chapel**, and **Byzantine Fresco Chapel Museum**, contributions by philanthropists John and Dominque de Menil. The

Renzo Piano–designed Menil building showcases changing exhibits of the de Menils' eclectic, 15,000-piece private art collection, which ranges from Byzantine to cubism to tribal art. In the adjacent block, the octagonal Rothko Chapel is a serene ecumenical center with works by the late Mark Rothko. Special events here have drawn such speakers as Nelson Mandela and the Dalai Lama. The Byzantine museum houses rare thirteenth-century frescoes from Cyprus.

Details: Menil Collection: 1515 Sul Ross St., 713/525-9400; Wed–Sun 11–7. Rothko Chapel: 3900 Yupon St., 713/524-9839; daily 10–6. Byzantine Fresco Chapel Museum: 4011 Yupon St., 713/521-3990; Wed–Sun 11–6. Free. (1½–2 hours)

★★★★ HOUSTON MUSEUM OF NATURAL SCIENCE

1 Hermann Circle Dr., 713/639-4600, www.hmns.mus.tx.us
With a planetarium, butterfly center, IMAX theater, and a museum with everything from dinosaurs to gemstones, this complex entertains all ages, making astrology, anthropology, and geology interesting even to the nonscientific. In the **Cockrell Butterfly Center**, some of the 2,000 live butterflies may light on your shoulder as you walk through their rain forest habitat in a six-story glass cone. At the **Burke Baker Planetarium** you can study the stars or see laser shows. The natural and cultural world comes to life in films shown on a six-story screen at the **Wortham IMAX Theater**. The museum itself has a variety of permanent and changing exhibits, and the gift shop has excellent selections.

Details: Mon–Sat 9–6, Sun 11–6 (until 8 p.m. during Daylight Savings Time months). IMAX Theatre, 713/639-4629, and Planetarium show times vary; call for specifics. Museum: $4 adults, $3 seniors and children ages 3–11, all free Tue beginning at 2 p.m.; IMAX: $6 and $4, respectively; planetarium and family laser shows: $4 and $3, respectively; butterfly center: $4 and $3, respectively; rock laser shows: $6/person. Prices are different for members. (3 hours minimum)

★★★★ MUSEUM OF FINE ARTS

1001 Bissonnet St., 713/639-7300, hirsch@mfah.org, www.mfah.org
Founded in 1900, the museum showcases a broad-based collection of 40,000 European, American, African, and Asian works, ranging from Renaissance to post-impressionist and including such names as Vincent van Gogh, Claude Monet, and Henri Matisse. It also houses a

collection of African gold, hosts special exhibits, and has a sculpture garden including works by Auguste Rodin. It's currently expanding its exhibit space to become sixth-largest in the country.

Details: *Tue–Sat 10–5 (Thu until 9), Sun 12:15–6. $3 adults; $1.50 seniors, college students, and ages 6–18; free Thu; extra fees for special exhibits. (1–2 hours)*

★★★ CONTEMPORARY ARTS MUSEUM
5216 Montrose Blvd., 713/284-8250, www.camh.org
In the spirit of its name, the museum is housed in a parallelogram-shaped, corrugated metal building. Changing exhibits feature painting, sculpture, photography, and other works by modern-day masters and emerging artists.

Details: *Tue–Sat 10–5 (Thu until 9), Sun noon–5. Free. (1 hour)*

★★★ HOLOCAUST MUSEUM HOUSTON
5401 Caroline, 713/942-8000, www.hmh.org
This museum, the third-largest of its kind in the country, was designed by the architect who created the U.S. Holocaust Memorial Museum in Washington, D.C. Besides permanent exhibits, it has a memorial area, a sculpture garden, and a film of oral history recounted by local Holocaust survivors and liberators.

Details: *Mon–Fri 9–5, Sat and Sun noon–5. Free. (1 hour)*

★★★ MUSEUM OF HEALTH & MEDICAL SCIENCE
1515 Hermann Dr., 713/521-1515, www.mhms.org
This is indeed a walk on the wild side—through the human body. An interactive tour of the **Amazing Body Pavilion** lets you see, feel, and hear what makes us tick.

Details: *Tue–Sat 9–5 (Thu until 7), Sun noon–5. $4 adults, $3 seniors and ages 4–11. (1 hour)*

★ HOUSTON ZOO
1513 N. MacGregor Way, Hermann Park, 713/523-5888 (recording) or 713/284-8300, krusso@houstonzoo.org, www.houstonzoo.org
A rare white tiger roams a natural habitat, and 200 exotic birds fly freely through an Asian jungle aviary at this popular zoo.

Details: *Daily 10–6. $2.50 adults, $2 seniors, 50¢ ages 3–12. (1 hour)*

GREATER HOUSTON AREA SIGHTSEEING HIGHLIGHTS

★★★★ GALLERIA

5075 Westheimer Rd., 713/621-1907
For shopaholics, this is the ultimate fix, and even those who aren't in the market to buy anything should see this truly Texas-sized emporium at Loop 610 West and Westheimer Road. Anchored by Neiman Marcus at one end and Macy's at the other, this three-story enclosed mall runs for about three blocks with a major portion wrapped around an ice-skating rink under a glass roof. Barney's New York, Tiffany & Co., Gucci, the Metropolitan Museum of Art Shop, and Saks Fifth Avenue are only a few of more than 300 establishments here. Numerous dining options allow shoppers to rest and refresh.

The Galleria-Uptown area, as this neighborhood has become known, is a destination in itself, encompassing a number of shopping plazas, restaurants and hotels. Across from the Galleria shops is the **Centre at Post Oak**, with such names as FAO Schwarz and Barnes & Noble, and farther down the street is the **Pavilion at Post Oak**, 1800 Post Oak, with upscale shops such as Hermes of Paris and Cartier.

While you're in the area, don't miss the **Transco Water Wall**, a 64-foot, U-shaped fountain with water cascading down all sides. It's just south of the Galleria, at Post Oak Road and Hidalgo Street.

Details: Galleria and other plaza stores usually open Mon–Sat 10–9, Sun noon–6. Free. (2 hours minimum)

★★★★ SPACE CENTER HOUSTON

1601 NASA Rd. 1, 800/972-0369, www.spacecenter.org
Take yourself out of this world at NASA's hands-on educational-entertainment complex, located at Clear Lake about halfway between Houston and Galveston. Roam at your own pace through exhibits that explore the past, present, and future of the space program, including a thrilling flight via an IMAX movie. See early space capsules, touch a moon rock, and test your skills landing a shuttle. **A Kids Space Place** has 17 activity areas where children can drive a Lunar Rover and launch a rocket. A guided tram tour takes visitors to Mission Control and training facilities.

Details: Memorial Day–Labor Day 9–7 daily; rest of year weekdays 10–5, weekends 10–7. $12.95 adults, $11.95 seniors, $8.95 ages 4–11. (4–5 hours)

HOUSTON REGION

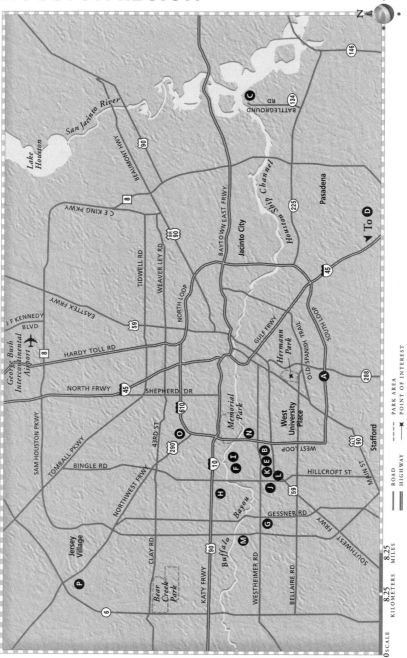

★★ ASTRODOME COMPLEX
Kirby Dr. at Loop 610 South
On the south side of the city, this complex includes the world-famous Astrodome, the first domed stadium; **Six Flags AstroWorld**, a 75-acre theme park; and **Six Flags WaterWorld**, a family water park. With 11 roller coasters and more than 100 rides, Six Flags AstroWorld promises a screaming good time, particularly on the new 112-foot-tall Taz's Texas Tornado with four loops, and Batman: The Escape, a stand-up roller coaster that takes you through a 360-degree loop. In summer's hot weather, it's cool to go to WaterWorld, with its surf pool, tubing, rafting, and water slides. Home of the Astros baseball team until the new downtown stadium opens in 2000, the Astrodome can be toured when events aren't scheduled.

Details: Astrodome: 8400 Kirby Dr., 713/799-9595, www.astros. com/dome.htm. Tours Tue–Sat 11 and 1, unless events are scheduled; $4 adults, $3 seniors and ages 4–11; $5 parking fee. Six Flags AstroWorld/WaterWorld: 9001 Kirby Dr., 713/799-8404, www.sixflags. com. AstroWorld: Memorial Day–mid-Aug daily 10–8 or 10, mid-Mar–May and mid-Aug–Oct weekends 10–6 or later; call for specifics. $32.95 for those 48 or more inches tall, $21.95 under 48 inches tall, under 3 free. WaterWorld: Memorial Day–mid-Aug daily 10–6, weekends 10–6 in May and mid-Aug–Labor Day; schedule may vary, so call for specifics. $16.95 for those 48 or more inches tall, $13.95 under 48 inches tall, under 3 free. Ask about combination passes. (full day)

★★ SAN JACINTO BATTLEGROUND STATE HISTORICAL PARK

SIGHTS
Ⓐ Astrodome Complex
Ⓑ Galleria
Ⓒ San Jacinto Battleground State Historical Park
Ⓓ Space Center Houston

FOOD
Ⓔ Café Lili
Ⓕ Carrabba's
Ⓖ Churrascos
Ⓗ Goode Company Barbeque
Ⓘ Grotto

FOOD (continued)
Ⓙ Kim Son
Ⓚ Pappas Brothers Steakhouse
Ⓛ Pappasito's Cantina
Ⓜ Rotisserie for Beef and Bird

LODGING
Ⓝ La Quinta Galleria Inn & Suites
Ⓞ Sheraton Houston Brookhollow

CAMPING
Ⓟ Traders Village

Off Hwy. 225, Deer Park, 281/479-2421, www.tpwd.state. tx.us or www.sanjacinto-museum.org
About 20 miles east of the city, General Sam Houston's army defeated Mexican General Antonio Lopez de Santa Anna in 1836 and won Texas' independence from Mexico. This state park commemorates that event with the **San Jacinto Monument and Museum of History**. An elevator goes to the top of the monument, an obelisk similar to the Washington Monument, rising 570 feet and topped with a lone star. Around the base, the museum houses excellent exhibits about the early history of Texas, and an award-winning slide show about the revolution is narrated by Charlton Heston. Also at the park, the battleship Texas from World Wars I and II is moored in the adjacent Ship Channel and open for touring.

Details: Monument/museum: daily 9–6, film shown hourly 10–5. Museum: free; elevator to top $3 adults, $2.50 seniors, $2 under age 12; show $3.50 adults, $3 seniors, and $2.50 under age 12; combination ticket $6 adults, $5 seniors, and $4 under age 12. (1–1 1/2 hours)

FITNESS AND RECREATION
Joggers will find lots of company at Memorial Park in the Galleria area west of downtown and on trails along North and South Braeswood Boulevards on either side of Brays Bayou, southwest of the Medical Center. The **Houstonian Hotel, Club & Spa**, 111 N. Post Oak Lane, 800/231-2759, has a fitness center and running trails through heavily wooded grounds in the Galleria area.

Among more than 100 public and private golf courses in the area are public courses at **Hermann Park**, 713/526-0077, and **Memorial Park**, 713/862-4033. For sporting events, here are helpful numbers: **Houston Aeros** (hockey), 713/627-AERO; **Houston Astros** (baseball), 800/ASTROS-2; **Houston Rockets** (basketball), 713/627-DUNK.

FOOD
Houstonians love to dine out, and with more than 8,000 restaurants, there's no end to choices of both cuisine and price. The problem, of course, is choosing from among so many places to eat. The following are only a taste.

For a memorable, upscale evening out ($30 or more per person), pick one of the following. **Café Annie**, 1728 Post Oak Boulevard, 713/840-1111, excels with innovative Southwestern cuisine in a quiet, elegant setting near the

Galleria. **Anthony's**, 4007 Westheimer Road, 713/961-0552, sets a slightly livelier scene, serving French and other continental favorites. The **Rotisserie for Beef and Bird**, 2200 Wilcrest Drive, 713/977-9524, has outstanding beef and game dishes in a more traditional fine-dining setting.

For slightly less expensive and perhaps slightly less dressy but still excellent dining, consider these choices. **Ruggles Grill**, 903 Westheimer Road, 713/524-3839, serves New American cuisine, including excellent grilled vegetables and desserts, in casual surroundings. Expect a wait. **Churrascos**, 2055 Westheimer Road, 713/527-8300, and 9705 Westheimer Road, 713/952-1988, introduced Houstonians to delicious, beef-oriented dishes from South America. The upscale **Pappas Brothers Steakhouse**, 5839 Westheimer Road, 713/780-7352, has excellent cuts and wine in a 1930s atmosphere. In a minimalist decor, **Sabine**, 1915 Westheimer Road, 713/529-7190, serves New American cuisine, drawing raves for its potato cakes infused with crawfish and shrimp. In one of the renovated brick buildings around Market Square downtown, **Tasca Kitchen and Wine Bar**, 908 Congress, 713/225-9100, brings New American dishes with a Spanish influence, including tapas and hors d'oeuvres of all types.

A longtime front-runner in Italian food is **Damian's Cucina Italiana**, 3011 Smith Street, 713/522-0439, which has a warm, cozy setting, good service, and innovative dishes. The lively and usually crowded **Grotto**, 6401 Woodway Drive, 713/782-3663, or 3920 Westheimer Road, 713/622-3663, turns out good pasta, seafood and grilled vegetables. A slightly less expensive and quite popular choice for pasta and grilled items is **Carrabba's**, 399 S. Voss Road, 713/468-0868, and other locations.

Houstonians love barbecue and Mexican (or Tex-Mex) food. **Goode Company Barbeque**, 8911 Katy Freeway (I-10 West), 713/464-1951, has tasty beef, ribs, and chicken. Fajitas and the whole enchilada are found at **Pappasito's Cantina**, 6445 Richmond Avenue, 713/784-5253, a crowd-pleaser popular for hefty servings at reasonable prices. In the Museum District, **Cafe Noche**, 2409 Montrose, 713/529-2409, serves specialties from interior Mexico and lighter Tex-Mex fare.

Ethnic restaurants abound. Try the cozy **Golden Room**, 1209 Montrose Boulevard, 713/524-9614, for fiery Thai food; the elegant **Hunan River Garden**, 2015 W. Gray Drive, 713/527-0200, for delicate Chinese; and **Khyber North Indian Grill**, 2510 Richmond Avenue, 713/942-9424, for its said fare. For Vietnamese and other Asian specialties, the leader is **Kim Son**, 300 Milam Street, 713/222-2790, and several other locations. **Café Lili**, 5757 Westheimer Road, 713/952-6969, serves freshly prepared Middle Eastern food in a small, family setting.

LODGING

On the luxury level downtown, the **Lancaster**, 701 Texas Avenue, 800/231-0336, a member of the elite Small Luxury Hotels of the World network, has intimate lodging in the Theater District starting at $200 weekdays, $120 weekends. The **Four Seasons Hotel-Houston Center**, 1300 Lamar Street, 713/650-1300, is an elegant 30-story hotel on the east side of downtown; rates start at $240 weekdays, $145 weekends. The **Hyatt Regency Houston**, 1200 Louisiana Street, 800/233-1234, has a soaring 30-story atrium; rooms start at $290 weekdays, $174 weekends.

Also luxurious, not far from downtown, and conveniently located for seeing the museums is the elegant **La Colombe d'Or**, 3410 Montrose Boulevard, 713/524-7999, a European-style inn with six suites in a restored mansion. Rates start at $195 and include continental breakfast. Another choice near the museums and Medical Center is the newly renovated **Park Plaza Warwick**, 5701 Main Street, 713/526-1991, a landmark Old World–style hotel on a tree-shaded boulevard. Rates range from $139 weekdays to $79 weekends.

In the Galleria-Uptown area, the top choice is the **St. Regis Houston** (formerly the Ritz-Carlton), 1919 Briar Oaks Lane, 800/325-3589, an elegant 12-story property with intimate lounge and swimming pool. Rates start at $250 weekdays, $115 weekends. In a secluded, wooded area, the **Houstonian Hotel, Club & Spa**, 111 N. Post Oak Lane, 800/231-2759, has a good fitness center and jogging trails; its rates start at $215 weekdays, $119 weekends. The **Doubletree Post Oak**, 2001 Post Oak Boulevard, 800/803-2582, convenient to Galleria shopping, is a large, 14-story hotel with amenities that include a pool. Rates start at $165 weekdays, $79 weekends.

Also near the Galleria, the **Sheraton Houston Brookhollow**, 3000 North Loop West (I-610 and U.S. 290), 713/688-0100, has a pool, spa, and popular restaurant, and weekend rates include breakfast. Its rooms run $119 weekdays, $59 weekends. La Quinta has 18 properties in the Houston area, among them the new **La Quinta Galleria Inn & Suites**, I-610 and San Felipe, 800/NU-ROOMS, with a pool, and exercise facilities. Room rates (including continental breakfast on weekends) range from $95 weekdays to $69 weekends.

For information and reservations at many Houston-area accommodations, call the **Greater Houston Convention & Visitors Bureau**, 800/4-HOUSTON.

CAMPING

On the west edge of the city, **Traders Village**, 7979 N. Eldridge Road, 281/890-5500, is a year-round RV park and huge marketplace on weekends.

The highly rated park has more than 200 full hookups and a number of amenities, including a pool.

NIGHTLIFE AND SPECIAL EVENTS

Beyond the theater scene, fine dining, special entertainment, and sports events, the two major scenes for nightlife are Bayou Place downtown and the Richmond Entertainment District in southwest Houston near the Galleria.

On the west end of the downtown Theater District, the old convention center has been transformed into **Bayou Place**, Texas Avenue, and Smith Street, a $23 million complex of restaurants, clubs, and theaters. Among its offerings: The **Aerial Theater**, 713/693-8600, is the setting for comedy acts and live theater and musical productions. The **Angelika Film Center**, 713/225-5232, has eight theaters screening foreign and independent films, and its **Angelika Cafe** is a fun spot for pre- or post-theater dining and coffee. Down-home cooking comes with soul music at **Harlon's Bayou Blues Bar-B-Que**, 713/230-0111.

Richmond Avenue from I-610 west to Hillcroft, about a two-mile stretch just southwest of the Galleria, hops with action at restaurants, clubs, outdoor cafés, and lounges. (Beware: The area can be congested with traffic.) **City Streets**, 5078 Richmond, 713/840-8555, has a number of nightspots under one roof. A little farther out, along both sides of Richmond Avenue, are clubs, pubs, sports bars, and lively restaurants, including **Dave and Buster's**, 6010 Richmond, 713/952-2233; **Billy Blues Bar & Grill**, 6025 Richmond, 713/266-9294; and **Joe's Crab Shack**, 6218 Richmond, 713/952-5400.

Entertainment moves outside in the summer. You'll find free concerts by the symphony and free performances during the Shakespeare festival at the **Miller Outdoor Theatre** in Hermann Park, 100 Concert Drive, 713/284-8350, and there are live concerts at the **Cynthia Woods Mitchell Pavilion** north of Houston, 281/363-3300.

For the latest information on nightlife, performances, and events, check listings in the *Houston Chronicle*, particularly its Weekend Preview section on Fridays.

Romantics, take note: Horse-drawn carriages make loops through the Theater District downtown and around the Transco Water Wall at the Galleria.

Of the many annual events, these are among the big crowd-pleasers: the **Houston Livestock Show & Rodeo**, 713/791-9000, mid-February through early March, a time when the city "goes Western"; the **Azalea Trail**, 713/523-2483, usually the first two weekends in March; and **Worldfest: Houston International Film Festival**, 713/965-9955, and **Houston International Festival**, 713/654-8808, both in April. The visitors bureau, 800/4-HOUSTON, can provide details about these and other events.

SHOPPING

While the **Galleria** (see Greater Houston Area Sightseeing Highlights) is the largest retail center in Houston, drawing 16 million visitors annually, it's only one of many shopping areas. Other neighborhoods for good shopping: **Highland Village**, 4000 block of Westheimer Road, 713/850-3100, has several blocks of individual boutiques and major retailers, including names such as Pottery Barn, Laura Ashley, and Williams-Sonoma. The **Village**, bounded by Kirby Drive, Rice Boulevard, University Boulevard, and Shepherd Drive in the Rice University area, 713/866-6000, bustles with shoppers who enjoy its cafés, coffee spots, well-known retailers, and specialty boutiques, which include Ann Taylor, the Gap, and Eddie Bauer stores. The art deco–design **River Oaks Shopping Center**, West Gray at Shepherd, 713/866-6000, has Talbots, Ann Taylor, and Garden Botanika shops among its wide selection. **Town & Country Mall**, Beltway 8 just south of I-10, 713/468-1171, has Neiman-Marcus, Saks Fifth Avenue, and Dillards. The **Victorian Heights** area has numerous antique shops along 19th and 20th Streets off Heights Boulevard; contact R & F Antiques, 713/861-7750, for more information on the area shops. **Old Town Spring**, 800/OLD-TOWN, about 20 miles north of Houston, is a turn-of-the-century village with 150 shops, galleries, and restaurants.

2
GALVESTON

Like a Southern belle, Galveston is a romantic flirt, with a multifaceted character and a colorful past. Located 50 miles southeast of Houston, the island boasts 32 miles of sandy beaches—a popular playground for all ages. In the city, tall oak trees, palms, and oleander bushes complement frilly "painted lady" Victorian homes.

Incorporated in 1839, Galveston eventually became the richest city in Texas, a major commercial and immigration center with its Strand business district dubbed "Wall Street of the Southwest."

On the night of September 8, 1900, a hurricane and tidal surge—the deadliest natural disaster in U.S. history—destroyed one-third of the city, killing more than 6,000 people. The city rebuilt, adding a seawall, now 10 miles long, but the state's commercial focus shifted to Houston. Galveston became a resort for high-rollers from the 1920s to the 1940s, but declined when gambling was shut down.

The island has shaken off the dust and now booms as a romantic retreat and family resort. The city has more than 550 designated landmarks on the National Register of Historic Places and more than 1,500 historic homes. Ships sail into the harbor, tying up at docks only a few feet from restored buildings, cafés, and old brick streets where visitors stroll. Beyond its Victorian districts, it boasts crowd-pleasing new attractions and resorts, such as the Moody Gardens entertainment complex.

GALVESTON

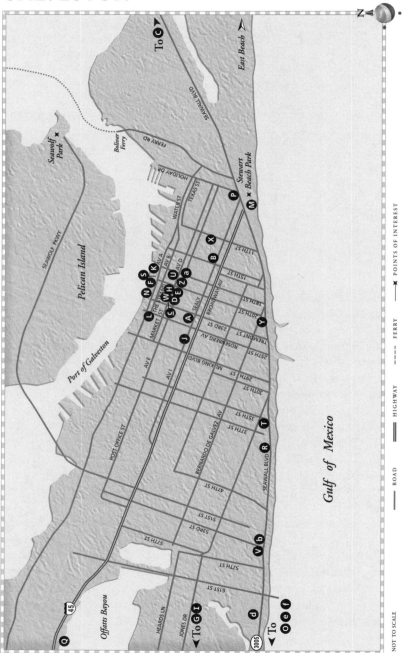

NOT TO SCALE   ROAD   HIGHWAY   FERRY   POINTS OF INTEREST

A PERFECT DAY IN GALVESTON

Visit Bishop's Palace and Ashton Villa, two of the city's historic homes, then spend the afternoon at Moody Gardens, a nature-oriented entertainment complex including a rain forest, aquarium, two IMAX theaters, and a white-sand lagoon. In the evening, browse through shops along the historic Strand and dine on the waterfront.

ORIENTATION

Beyond the beaches running along the Gulf, Galveston's main attractions are around the Strand National Historic Landmark District next to the port and toward the west end of the city, around Offatts Bayou beyond 61st Street.

HISTORIC HOME SIGHTSEEING HIGHLIGHTS

Turrets, towers, and frills accent Galveston's historic homes dating back to the mid-1800s. A number welcome visitors year-round, while others can be seen during the Galveston Historic Homes Tour the first two weekends each May. There are two

SIGHTS

- **A** Ashton Villa
- **B** Bishop's Palace
- **C** East Beach/R.A.Apffel Park
- **D** Galveston County Historical Museum
- **E** Grand 1894 Opera House
- **F** The Great Storm
- **G** Lone Star Flight Museum
- **H** Mardi Gras Museum
- **I** Moody Gardens
- **J** Moody Mansion and Museum
- **K** Offshore Energy Center
- **L** Railroad Museum
- **M** Stewart Beach Park

SIGHTS *(continued)*

- **N** Texas Seaport Museum & Elissa
- **O** West Beach

FOOD

- **P** Christie's Beachcomber
- **Q** Clary's
- **N** Fisherman's Wharf Seafood Grill
- **R** Gaido's
- **S** Hill's Pier 19 Restaurant, Bar and Fish Market
- **T** Joe's Crab Shack
- **U** La Mixteca
- **V** Landry's Seafood
- **E** Rudy and Paco
- **W** Wentletrap
- **F** Willie G's

LODGING

- **X** Away at Sea
- **V** Galveston Island Hilton Resort
- **F** Harbor House
- **Y** Hotel Galvez
- **Z** Inn at 1816 Postoffice
- **a** Madame Dyer's B&B
- **I** Moody Gardens Hotel
- **b** San Luis Resort
- **C** Tremont House
- **d** Victorian Condo-Hotel
- **a** Victorian Inn

CAMPING

- **e** Dellanera RV Park
- **f** Galveston Island State Park

Note: Items with the same letter are located in the same area.

designated historic neighborhoods, the East End and the Silk Stocking District. For a good overview, drive through the East End between Broadway and Harborside Drive from 19th to 10th Streets.

★★★★ **ASHTON VILLA**
2328 Broadway Ave., 409/762-3933, foundation@ galvestonhistory.org, www.galvestonhistory.org
This 1859 Italianate mansion exudes Southern hospitality, offering intimate glimpses into the lifestyle of old Galveston's wealthy merchants. Family heirlooms and original art personalize the home. This tour is especially fun for the stories that docents share about the owner's daughter, Bettie Brown, who was extremely independent and rather risqué for her time.

> **Details:** *Mon–Sat 10–4, Sun noon–4. $4 adults, $3.50 seniors and ages 7–18, $12.50 combination ticket with other homes. Wheelchair accessible on the first floor only. (1–1 1/2 hours)*

★★★★ **BISHOP'S PALACE**
1402 Broadway Ave., 409/762-2475
Built as a private home and later bought by the Galveston-Houston Catholic Diocese for Bishop Byrne, this mansion is one of the nation's premier Victorian homes. It's on the American Institute of Architects' list of 100 outstanding buildings in the country. Construction began in 1886, took seven years, and cost $250,000. The interior is distinguished by beautiful woodwork, a spiral staircase with a rotunda and stained-glass windows, and 11 fireplace mantels collected from all over the world.

> **Details:** *Memorial Day–Labor Day Mon–Sat 10–5, Sun noon–5; rest of year daily noon–4. $5 adults, $4 seniors, $3 ages 13–18, $1 12 and under, $12.50 combination ticket with other homes. (1–1 1/2 hours)*

★★★ **MOODY MANSION AND MUSEUM**
2618 Broadway Ave., 409/762-7668
Of the many island entrepreneurs, William L. Moody Jr. stands out for his wealth and, in recent years, the generous contributions to historical, cultural, and educational causes by his daughter, Mary Moody Northen. The 31-room mansion echoes the family's lifestyle in the early twentieth century, with the first floor decorated in preparation for Mary Moody Northen's debut party on December 12, 1911.

> **Details:** *Mon–Sat 10–4, Sun 1–4:30. $6 adults, $5 seniors and*

ages 6–18, $12.50 combination ticket with other homes. Wheelchair accessible. (30 minutes)

THE STRAND/HARBORFRONT AREA SIGHTSEEING HIGHLIGHTS

The heart of Galveston, fronting the port, once again bustles with business, its historic two- and three-story iron-front buildings beautifully restored and housing shops, restaurants, galleries, pubs, and antiques stores. Horse-drawn carriages rattle along brick streets lit with restored gaslights, and an old-fashioned fixed-rail trolley glides around the area. Within sight, big freighters and an occasional cruise ship tie up at the dock beside restaurants with sidewalk cafés.

Considered one of the nation's finest collections of nineteenth-century architecture, the Strand National Historic Landmark District runs along Water, Strand, and Mechanic Streets between 20th and 25th Streets. Adjacent to Water Street is the harborfront. The Strand Visitors Center, 2016 Strand, 409/765-7834, is a good starting point and can provide information on all attractions in Galveston.

✦

BOLIVAR FERRY

One of Galveston's most fun attractions is totally free—a ride on the Bolivar Ferry, which carries cars and passengers from the upper tip of Galveston Island to Bolivar Peninsula. The run takes about 20 minutes. Seagulls love to follow the ship, and you usually pass ocean-going freighters and occasionally see dolphins.

★★★★ **RAILROAD MUSEUM**
Strand and 25th Sts., 409/765-5700,
www.tamug.tamu.edu/rrmuseum
Housed in a restored, 1932 art deco Santa Fe railroad depot, the museum lures train buffs and kids, who will enjoy exploring vintage rolling stock and listening to "ghosts of travelers past," life-size figures in 1930s dress who "chat" (via recordings) while they wait in the depot.

Details: *Memorial Day–Labor Day daily 10–5; rest of year until 4. $5 adults, $4.50 seniors, $2.50 ages 4–12. (1–2 hours)*

THE *ELISSA*

Texas Department of Transportation

★★★ GRAND 1894 OPERA HOUSE
2020 Postoffice St., 800/821-1894, www.thegrand.com
If possible, catch a performance at this ornate, intimate theater, considered one of the country's finest restorations. No seat is farther than 70 feet from the stage. Located near the Strand, it's also open for self-guided tours.

Details: Mon–Sat 9–5, Sun noon–5 (except during performances). $2 ages 12 and older. (30 minutes)

★★★ THE GREAT STORM
Pier 21 Theater/Harborside Dr., 409/763-8808, foundation@galvestonhistory.org, www.galvestonhistory.org
This film, including stills and rare movie footage, captures the terrifying story of the 1900 hurricane that devastated the island, killing more than 6,000 people.

Details: Sun–Thu 11–6, Fri and Sat until 8; shows begin on the hour. $3.50 adults, $2.50 ages 7–18. (30 minutes)

★★★ OFFSHORE ENERGY CENTER
Pier 19, 409/766-STAR, oecstar@aol.com, www.oceanstaroec.com
You can't miss seeing this attraction, a refurbished three-deck drilling rig by dockside. You can tour it and learn about the offshore drilling process and production of oil and gas around the world.

Details: Memorial Day–Labor Day daily 10–5; rest of year daily 10–4. $5 adults, $4 seniors and ages 7–18. (1 hour)

★★★ TEXAS SEAPORT MUSEUM AND ELISSA
Harborside Dr. at Pier 21, 409/763-1877, foundation@ galvestonhistory.org, www.galvestonhistory.org
Galveston's tall ship, the circa-1877 *Elissa*, is the star of this museum, which tells the island's history as a port and recounts the rescue and restoration of the *Elissa*. The museum also has a database of more than 133,000 immigrants who were processed here when Galveston was second only to Ellis Island as an entry point into the United States.

Details: Memorial Day–Labor Day daily 10–5:30; rest of year until 5. $5 adults, $4 seniors and ages 7–18. (1 hour)

★★ GALVESTON COUNTY HISTORICAL MUSEUM
2219 Market St., 409/766-2340, foundation@

galvestonhistory.org, www.galvestonhistory.org

Occupying a 1919 bank building near the Strand, this museum has permanent and changing exhibits and unique film footage of the 1900 hurricane—shot with one of Thomas Edison's early cameras.

Details: Memorial Day–Labor Day Mon–Sat 10–5, Sun noon–5; rest of year until 4. Free, $1 donation suggested. (30 minutes)

★★ **MARDI GRAS MUSEUM**
2211 Strand, 409/763-1133, foundation@galvestonhistory. org, www.galvestonhistory.org

Three galleries of exhibits show the glittering costumes, masks, and crowns from the island's history of Mardi Gras celebrations dating back to 1867.

Details: Memorial Day–Labor Day Wed–Sun noon–6; rest of year Wed–Fri noon–5, Sat and Sun noon–6. $2 adults, $1 ages 7–18. (45 minutes)

OTHER SIGHTSEEING HIGHLIGHTS

★★★★ **GALVESTON BEACHES**

Boasting 32 miles of beaches fronting the Gulf of Mexico and a warm climate most of the year, Galveston Island draws sun-and-sea enthusiasts, from the college spring-break crowd to families, anglers, and snowbirds escaping winter. Don't expect Florida except for the warm sun. The sand here is tannish-brown, and the water ranges from a murky tea color to deep blue. The Gulf is normally gentle, though there sometimes are good breakers, and in the summer it's bathwater warm. A highway running the length of the island provides access to beaches, the best being toward the east end of the island and on the west end beyond the seawall.

For beach areas with services, options are: On the east end, **Stewart Beach Park**, Sixth Street and Seawall, 409/765-5023, is the family-oriented waterfront, with a children's playground, umbrella and chair rentals, food stands, rest rooms, a bathhouse, water slide, and mini-golf course. **East Beach/R. A. Apffel Park**, at the upper tip of the island, 409/762-3278, has facilities and offers live music on weekends during summer. On West Beach beyond the seawall, there are several county **Beach Pocket Parks**, 409/770-5355, that offer pavilions with rest rooms and showers.

There also are long stretches of beach across from the east end of the island on Bolivar Peninsula, reached by a free ferry that's part of the highway system. The Bolivar beaches are often not very crowded, but vacationers should be alert for cars.

Details: *Stewart Beach Park and East Beach/R. A. Apffel Park: mid-Mar–mid-Oct daily 8–6. $5/vehicle each park. Beach Pocket Parks: Memorial Day–Labor Day daily 8–6. $5/vehicle. (half–full day)*

★★★★ **MOODY GARDENS**

One Hope Blvd., 800/582-4673, www.moodygardens.com

The island's hot attraction, this expanding entertainment/educational complex provides a variety of action for all ages. Walk through a rain forest with exotic plants, birds, fish, waterfalls, and caverns inside a 10-story glass pyramid. Experience the thrills and chills of exciting films in the IMAX 3D Theater, which brings the action right off the big screen into your face. Get out of this world at the Discovery Pyramid, where you sample future life in outer space, and buckle up for a moving, shaking Asteroid Adventure in the 180-degree wrap-around IMAX Ridefilm Theater. See Antarctica penguins, Alaska seals, South Pacific coral, and Caribbean fish in the underwater world of the aquarium pyramid. Soak up some sun on Palm Beach in the la-goon or board the triple-deck Colonel paddle wheeler for sightseeing or a meal. The complex, facing Offatts Bayou, also has a hotel.

Details: *Memorial Day–Labor Day daily 10–9; rest of year Sun–Thu 10–6, Fri and Sat 10–9. $6 adults, $5 ages 4–12 for each at-traction, except $7 for IMAX theaters. Combination tickets at reduced prices. (3 hours minimum)*

GALVESTON ISLAND TROLLEY

You can see many sights—and get a sense of nineteenth-century lifestyles—by taking the Galveston Island Trolley, replica 1900-vintage cars that run on fixed rails around the Strand and to the seawall. The fare is 60¢ adults, 30¢ students. It usually runs from 9 to 6 on weekends and slightly longer on weekdays, but check locally for the schedule.

★★★ LONE STAR FLIGHT MUSEUM
2002 Terminal Dr., 409/740-7722, www.lsfm.org
Aviation buffs could spend hours here inspecting more than 40 restored vintage aircraft, many from World War II. Aircraft take to the air on Flying Days. The museum also has an impressive collection of pictures and handwritten letters from decorated pilots who've flown some of the aircraft (or ones like them).

    Details: Located by the airport. Daily 10–5. $6 adults, $2.50 ages 4–13. (1–2 hours)

FITNESS AND RECREATION
Walkers and joggers can join the crowd along the seaside sidewalk, which runs along Seawall Boulevard from Broadway to 61st Street. Those who like to run on long stretches of beach with fewer people should head toward the west end of the island beyond the seawall to some of the county parks, 409/770-5355. Anglers can try their luck in the surf from **West Beach** or public fishing piers, such as **Galveston Fishing Pier**, 90th Street and Seawall Boulevard, 409/744-2273, and **61st Street Fishing Pier**, 61st Street and Seawall Boulevard, 409/744-8365. **Galveston Party Boats**, Pier 19, 409/763-5423, runs charter boats on deep-sea fishing trips.

FOOD
Though everything from burgers to prime rib is available on the island, this is the place to eat your fill of seafood, from shrimp, oysters, and crawfish to red snapper and flounder. Dress is quite casual, except at the most upscale restaurants and for special events.

    In the Strand/harbor area, the **Wentletrap**, 2301 Strand Street, 409/765-5545, offers the premier fine-dining experience in a historic building. Duck, venison, shrimp, and snapper are popular, with Asian influences adding an innovative touch. Expect a tab of $20 to $30 a person for dinner. At Pier 21, **Willie G's**, 409/762-3030, has both a seafood place and oyster bar, offering indoor and outdoor tables with views. **Fisherman's Wharf Seafood Grill**, Harborside Drive at Pier 22, 409/765-5708, has casual indoor and patio dining overlooking the Texas Seaport Museum's *Elissa*. The house salad has fried goat cheese and slivers of fried onion rings, and an order of crispy calamari is plenty for two. **Hill's Pier 19 Restaurant, Bar and Fish Market**, Pier 19 at Harborside Drive, 409/763-2929, has great fried shrimp and oyster po'boy sandwiches. Prices for these three are moderate, usually under $20.

Local favorites are casual **Christie's Beachcomber**, 401 Broadway Avenue, 409/762-8648, for home-style food on the beach; the upscale **Clary's**, 8509 Teichman Road, 409/740-0771, overlooking Offatts Bayou; and also-upscale **Gaido's**, 3800 Seawall Boulevard, 409/762-9625, overlooking the Gulf, for a wide array of tempting seafood. Also along the Gulf are **Landry's Seafood**, 5310 Seawall Boulevard, 409/744-1010, and **Joe's Crab Shack**, 3502 Seawall Boulevard, 409/766-1515, which serves fresh seafood in a casual but festive atmosphere.

Rudy and Paco, 2028 Postoffice Street, 409/762-3696, puts a Latin American touch on seafood, steaks, and other dishes. It's moderately expensive and popular enough that you need reservations. **La Mixteca**, 1818 Mechanic Street, 409/762-2235, blends Mexican spices and sauces with seafood and offers popular Mexican dishes.

LODGING

Once home to mainly mom-and-pop motels and beach houses, Galveston now offers a wide variety of accommodations, from romantic bed-and-breakfasts in old Victorian homes to family-friendly condos, historic hotels, and luxury lodging in the downtown area and along the seashore. Most hotels along the Gulf are not built directly on the beachfront but along a wide boulevard on the raised seawall.

In the historic area downtown, the top choice is the **Tremont House**, 2300 Ship's Mechanic Row, 800/874-2300, a new hotel built in a beautifully restored 1879 property with an atrium. A black-and-white theme is carried throughout the 117 guest rooms and suites, which have vaulted ceilings, white enamel-and-brass beds, white linens, armoires, and Italian marble bathrooms with towel warmers. Rates start at about $135; ask about midweek specials. Adjacent to the historic downtown, the **Harbor House**, No. 28 at Pier 21, 800/874-3721, has 42 rooms overlooking the wharf (an oceangoing ship may be just outside your room), with rates from $155 that include continental breakfast; ask about specials.

Along the Gulf, the early-1900s Spanish colonial–style **Hotel Galvez**, 2024 Seawall Boulevard, 800/392-4285, is the grand dame of island lodging, with 228 rooms, a swim-up bar, lounge, and restaurant. Rates start at about $130, but specials may be available. Farther west are two newer large properties with tropical landscaping and full amenities: the **Galveston Island Hilton Resort**, 5400 Seawall Boulevard, 800/HILTONS, and the recently renovated **San Luis Resort**, 5222 Seawall Boulevard, 800/445-0090; both have rates starting slightly under $100. For families, a good choice is the **Victorian Condo-Hotel**,

6300 Seawall Boulevard, 800/231-6363, which has suites of varying sizes with kitchens; rates start at $59 in winter and $99 in summer.

The newest lodging on the island is the **Moody Gardens Hotel**, One Hope Boulevard, 888/388-8484, which has 300 rooms (including some Jacuzzi suites), a spa, and two restaurants. It overlooks the Moody Gardens entertainment complex of glass pyramids and a lagoon. Rates run about $200.

The island has about a dozen bed-and-breakfasts in restored Victorian homes furnished in antiques. Among the options: **Madame Dyer's B&B**, 1720 Postoffice Street, 409/765-5692, is an 1889 home with wraparound porches overlooking a lovely small garden. The three guest rooms have private baths; rates start at $100. The **Victorian Inn**, 511 17th Street, 409/762-3235, is a large 1899 Italianate villa with fireplaces and balconies; rates for its guest rooms start at $100. The **Inn at 1816 Postoffice**, 409/765-9444, an 1886 home behind a wrought-iron fence, has two guest rooms on a veranda and a third with a Jacuzzi. Rates start at $125. A small cottage, **Away at Sea**, 1127 Church Street, 800/762-1668, offers three guest rooms, two with Jacuzzis; rates start at $85.

The **Galveston Convention & Visitors Bureau**, 888/GAL-ISLE, cvb@galvestontourism.com, www.galvestontourism.com, offers a helpful information sheet giving names, addresses, phone numbers, and prices for all types of island accommodations.

CAMPING

On the western end of the island, outside the city, are two RV parks. **Dellanera RV Park**, Route 3005 at 7 Mile Road, 409/740-0390, is located on the beachfront. It offers umbrella and chair rentals, rest rooms, a bathhouse, a children's play area, picnic sites, and a pavilion with groceries, a snack bar, laundry facilities, and a recreation room. It has 84 spaces with hookups.

Galveston Island State Park, 14901 Route 3005, 409/737-1222, also by the water, has picnic tables, barbecue pits, rest rooms, showers, and 180 spaces—170 of them with full hookups.

NIGHTLIFE AND SPECIAL EVENTS

Summer ushers in the liveliest action, from beachfront to restaurants and nightspots. Check out **East Beach**, 409/762-3278, for seaside concerts. Summer band concerts, 409/744-2174, are each Tuesday evening at the **Sealy Gazebo**, 23rd and Sealy Streets. Concerts and outdoor musicals are staged at the **Mary Moody Northen Amphitheater**, 800/54-SHOWS, toward the western end of the island; and the **Grand 1894 Opera House**,

2020 Postoffice Street, 800/821-1894, has productions year-round. A **Historic Homes Tour** is scheduled each May by the **Galveston Historical Foundation**, 409/765-7834, and every six weeks the **Galveston ArtWalk**, 409/763-2403, showcases varying city galleries in the historic downtown area.

At night in the Strand area, **Yaga's Tropical Café**, 2314 Strand Street, 409/762-6676, draws crowds to its fun setting for cocktails and dinner. The **Strand Brewery**, 111 23rd Street, 409/763-4500, serves beer, pizza, and other items on three floors with outdoor decks. For a quieter spot, drop by the atrium bar at the **Tremont House**, 2300 Ship's Mechanic Row, 800/874-2300, a lovely courtyard lounge with palm trees, a massive hand-carved mahogany bar, and a pianist. Along the beachfront, **Joe's Crab Shack**, 3502 Seawall Boulevard, 409/766-1515, boasts a festive air with live entertainment and views of the Gulf.

Twice a year the island becomes a big party scene. During **Mardi Gras**, preceding the season of Lent, crowds estimated at 250,000 jam the island for merrymaking. Parades, masked balls, art exhibits, and entertainment stretch over 12 days. The festivities usually fall in February, when weather can change from balmy to chilly but spirits are never dampened. Advance reservations for lodging are a must. Call the visitors bureau, 888/GAL-ISLE, cvb@galvestontourism.com, www.galvestontourism.com, for information.

Dickens on the Strand, the first weekend in December, draws about 100,000 people as costumed characters, entertainers, and vendors re-create Queen Victoria's London. Many partygoers wear period dress. The Friday preceding the Dickens Festival, the East End Historic District celebrates a **Victorian Christmas** with horse-drawn carriage rides to historic homes. Advance reservations are advised for the Dickens festival. For information, contact the **Galveston Historical Foundation**, 409/765-7834, foundation@ galvestonhistory.org, www.galvestonhistory.org.

SHOPPING

From bargain outlets to specialty boutiques and art galleries, Galveston Beach tempts shoppers with an unexpected bonanza, most of it in and around the historic **Strand** area by the harborfront. Generally, between Harborside Drive and Market Street from 20th to 25th Streets, you will find numerous antiques shops and malls, gift boutiques, and several major outlet stores. Among the notable stores: **Peanut Butter Warehouse**, 100 20th Street, with three floors of antiques and collectibles; **Hendley Market**, 2010 Strand Street, specializing in Victorian jewelry, early books and laces; and **Eiband's Gallery**, 2201 Postoffice Street, with art, antiques, rugs, and gift items.

Outlets include **Bass Outlet**, 2314 Harborside Drive, with shoes and clothes; **Mikasa Factory Outlet**, 2225 Strand Street, with china and housewares; **New York Dress Outlet**, 2228 Mechanic Street, with name-brand clothing. The city also has more than a dozen art galleries, most of which are located in the historic district on Postoffice Street, known as **Gallery Row**, and on the Strand.

3
CRADLE OF TEXAS

In the south-central region of the state, you're deep in the heart of Texas history. Some of the state's oldest towns, predating the colonization by Stephen F. Austin in the 1820s, still thrive here. It was on this rolling land that the first shots were fired in the battle for freedom from Mexico and where the Texans signed their own declaration of independence.

Our route loosely follows some of La Bahia Road and the old San Antonio Road, known as El Camino Real, used by explorers, Indians, and early settlers. From the 1749 Presidio La Bahia outside Goliad, we wind through cattle and farming country to Washington-on-the-Brazos, considered the birthplace of Texas. The towns here are small and friendly, boasting everything from restored Old West jails to turn-of-the-century opera houses. Antiquing and arts-and-crafts fans will want to brake often for browsing.

This chapter focuses on a select few towns, but others also beckon travelers to slow down, drive through historic neighborhoods, poke through attractive shops and antiques stores, and enjoy good food. Explore the back roads and discover your own Texas treasure.

A PERFECT DAY IN THE CRADLE OF TEXAS

Poke around downtown Bastrop, one of the oldest communities in the state, exploring its River Walk and restored buildings. Head east via the scenic drive through Bastrop and Buescher State Parks to Washington-on-the-Brazos, known as the birthplace of Texas. End your day with dinner at Royers' Café in Round Top and overnight in one of the many bed-and-breakfasts dotting the countryside nearby.

ORIENTATION
The towns within this chapter could be combined in a history-oriented tour of the state, but they also make good short getaways from urban areas. For instance, Goliad is an easy day trip from Corpus Christi or San Antonio, and Gonzales is also close to San Antonio. Bastrop and nearby Smithville make an easy day's outing from Austin or a weekend trip from Houston. Brenham, Columbus, Round Top, and Washington-on-the-Brazos are popular day trips and weekend getaways from Houston.

BRENHAM AREA SIGHTSEEING HIGHLIGHTS
For information about this area, contact Washington County Chamber of Commerce/Convention & Visitor Bureau, 888/BRENHAM, tourinfo@brenhamtx. org, www.brenhamtx.org.

★★★★ **WASHINGTON-ON-THE-BRAZOS STATE HISTORICAL PARK**
Rte. 1155 off Rte. 105 about 7 miles southwest of Navasota, 409/878-2214, www.tpwd.state.tx.us
Called "the birthplace of Texas," the once-bustling community known as Washington-on-the-Brazos and Old Washington was the site of the signing of the Texas Declaration of Independence and served as the republic's capital for a time.

Washington-on-the-Brazos State Historical Park contains part of the old town site, a replica of the Independence Hall, and the Star of the Republic Museum, which has excellent exhibits explaining the Spanish and Mexican history of the area, the colonization years, the fight for independence from Mexico, and Texas' republic years (1836–1945). A living-history farm is under construction for late 2000.

Details: *Grounds open daily 8–dusk, visitors center daily 9–5, museum and hall 10–5. $4 adults, $2 children each for museum and hall; or $6 and $3, respectively, for combination ticket; or $15/family. (1–2 hours)*

CRADLE OF TEXAS

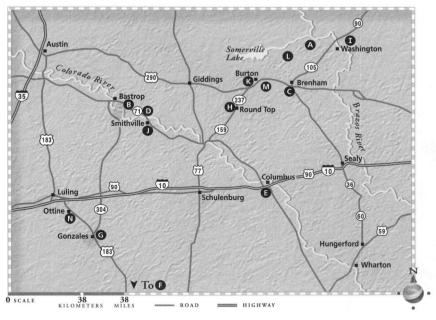

SIGHTS

Ⓐ Antique Rose Emporium
Ⓑ Bastrop State Park
Ⓒ Blue Bell Creameries
Ⓓ Buescher State Park
Ⓔ Columbus
Ⓕ Goliad
Ⓖ Gonzales
Ⓗ Round Top
Ⓘ Washington-on-the-Brazos State Historical Park

FOOD

Ⓙ Back Door Café
Ⓚ Brazos Belle
Ⓚ Burton Cafe
Ⓔ ...Of the Day, a Café
Ⓗ Royers' Café

LODGING

Ⓒ Ant Street Inn
Ⓗ Heart of My Heart Ranch
Ⓔ Magnolia Oaks
Ⓛ Mariposa Ranch Bed & Breakfast

LODGING (continued)

Ⓜ Nueces Canyon B&B Resort & Inn
Ⓕ Presidio La Bahia
Ⓖ St. James Inn
Ⓗ Texas Pioneer Arts Foundation

CAMPING

Ⓑ Bastrop State Park
Ⓕ Goliad State Historical Park
Ⓝ Palmetto State Park

Note: Items with the same letter are located in the same area.

★★★ ANTIQUE ROSE EMPORIUM
About 12 miles north of Brenham on Hwy. 50, just south of intersection with Hwy. 390, Independence, 409/836-5548

Eight acres of gardens combine with a historic homestead for a pleasant country outing in a scenic area north of Brenham. Pathways lead past gardens with antique roses (some classes dating back to the early pioneers), wildflowers, herbs, and native plants and flowers. An 1800s stone kitchen and Victorian home are among restored properties at this site outside the historic community of Independence, which includes the homesite of Sam Houston and grave of Mrs. Margaret Houston.

Details: Mon–Sat 9–6, Sun 11–5:30. Free. (1–1½ hours)

★★ BLUE BELL CREAMERIES
**2 miles southeast of Brenham on Rte. 577
800/327-8135**

Texans love their Blue Bell ice cream, which ranks with the nation's top scoops. Shop at the Blue Bell store, tour the plant, and get a free scoop of the good stuff.

Details: Store: Mar–Dec Mon–Fri 8–5, Sat 9–3. Tours: Mar–Oct Mon–Fri 10, 11, 1, 1:30, 2, and 2:30; Nov–Feb call for times. $2 adults, $1.50 seniors and ages 6–14. (45 minutes)

OTHER SIGHTSEEING HIGHLIGHTS

★★★★ BASTROP
Chamber of Commerce, 927 Main St., 512/321-2419, www.bastrop.com

Founded on the site where El Camino Real crossed the Colorado River, this community, about 30 miles southeast of Austin, was bustling in 1836. The surrounding area became one of the 10 original counties created when Texas became an independent nation. Today Bastrop is a charming small town with more than 125 structures on the National Register of Historic Places. In recent years it has been revitalized with development along the riverfront and Main Street, where buildings now house specialty shops, antiques stores, and restaurants. The two-story 1889 **Bastrop Opera House** on Main Street serves as the visitors center and stages live productions (see Nightlife and Special Events), and a new **River Walk** with antique lampposts invites strolling along the banks of the Colorado, which is popular for canoeing and rafting in the summer. Also by the river, it's fun to browse among a group of pioneer buildings that form a village of shops, cafés, and accommodations called **The Crossing**, 601 Chestnut Street, 512/321-7002.

On the edge of town, **Bastrop State Park**, www.tpwd.state. tx.us, sits on a section of rolling land covered in heavy woods known as the Lost Pines, an isolated region of loblolly pine trees. Park Road 1, a scenic 13-mile roller-coaster ride through the woods, connects Bastrop to **Buescher State Park**.

Details: *Bastrop State Park, 512/321-2101, and Buescher State Park, 512/237-2241, open year-round. $3 ages 13 and older, seniors free; one state park fee admits you to other state parks within the same day. (1–3 hours, 1 hour for drive)*

★★★★ **COLUMBUS**
Area Visitor Center/Chamber of Commerce
425 Spring St., 409/732-8385, ccvb@intertex.net,
www.intertex.net/users/ccvb
Settled in 1823, Columbus is considered the oldest continuously occupied Anglo American town in the state. Huge oak and magnolia trees shade Victorian mansions, some now serving as bed-and-breakfast inns, and at the heart of town is one of the state's prettiest courthouses, which has a stained-glass dome. A restored 1886 opera house still presents live productions, and there are a few small museums, including an extensive Santa Claus collection. On the town square, visit the Chamber of Commerce in the opera house to get maps noting sightseeing attractions. Most historic homes are open only during a tour in mid-May or for other special events, but you can do a self-guided driving tour of the town's "talking homes," where descriptions are accessed via your car's AM radio. Plan a visit on Thursday, Friday, or Saturday, when more attractions are open.

The rural area west of Columbus around Schulenberg is dotted with old German–Czech–Moravian churches. You can spot them by their classic steeples rising above the farmlands. Inside, four churches are adorned with painted vaulted ceilings, intricate stenciling, and frescoes. Several of these painted churches are on the National Register of Historic Places. For more information, contact the Schulenberg Visitor Center, 101-B Kessler Avenue (U.S. 77), 409/743-4514.

Details: (1–3 hours)

BASTROP

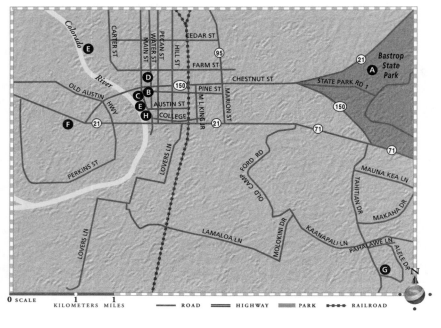

SIGHTS
Ⓐ Bastrop State Park
Ⓑ Chamber of Commerce
Ⓒ The Crossing
Ⓓ Bastrop Opera House
Ⓔ River Walk

FOOD
Ⓕ Cartwright's BBQ
Ⓖ Chabot's Italian Cafe
Ⓒ Yacht Club at the Crossing

LODGING
Ⓒ Cabins on the Colorado
Ⓗ The Colony

Note: Items with the same letter are located in the same area.

★★★★ **GOLIAD**

**Chamber of Commerce, Market and Franklin Sts.,
512/645-3563, gedc@icsi.net, www.goliad.org**

The site of Indian settlements before the Spaniards established a mission and protective fort, or *presidio*, here in 1749, Goliad is also dear to Texans for the role it played in the revolution against Mexican rule.

The town itself has one of the prettiest courthouse squares in the state, accented by huge oak trees with long, sprawling branches. One is known as "the hanging tree," where sentences were carried out swiftly in the mid-1800s. Many restored buildings date to the middle or late 1800s.

The majestic reconstructed **Presidio La Bahia**, 512/645-3752, located about two miles south of Goliad on U.S. 183, is considered one of the finest examples of a Spanish frontier fort and crowns a hill in a quiet, rural setting. Its small **Our Lady of Loreto Chapel**, the only original section, has held regular services since the 1700s and has a beautiful fresco behind the altar and an unusual vaulted ceiling. A block or so beyond the compound are the graves and a monument to Colonel James Fannin and about 340 men who surrendered near here after losing a battle to the Mexican army, then were massacred at the presidio on Palm Sunday, March 27, 1836, by order of General Santa Anna. Also near the fort is the reconstructed birthplace and statue honoring General Ignacio Zaragoza, a Mexican hero of the mid-1800s.

At nearby **Goliad State Historical Park**, 512/645-3405, www.tpwd.state.tx.us, honoring the men killed in the Battle of Goliad, a small museum depicts area history; visitors may tour the reconstructed *Mission Espíritu Santo*, founded here in 1749 and site of the first large cattle ranch in Texas.

Details: Presidio: open daily 9–4:45, state park open daily 8–5. $3 adults, $1 ages 6–12, state park $2 ages 13 and older, seniors free. (2–3 hours)

★★★★ **ROUND TOP**
Chamber of Commerce, 409/249-4042
www.rtis.com/reg/roundtop
A little country mixes with culture in this tiny community of fewer than 100 people (that number mushrooms on weekends for the many special events in the area). In town, you will find Texana-antiques shops, several cafés, bed-and-breakfasts, and an 1866 German Lutheran church that's still active. A split-rail fence encloses a restored nineteenth-century village known as **Henkel Square**, 409/249-3308, which illustrates pioneer Anglo American and German lifestyles.

On summer weekends, classical music resounds from the hills around Round Top. The **International Festival-Institute**, Route 237, 409/249-3129, a teaching campus and conference center located in a collection of restored Victorian buildings, presents a series of classical concerts (both chamber and symphony) from May through July. The rest of the year the International Festival-Institute performs monthly concerts.

At **Winedale Historical Center**, 409/278-3530, a nineteenth-century farmstead and study center, Shakespeare goes on stage in spring and late summer. Grounds include a nature trail and picnic area, and visitors may tour historic buildings. The center is located four miles east of Round Top via Routes. 1457 and 271.

Details: *Henkel Square is open Thu–Sun noon–5. Tours $5 adults, $2.50 students, free under 12. May–Sep Sat 10–6 and Sun noon–6, Oct–Apr Sat 9–5 and Sun noon–5. $3 adults, $1 students, under 6 free. (1 hour)*

★★★ GONZALES

Chamber of Commerce, 414 St. Lawrence St., 830/672-6532, info@gonzalestexas.com, www.gonzalestexas.com

You have to salute a little town that, back in 1835 with minimal manpower, stood up against more than 100 Mexican soldiers who were trying to take their cannon—even taunting the soldiers with a homemade flag that said "Come and Take It." The Gonzales men fired the cannon, the Mexicans retreated, and that was the first shot of the battle for independence from Mexico. It earned the town of Gonzales the title of Lexington of Texas.

On the courthouse square, drop by the 1887 **Gonzales County Jail**, 414 St. Lawrence Street, 830/672-6532, which is open for touring and houses the visitors center. Both St. Lawrence and St. Louis Streets, running off the square, have pretty homes and lead to the **Gonzales Memorial Museum**, Smith and St. Lawrence Streets, 830/672-6350, which houses the small cannon that supposedly is the historic weapon. The "Come and Take It" Battleground is seven miles southwest of town on Route 97. If time allows, stop by the **Gonzales Pioneer Village**, north on U.S. 183, 830/672-2157, a living-history center with eight restored buildings from the mid-1800s.

Palmetto State Park, 12 miles north of Gonzales on U.S. 183, between Luling and Gonzales, 830/672-3266, www.tpwd.state.tx.us, is a small tropical wonderland in an otherwise dry area. Its rich diversity of plants, including the namesake palmetto, creates an environment that's great for bird-watching, with an estimated 240 species spotted here. The park is open year-round and offers a short scenic drive, hiking, swimming, and camping.

Details: *(1–2 hours)*

FITNESS AND RECREATION

Bicycling, hiking, and canoeing are popular in the area. **Palmetto State Park**, north of Gonzales, 830/672-3266, has hiking and biking trails, fishing, and swimming in a tropical setting. On the edge of Bastrop, bicyclists enjoy the hilly, wooded terrain of **Bastrop and Buescher State Parks**, 512/321-2101 and 512/237-2241, respectively, and Park Road 1, which connects them. Lakes at both parks and nearby Lake Bastrop offer good bass fishing. While canoeists paddle along the slow-moving Colorado River from north of Bastrop down to Smithville, there was no local equipment rental at press time, though river outfitters previously had shops at Bastrop. Bicyclists wander along the many rolling back roads around Brenham, Chappell Hill, Round Top, and Columbus. Most visitors bring their own bikes; no local rentals are available.

FOOD

Forget the diet and indulge in finger-lickin' good barbecue and home cooking in this area. Along with little hometown cafés, you'll also find some excellent New American cuisine. Check days and hours of operation of the restaurants in these small towns because they're often open at specified times only.

In Bastrop, the **Yacht Club at the Crossing**, 601 Chestnut Street, 512/321-2545, serves burgers, Tex-Mex, steaks, and sandwiches in a casual atmosphere overlooking the Colorado River. **Cartwright's BBQ** (formerly Bastrop BBQ), 409-A Highway 71, 512/321-7719, is a longtime favorite for brisket and ribs. Upscale **Chabot's Italian Cafe**, 1001 Tahitian Drive, 512/303-4863, presents the creative flair of Chef John Chabot (pronounced shah-bow) who made a name for himself at Austin's trendy Mezzaluna restaurant.

In Smithville, about 12 miles southeast of Bastrop on Highway 71, the **Back Door Café**, 117 Main Street, 512/237-3128, combines home-grown herbs with fresh ingredients for gourmet dishes, including a popular beef tenderloin.

In the Columbus-Brenham area, head for lunch or dinner at **Royers' Café** on the square in Round Top, 877/866-PIES, where you'll probably endure a long wait on the front porch (go browse through the shops around the square). It's a fun spot with great food—from rainbow trout to stuffed quail, a marvelous beef tenderloin plate, and fresh pasta at moderate to moderately expensive prices. Save room for a slice of pie.

In the nearby blink-and-you'll-miss-it town of Burton, west of Brenham, the **Brazos Belle**, Main Street, 409/289-2677, serves country-French cuisine (usually open only on Friday and Saturday evenings and for Sunday lunch). The **Burton Cafe**, Washington Street, 409/289-3849, has been a longtime favorite as a casual gathering spot for its home cooking—including freshly baked pies—and live entertainment on Saturday nights.

In Columbus, one of the restored buildings on the town square now houses a snappy, modern restaurant called **... Of the Day, a Café**, 1114 Milam Street, 409/732-6430, which serves freshly prepared sandwiches, soups, specials, and desserts prepared from scratch.

Most restaurants in this area are inexpensive, but the tab will be $20 or so at the more upscale. Also, it's always wise to ask about credit cards; many restaurants take only cash.

LODGING

This area is a haven for bed-and-breakfast lodging and small inns. Goliad offers unique accommodations—two-bedroom quarters at the restored **Presidio La Bahia**, south of town on U.S. 183, 512/645-3752. Stone walls, open beam ceilings, and heavy Spanish-style furnishings accent the bedrooms, living area, kitchen, and bathroom. Guests have access to the inner quadrangle of the fort even after closing. The lodging can sleep four and costs $150 a night. In Gonzales, the **St. James Inn**, 723 St. James Street, 830/672-7066, a 1914 mansion built for a cattle baron, blends antiques with modern furnishings. Rates for its five bedrooms start at $85 with full breakfast.

Spend the night like a pioneer in the **Cabins on the Colorado**, 601 Chestnut Street, Bastrop, 512/321-7002. This collection of old Texas homes on the river bank downtown is part of a village of shops and restaurants called the Crossing. Three of the four cabins have porches with swings or rocking chairs overlooking the river, and all are furnished country style, each with private bath. Rates start at $75, including a $10 credit for breakfast (or another meal) at the adjacent Yacht Club Restaurant. Among the bed-and-breakfasts in Bastrop's historic homes, **The Colony**, 703 Main Street, 512/303-1234, has several themed rooms, one honoring the town namesake Baron de Bastrop. Rates start at $99 (with private bath), including full breakfast.

In Columbus, the **Magnolia Oaks**, 634 Spring Street, 409/732-2726, an 1890 gingerbread Victorian set amid huge trees, has four rooms and a loft apartment furnished with antiques and Texana. An adjacent saltbox-style cottage has three rooms with private entrances. All rooms have private baths. Rates start at $80, including full breakfast.

In Round Top, the **Texas Pioneer Arts Foundation**, Henkel Square, 409/249-3308, has several accommodations, including a rustic one-bedroom cabin with fireplace and claw-foot tub and a restored nineteenth-century home. Rates start at $70, with proceeds helping preserve and share the German-Texan culture of the area. The **Heart of My Heart Ranch** outside Round Top, 403 Florida Chapel Road (off Route 237), 800/327-1242, satisfies the desire to escape to the country without giving up any desirable amenities. On property that dates back to early Texas pioneer days, this inn has a new farmhouse with a long porch overlooking the pond, a 1900s cottage, an 1836 log cabin, and an 1828 frontier home, all with guest rooms and private baths, starting at $135 with a bountiful buffet breakfast that includes heart-shaped waffles. In a peaceful setting, the ranch offers a pool, hot tub, hiking, horseback riding, fishing, boating, biking, a driving range—and massages.

Outside Brenham, not far from the community of Independence, the **Mariposa Ranch Bed & Breakfast**, 8904 Mariposa Lane (on Route 390), 409/836-4737, has accommodations in historic properties ranging from an 1836 Greek Revival home to an 1825 log cabin with stone fireplace and a 100-year-old farmhouse. Rates start at $80 with a full breakfast. Horseback-riding enthusiasts should check out **Nueces Canyon B&B Resort and Inn**, 9501 U.S. 290 West., Brenham, 800/925-5058, which is a working ranch with an equestrian center, hiking and riding trails, and lakes. Near Burton, Nueces Canyon has a cottage with three guest rooms and an inn with country antiques in its 12 bedrooms, all with private baths and terry robes. Rates start at about $80, including continental breakfast.

In downtown Brenham, the **Ant Street Inn**, 107 W. Commerce Street, 800/481-1951, is a 14-room hotel in a restored turn-of-the-century mercantile building. Exposed brick walls, oriental rugs, antiques, and stained-glass windows accent the rooms, which start at $85, including full breakfast.

CAMPING

Visitors can camp amid big shade trees at **Goliad State Historical Park**, on the south edge of Goliad on U.S. 183, 512/645-3405. The park has showers, rest rooms, tent camping, and hookups. **Palmetto State Park**, 12 miles north of Gonzales, 830/672-3266, has swimming, fishing, tent camping, hookups, and a large historic pavilion available to rent for picnics. **Bastrop State Park**, on the edge of Bastrop, 512/321-2101, is unique in offering historic lodging in 1930s buildings of stone and wood, a dozen cabins of varying sizes, and a lodge accommodating eight. Rates are $50 to $80. The lodging is quite popular and books up early; reservations are accepted 11 months in advance. The park also has tent camping and hookups, a swimming pool, fishing lake, and golf course. For all state park reservations, call 512/389-8900.

NIGHTLIFE AND SPECIAL EVENTS

In Gonzales, the turn-of-the-century **Crystal Theatre**, 511 St. Lawrence Street, has both local productions and visiting shows. Call the Gonzales Chamber of Commerce, 830/672-6532, for information.

The 1889 **Bastrop Opera House**, 711 Spring Street, Bastrop, 512/321-6283, has all types of entertainment, from plays to vaudeville, murder mysteries in which the audience participates, and community events such as arts and crafts fairs. It even does a "poke bonnet and pantaloon" vintage clothing show.

In Columbus, the 1886 **Stafford Bank and Opera House**, 425 Spring Street, 409/732-5135, has a season of dinner theater and other live productions. On Saturday nights, the **Columbus Opry**, 715 Walnut Street, 409/732-9210, is hopping with country-western music. The area's German heritage is celebrated with live oompah music on most weekends at **Hofbrauhaus Restaurant**, 10 miles north of Columbus on Route 109, 409/732-6321.

Outside Round Top, the **International Festival-Institute** at Festival Hil on Route 237, 409/249-3129, presents an acclaimed series of summer concerts from May through July, then has monthly concerts from August through April. At nearby **Winedale Historical Center**, about four miles east of Round Top on Route 2714, 409/278-3530, what was once a hay barn now is the stage for a Shakespeare festival with performances in late July and early August.

In Brenham, **Unity Theatre**, in an old bank building at the Courthouse Square, 409/830-8358, presents plays and musicals year-round, usually offering five productions that run three to four weeks each.

Outside Round Top, the twice-yearly **Texas Antiques Fair**, 281/493-5501, draws crowds of about 8,000 people the first weekend in April (if that's Easter, the second weekend) and in October.

4
AUSTIN

Once mainly a laid-back college town where political sparks flew every two years when the legislature met, Austin has blossomed into a multifaceted capital ranked as one of the best places to live in America. Texans themselves love Austin—thousands of students who come here to the mammoth University of Texas like the city so much they never want to leave. And with the infusion of high-tech industries, many graduates do indeed stay to work.

Located in central Texas, Austin is a green haven where farmlands give way to tree-covered hills and blue lakes shimmering beneath limestone bluffs. The city of approximately 570,000 nestles up to the winding Colorado River, now tamed with dams to form a chain of seven lakes stretching from the foot of downtown Austin northwest through the hills for more than 150 miles.

Natural springs dot the area, one of them forming a popular town swimming hole, the Barton Springs Pool. Austinites tend to be nature lovers, enjoying recreation, dining, and entertainment outdoors most of the year since winters are relatively mild.

Founded in 1839, the city was named for Stephen F. Austin, the Father of Texas, and played a tug-of-war with Houston to become the permanent capital. The 1888 domed Capitol crowns a hill downtown. Nearby, a historic area now turned into an entertainment district has helped make the city into a different kind of capital—the Live Music Capital of the World.

A PERFECT DAY IN AUSTIN

Start with a guided tour of the Capitol, walk over to the nearby Governor's Mansion to see its formal rooms, and lunch at one of the restaurants in the West Sixth Street area. In the afternoon, visit the Lyndon B. Johnson Library and Museum, then drive to Barton Springs for a dip in the pool or a walk through the Botanical Gardens. Toast the sunset on a deck at the Oasis on Lake Travis and cap the evening with a visit to one or more clubs or cafés with live music.

ORIENTATION

The dome of the state Capitol and the University of Texas Tower and football stadium are dominant landmarks on the downtown skyline, helping define the major sightseeing area. Across the Colorado River at the foot of downtown lies popular Zilker Park, with its Barton Springs Pool, botanical garden, and Umlauf Sculpture Garden and Museum. Other sights are scattered about or on the outskirts of the city.

Visitors can hop aboard the free trolley-like 'Dillo (short for armadillo) shuttle buses to see a number of sights, from the University of Texas south to the Capitol and Governor's Mansion, or to reach popular restaurants around lower Congress Avenue and entertainment and dining venues along Sixth Street. UT also has a shuttle system within the university area. For schedules and other information, call Capital Metro at 800/474-1201. It's best to have a car for getting around in the evening and for touring elsewhere in the city and area.

DOWNTOWN/UNIVERSITY AREA
SIGHTSEEING HIGHLIGHTS

★★★★ LYNDON B. JOHNSON LIBRARY AND MUSEUM
2313 Red River St. on the east edge of the UT campus, 512/916-5137, www.lbjlib.utexas.edu

A powerful, moving experience, this museum transports visitors back to the turbulent 1960s through audio recordings, film footage, historical photographs, and exhibits. Visitors walk through 60 years of history, starting with the childhood days of both the former president and Lady Bird Johnson, but the exhibits relating to the 1960s are the most compelling. Well-done educational exhibits, which may bring a tear to the eyes of older visitors, chronicle the assassination of President Kennedy, the swearing in of LBJ, the Great Society, the Civil Rights movement, '60s rock music and fashions, the Vietnam War, the antiwar movement, and LBJ's decision to withdraw from politics. On the lighter side, there are recordings of "The Humor of LBJ," a collection of ceremonial gifts given to the Johnsons from other countries, and many family pictures.

Details: Daily 9–5. Free. (2 hours)

★★★★ TEXAS CAPITOL
Congress Ave. at 11th St., 512/463-0063, www.capitol.state.tx.us

Completed in 1888, this soft-pink granite building topped with a 15-foot Goddess of Liberty statue is a National Historic Landmark. On extensive wooded grounds atop a hill, the Capitol enjoys a commanding presence, overlooking a complex of government buildings and Congress Avenue, the main thoroughfare sloping to the Colorado River. A recent four-year, $67 million renovation project has restored the building's original fine workmanship. Inner walls are limestone with dark wainscoting and tall doors of oak, pine,

Locally, Guadalupe Street, running along the west side of the University of Texas campus, is known as the Drag. Loop 1 is also called Mo-Pac Boulevard, and the Capital of Texas Highway is Loop 360.

and other woods. The most impressive area, from bottom to top, is the rotunda, soaring more than 300 feet above a terrazzo floor featuring the seals of the six nations that have governed the state, including the Republic of Texas. Balconies of the building's three upper floors overlook the rotunda. Senate and House of Representative chambers are here, as are the offices for the governor and other state officials. Paintings and other artwork throughout the Capitol depict historic events. The renovation project included a four-story underground Extension, with eight skylit courts and a two-story rotunda. Tunnels connect the Extension to other state buildings.

Details: Mon–Fri 7 a.m.–10 p.m., Sat and Sun 9–5; free guided tours every 15 minutes 8:30–4:30 (Sat and Sun 9:30–4:15). Free. (1–1 1/2 hours)

AUSTIN

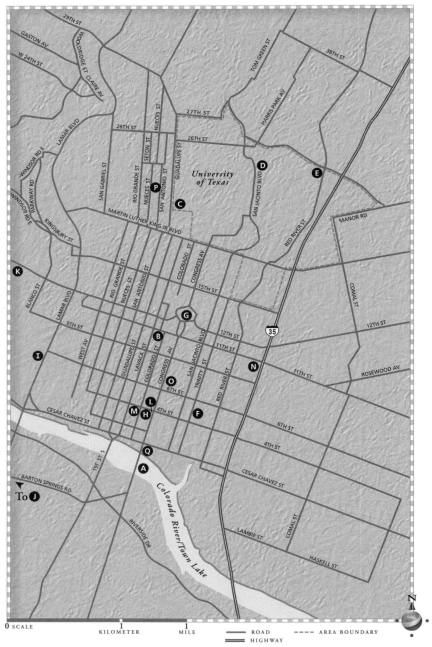

29TH ST
GASTON AV
W 24TH ST
WOOLDRIDGE ST
CLAIRE AV
LAMAR BLVD
WINDSOR RD E
PARKWAY RD
WINDSOR RD E
KINGSBURY ST
BLANCO ST
LAMAR BLVD
9TH ST
WEST AV
CESAR CHAVEZ ST
BARTON SPRINGS RD
To **J**
1ST ST S
RIVERSIDE DR

26TH ST
NUECES ST
27TH ST
26TH ST
SAN GABRIEL ST
RIO GRANDE ST
SETON ST
NUECES ST
SAN ANTONIO ST
GUADALUPE ST

University of Texas

TOM GREEN ST
36TH ST
HARRIS PARK AV

D
E
SAN JACINTO BLVD
RED RIVER ST
MANOR RD

MARTIN LUTHER KING JR BLVD
P
C

COLORADO ST
CONGRESS AV
15TH ST
COMAL ST
12TH ST

K
RIO GRANDE ST
NUECES ST
SAN ANTONIO ST
G
12TH ST
35
B
11TH ST
I
GUADALUPE ST
LAVACA ST
COLORADO ST
CONGRESS AV
SAN JACINTO BLVD
TRINITY ST
RED RIVER ST
N
11TH ST
ROSEWOOD AV
O
6TH ST
L
M **H** 4TH ST
F
6TH ST
4TH ST
Q
A
CESAR CHAVEZ ST
Colorado River/Town Lake
LAMBIE ST
COMAL ST
HASKELL ST

N

0 SCALE   1   1
        KILOMETER   MILE   ——— ROAD   - - - - AREA BOUNDARY
                                     ═══ HIGHWAY

★★★ BAT WATCHING

From late March through October, Austin goes batty, as more than a million little Mexican free-tailed bats migrate here and roost under the Congress Avenue Bridge at Town Lake. About dusk, they swarm out like a big cloud of smoke. Fear not; this largest urban colony is an insect-eating friend, heading out nightly for a main course of mosquitoes. A "Save the Bats" campaign has helped make the nocturnal flights a big attraction. Head to one of the watering holes in lower downtown or around Town Lake and join in the bat-watch.

Details: *For information, call the Visitors Bureau, 800/926-2282 or 512/478-0098, or Bat Conservation International, 512/327-9721. (45 minutes–1 hour)*

★★★ GOVERNOR'S MANSION

1010 Colorado St., 512/463-5518, thc@thc.state.tx.us, www.thc.state.tx.us/mansion.html
This National Historic Landmark, built in 1856 and little changed since, sits on a tree-shaded hill just west of the Capitol. Its two-story white facade with six Ionic columns is reminiscent of a stately Southern mansion.

Inside, Federal and Empire furnishings give public rooms an elegant feeling, and memorabilia from former governors add a personal touch.

Details: *Mon–Fri 10 a.m.–11:40 a.m., with free tours about every 20 minutes; the home may be closed as needed for functions. (1 hour)*

SIGHTS
Ⓐ Bat Watching
Ⓑ Governor's Mansion
Ⓒ Jack S. Blanton Museum of Art/Harry Ransom Center
Ⓓ Jack S. Blanton Museum of Art/UT Art Building
Ⓔ Lyndon B. Johnson Library and Museum
Ⓕ O. Henry Home and Museum
Ⓖ Texas Capitol
Ⓖ Walking Tours

FOOD
Ⓗ Bitter End Bistro and Brewery
Ⓘ Castle Hill
Ⓙ Green Mesquite
Ⓚ Jeffrey's
Ⓛ Manuel's
Ⓜ Mezzaluna

LODGING
Ⓝ Austin Marriott
Ⓞ Driskill
Ⓟ Governor's Inn
Ⓠ Radisson Hotel & Suites

Note: Items with the same letter are located in the same area.

★★★ WALKING TOURS
Austin Convention & Visitors Bureau, 201 E. 2nd St., 512/478-0098, gspain@austintexas.org, www.austintexas.org

More than just a tour of interesting buildings and homes, these walks through Austin's past give you a peek into the lives of the statesmen, cattle barons, bankers, politicians, and outlaws who helped shape the city. The **Historic Congress Avenue and Sixth Street** tour goes through downtown, where restored nineteenth-century buildings mingle with modern skyscrapers. The **Historic Bremond Block** tour shows off a neighborhood of stately Victorian homes, and there's a **Capitol grounds** tour. Ask about maps for other self-guided tours at the Austin Convention & Visitors Bureau.

Details: Tours Mar–Nov. Congress Ave. tours: Thu–Sat at 9, Sun at 2. Bremond tours: Sat and Sun at 11. Capitol grounds tours: Sat at 2, Sun at 9. Tours meet on the south steps of the Capitol and are free. (1 1/2 hours)

★★ UNIVERSITY OF TEXAS
I-35 and Martin Luther King Blvd., 512/471-3434, www.utexas.edu

As you drive around Austin you can't miss this renowned school with its tall tower and huge football stadium as landmarks dear to students and alumni. On the edge of downtown, the campus, with about 48,000 students, sprawls for about 10 blocks north of Martin Luther King Boulevard between I-35 and Guadalupe Street, the latter known locally as the Drag.

On campus, a major attraction is the **Jack S. Blanton Museum of Art** (formerly the Huntington Art Gallery), 512/471-7324, www.utexas.edu/cofa/hag. At the **Harry Ransom Center**, the permanent exhibits range from rare books—including a Gutenberg Bible printed in 1455—to several large art collections, from newly acquired Renaissance and Baroque pieces to Latin American and twentieth-century works. Temporary exhibits are shown at the **UT Art Building**. A new facility to combine all exhibits is planned by 2002 at a site on Martin Luther King Boulevard.

Details: Harry Ransom Center, 21st and Guadalupe Sts., and UT Art Building, 23rd and San Jacinto; Mon–Fri 9–5 (Thu until 9), Sat and Sun 1–5. Free. (30 minutes–1 hour)

★ **O. HENRY HOME AND MUSEUM**
409 E. Fifth St., 512/472-1903, www.ci.austin.tx.us/parks/
ohenry.htm
Short-story writer William Sidney Porter, who used the pen name
O. Henry, lived and worked in this Victorian cottage in the mid-
1890s. The home still has some original furnishings and his personal
effects.
Details: Wed–Sun noon–5. Donation requested. (30 minutes)

GREATER AUSTIN AREA SIGHTSEEING HIGHLIGHTS

★★★★ **ZILKER PARK**
2100 Barton Springs Rd., 512/499-6700 or 512/478-0098
Few cities have such a beautiful playground as this, and Austinites
take advantage of this greenbelt along the south shore of Town Lake
just southwest of downtown. The don't-miss attraction is everyone's
favorite swimming hole, **Barton Springs Pool**, 2100 Barton Springs
Road, 512/476-9044 or 512/867-3080, a 1,000-foot-long aquama-
rine spring-fed pool that stays at 68 degrees year-round. On hot
summer days it's the place to cool off—float on a raft or swim laps,
then relax on grassy slopes under big shade trees. Though it looks
similar to an Olympic pool, it's natural, and the bottom can be slippery. Call ahead to verify hours; the pool sometimes closes because
of heavy rains or cleaning. There's a bathhouse, and refreshments
are available.

Also at the park, across Barton Springs Road from the pool, slip
into the quiet beauty of **Zilker Botanical Gardens**, 2220 Barton
Springs Road, 512/477-8672, which meanders along a bluff above
the lake. Paths lead through nine types of gardens, including a lovely
Asian retreat with great views through the trees of the downtown
skyline. Ask about tours to see the dinosaur tracks, offered on
Saturdays from May through Thanksgiving. Adjacent to the park,
Umlauf Sculpture Garden and Museum, 605 Robert E. Lee
Road, 512/445-5582, www.io.com/~tam/umlauf, entices outdoor
enthusiasts as well as art lovers with the work of nationally acclaimed
sculptor Charles Umlauf. The park also has a miniature train; a hillside
theater where free concerts, musicals, and movies are presented in
summer; and canoe rentals.

GREATER AUSTIN

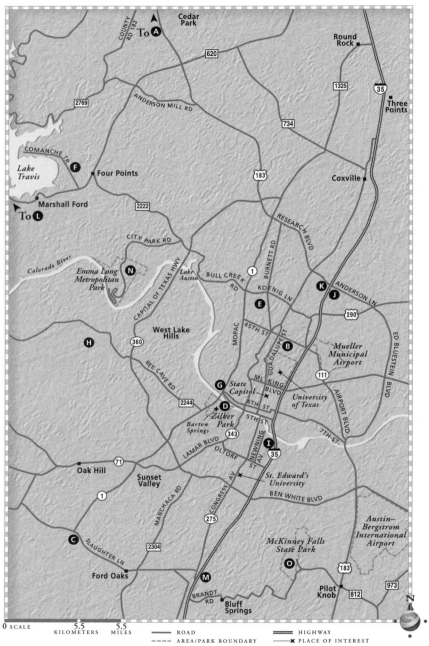

0 SCALE

KILOMETERS 5.5   MILES 5.5

ROAD
AREA/PARK BOUNDARY

HIGHWAY
PLACE OF INTEREST

Details: Hours and fees vary for different destinations within the park. (1 hour minimum)

★★★ AUSTIN & TEXAS CENTRAL RAILROAD

Cedar Park, 512/477-8468, www.main.org/flyer

The Austin Steam Train Association runs excursions into the countryside northwest of Austin and from downtown to east Austin, using restored cars with windows that open and air-conditioned lounge cars. The **Hill Country Flyer** goes from Cedar Park through scenic country to the small town of Burnet, where passengers have about three hours to browse before the return trip. The outing takes six to seven hours total; diesel engines run January and February, steam engines the rest of the year. The **River City Flyer** makes 60- to 90-minute excursions from downtown Austin June through October, and the **Twilight Flyer** makes occasional evening runs with entertainment. The trip to Burnet is particularly pretty in spring and early summer when wildflowers are in bloom.

Details: Cedar Park Depot at U.S. 183 and Rte. 1431, downtown depot at Fourth and Red River Sts. Trains operate on weekends; call for schedules. (1 1/2–7 hours)

★★★ LADY BIRD JOHNSON WILDFLOWER CENTER

4801 LaCrosse Ave., 512/292-4100, nwrc@onr.com, www.wildflower.org

Founded by the former First Lady, a wildflower enthusiast, this educational center is dedicated to preserving and promoting the use of native wildflowers, plants, grasses, shrubs, and trees. Attractive for touring, the gardens also offer economically and ecologically

---

SIGHTS

Ⓐ Austin & Texas Central Railroad
Ⓑ Elisabet Ney Museum
Ⓒ Lady Bird Johnson Wildflower Center
Ⓓ Zilker Park

FOOD

Ⓔ Fonda San Miguel
Ⓕ Oasis
Ⓖ Zoot

LODGING

Ⓗ Barton Creek Resort
Ⓘ Fairview
Ⓙ Hampton Inn North
Ⓚ Holiday Inn Express
Ⓛ Lakeway Resort

CAMPING

Ⓜ Austin Lone Star RV Resort
Ⓝ Emma Long Metropolitan Park
Ⓞ McKinney Falls State Park

AUSTIN-BERGSTROM INTERNATIONAL AIRPORT

The new Austin-Bergstrom International Airport opens in 1999, located on the southeast edge of the city at the site of the closed Bergstrom Air Force Base. About 15 minutes from downtown, the airport includes a courtyard Market Place that houses shops selling Texas products; Market Place restaurants include the Cybersmith Cafe, where travelers can check their e-mail. There's also a stage where local musicians will perform.

oriented ideas for homeowners. In its rocky Hill Country setting, the center's nature trail leads through a wildflower meadow to a cave. While it has year-round exhibits, the center is particularly colorful from March into early summer with yellow, blue, red, orange, purple, and pink wildflowers. It has picnic grounds, a café, and an excellent gift shop.

Details: Off Slaughter Ln. and Loop 1 southwest of the city. Grounds open Tue–Sun 9–5:30. $3.50 adults, $2 students and seniors, $1 ages 18 mos.–5 years. (1 hour)

★★ ELISABET NEY MUSEUM

304 E. 44th St., 512/458-2255, elisabetney@earthlink.net

Art lovers will appreciate the extensive collection of sculptures by this unusual woman, who immigrated to Texas from Germany in the 1870s and became an eminent sculptor whose works grace the Smithsonian, among other places. The museum is located in her castle-like 1892 home and studio in a wooded, historic neighborhood.

Details: Wed–Sat 10–5, Sun noon–5. Donation requested. (30 minutes–1 hour)

FITNESS AND RECREATION

With a chain of Highland Lakes extending northwest from the city and the Colorado River twisting through downtown, Austin abounds with outdoor activities. At the foot of downtown, **Town Lake**, 512/499-6700, a part of the Colorado River, draws fitness enthusiasts and fun-seekers. Canoeists and paddleboaters join rowing teams practicing their sculling techniques and river-boats on sightseeing and sunset cruises. Joggers, cyclists, and skaters will find plenty of company—and great skyline views—along the 10.1-mile **Town Lake Hike and Bike Trail** by the lakeshore.

Joggers who like hills and mountain bikers looking for some tough terrain should head to **Zilker Park** and the start of the **Barton Creek Greenbelt** trail through the surrounding woods. Bordering the city are a number of parks and preserves with hiking, biking, and nature trails, swimming, and sometimes fishing. Among the options are **Emma Long Metropolitan Park**, 512/346-1831, on Lake Austin, and **McKinney Falls State Park**, 512/243-1643, to the southeast.

Farther up the Colorado River, on the western edge of the city, Lake Austin winds along limestone bluffs to create a scenic boating, water-skiing, and sailing venue. Farther out, drop a line and reel in bass from **Lake Travis**. For information on the Highland Lakes, call 512/478-0098.

Besides public golf courses, there are two major golf resorts in the area: **Lakeway Resort**, 101 Lakeway Drive, 800/LAKEWAY, and **Barton Creek Resort**, 8212 Barton Club Drive, 800/336-6158.

FOOD

Austinites love their chips, salsa, fajitas, and enchiladas. But besides the traditional Tex-Mex food, restaurants often serve specialties from the interior of Mexico. The city also has embraced spicy Southwestern cuisine and organic foods.

Manuel's, 310 Congress Avenue, 512/472-7555, serves sizzling fajitas and lets you mix and match five fillings and six sauces for your enchiladas. The upscale menu includes more than Tex-Mex, offering fish and steaks with Southwestern sauces. It's a popular downtown spot, so expect crowds. **Fonda San Miguel**, 2330 W. North Loop Boulevard (west of Burnet Road), 512/459-4121, in a lovely hacienda setting, has both Tex-Mex and traditional Mexican dishes prepared with flair. Meals run $10 to $20.

Among the city's top restaurants, the menus successfully "fuse" several cuisines. Southwestern, Tuscan, New American and even some Pacific Rim dishes show up on the changing menu at **Castle Hill**, 1101 W. Fifth Street, 512/476-0728, a local favorite in a converted 1890s grocery store. Go early or late to beat the crowds. Considered by many to be the city's finest restaurant, **Jeffrey's**, 1204 W. Lynn Street, 512/477-5584, leans toward New American, with Asian and Southwestern influences in its changing menus. **Zoot**, 509 Hearn Street, 512/477-6535, calls itself an American bistro and wine bar, and delivers sophisticated New American cooking in a warm setting in a renovated old house. Service is excellent at these restaurants, which are moderately expensive to expensive.

In the Warehouse District of lower downtown, upscale **Mezzaluna**, 310 Colorado Street, 512/472-6770, has earned a reputation for excellent Italian dishes, with seafood often accompanying pasta. The **Bitter End Bistro and Brewery**, 311 Colorado Street, 512/478-2337, keeps fans returning not only for its varied brews but also for its good food, which shows Southwestern touches. Prices are moderately expensive.

For barbecue and burgers at low prices, a favorite "Bubba"-type restaurant is **Green Mesquite**, 1400 Barton Springs Road, 512/479-0485 (one of several locations).

No trip to Austin is complete without raising a 'rita (that's Texan for margarita) and applauding the sunset high above Lake Travis at the **Oasis**, 6550 Comanche Trail, 512/266-2442, a restaurant with 28 outdoor decks cascading down the hillside.

LODGING

One of the state's legendary hotels, the **Driskill**, 604 Brazos, 800/252-9367, has been the site for political wheelin' and dealin' and gala parties since 1886. Beautifully restored, the original five-story building has ornate arches and porticoes; a 12-story annex was added in the late 1920s. The hotel is located downtown, close to the Capitol.

Also, ask for one of the renovated rooms. Rates start at $145. Also convenient for downtown and UT sights, **Austin Marriott at the Capitol**, 701 E. 11th Street, 800/228-9290, offers a pool and other large-hotel amenities at rates of $175 weekdays and $105 weekends. South of downtown, **Radisson Hotel & Suites**, 111 E. First Street, 800/333-3333, overlooks the popular Town Lake recreational area; its rooms start at $145, or $120 on specials including breakfast.

Many less-expensive options are located in the Highland Mall area north of downtown. Among them are **Hampton Inn North**, 7619 N. I-35 (Exit 240A), 800/426-7866, with rooms for $79 including continental breakfast; and **Holiday Inn Express**, 7622 N. I-35, 800/HOLIDAY, with rooms for $79, including continental breakfast, and specials for $65. There are many economy and midpriced chain hotels/motels in the city.

Among a number of bed-and-breakfasts, the **Fairview**, 1304 Newning Avenue, 512/444-4746, a 1910 landmark, offers a quiet residential setting with gardens. It has four rooms in the main home and two in a carriage house, with rates starting at $99 including a full breakfast. In a tree-shaded area near the UT campus, the **Governor's Inn**, 611 W. 22nd Street, 800/871-8908, is a turn-of-the-century Victorian home with rockers and swings on the porch. Inside, guests find an English country decor and 10 guest rooms, each with private bath and bathrobes. Rates start at $79 including full breakfast.

For vacationers who want a deluxe recreational setting, **Barton Creek Resort**, 8212 Barton Club Drive, 13 miles west of downtown, 800/336-6158, has a spa, three golf courses, restaurants, and other amenities; rooms start at $225. **Lakeway Resort**, 101 Lakeway Drive, 800/LAKEWAY, on Lake Travis about 20 miles northwest of the city, has a marina, three golf courses, tennis courts, and 138 rooms, starting at $110.

CAMPING

Southeast of town off U.S. 183, **McKinney Falls State Park**, 7102 Scenic Loop Road, 800/792-1112 or 512/389-8900 for reservations, offers a scenic setting with clear pools and waterfalls amid old cypress trees. You'll find hiking and biking trails, swimming, fishing, a visitors center and historic homestead, tent sites, hookups, and facilities. **Emma Long Metropolitan Park**, 512/346-1831, on Lake Austin about 17 miles outside town, has mountain bike trails, swimming, fishing, tent camping, hookups, and full amenities. The **Austin Lone Star RV Resort**, 7009 S. I-35, 800/284-0206, has about 150 hookups, a tent village, eight cabins, and full amenities.

NIGHTLIFE AND SPECIAL EVENTS

Though music clubs are dotted throughout the city, much of the action centers around downtown. Historic **Sixth Street** from Congress Avenue east to I-35 is known as the entertainment district, with music pulsating from the many clubs and cafés in the restored buildings. Another lively spot is the **Warehouse District**, a few blocks southwest of the Sixth Street district in lower downtown. Park the car and stroll through one or both districts, stopping wherever the music suits your taste—but take the usual personal safety precautions you would in any city at night.

The popular PBS series "**Austin City Limits**," featuring live music, is taped at the UT campus September through February. For information about tickets, call 512/475-9077 or 512/471-4811.

Toe-tappin' country music comes alive at the legendary **Broken Spoke**, 3201 S. Lamar Boulevard, 512/442-6189; and at **Hang 'Em High Saloon**, 201 E. Sixth Street, 512/322-0382. **Maggie Mae's**, 323 E. Sixth Street,

HIGHLAND LAKES AND WINERIES

About a dozen wineries are located around Austin, particularly to the west in the scenic Hill Country and around the Highland Lakes. Start by packing a picnic of cheeses, meats, fruits, and anything else you want to eat from **Central Market**, 4001 N. Lamar Boulevard, 512/206-1000. Then make a day trip, meandering the back roads, enjoying the expansive views of green hills and canyons, and stopping for tastings at several wineries. It's wise to call ahead and confirm the visitor center locations, directions, and hours of operation.

From Austin, take Loop 1 south, then Route 71 northwest through the Hill Country, skirting the southern edge of the chain of lakes. At Llano, take Route 29 east, then Route 261 north to Bluffton and Route 2241 northeast past Tow about two miles to **Fall Creek Vineyards**, 512/476-4477, overlooking **Lake Buchanan**. This 65-acre estate winery, a winner of international awards, is open for tours, tastings, and sales Monday through Friday 11 a.m. to 3 p.m., Saturday noon to 5 p.m., and Sunday noon to 4 p.m. (closed Sunday December through February). Buy a bottle and have your lunch at the winery's picnic grounds or at nearby **Inks Lake State Park**, 800/792-1112, which is farther east on Route 29 across Buchanan Dam and south on Park Road 4.

After lunch, follow Route 29 (or the park road) to U.S. 281, go south to **Marble Falls**, and take Route 1431 east along the lakes to Cedar Park and **Hill Country Cellars**, 1700 N. Bell Boulevard, 512/259-2000, off U.S. 183 about a mile north of Route 1431. The winery, known for its prize-winning Chardonnays, has a tasting room in its 50-year-old, native stone ranch house. It's open daily noon to 5 p.m., with tours Monday through Thursday at 1 and Friday through Sunday 1 to 4 on the hour.

You can follow U.S. 183, a major artery, back into Austin or, if time allows, visit one more winery. Take U.S. 183 southeast, then Route 620 south to **Slaughter-Leftwich Vineyards**, 512/266-3331, overlooking **Lake Travis** at 4209 Eck Lane, off Route 620, one mile south of Mansfield Dam. The winery is open for tastings Thursday through Sunday 1 to 5, with tours Thursday and Friday at 3 and Saturday and Sunday at 1:30 and 3:30.

512/478-8541, has rock and pop; and **Cedar Street**, 208 W. Fourth Street, 512/708-8811, serves up jazz. **Antone's**, 2915 Guadalupe Street, 512/474-5314, known as Austin's Home of the Blues, has been the place for top names to perform for two decades. Another blues favorite is **Pearl's Oyster Bar**, 9033 Research Boulevard, 512/339-7444; and there are more blues clubs on Sixth Street. Mix in a little comedy with a stop at **Esther's Follies**, 525 E. Sixth Street, 512/320-0553. For a variety of music styles, stop by **Top of the Marc**, 618 W. Sixth Street, 512/472-9849.

Austin also hosts many touring performers, often for outdoor concerts at **Zilker Hillside Theatre and Auditorium Shores**. For information on what's happening, call 512/832-4094, an entertainment hotline.

Austin parties at numerous fun events. Among them: In March, the **South by Southwest Music, Film and Multimedia Conferences and Festival** brings together critics, producers, and several hundred big-name and new musical acts for a 10-day event; **Jerry Jeff Walker's Birthday Celebration** attracts several thousand fans for several events, including a performance by the songwriter honoree.

In April, the **Texas Hill Country Wine & Food Fest** showcases chefs and vintners, and **Spamarama** features zany recipes, fun, and music centered on the potted meat called Spam.

In May and September, the **Old Pecan Street Arts Festival** has live music, arts, and crafts along Sixth Street (formerly Pecan Street). The **Austin Aqua Fest** in July includes outdoor concerts, boat races, and other events focused around the city's waterfront setting. For information call the **Austin Convention & Visitors Bureau**, 800/926-2282.

5
HILL COUNTRY

A part of Texas where the deer and antelope—and even a few buffalo—still roam, the Hill Country graces the state with rolling terrain, expansive skies, canyons, limestone bluffs, caves, and clear cool rivers. This is the beloved land of the late President Lyndon B. Johnson and the home of many summer camps for children.

Located northwest of San Antonio and west-southwest of Austin, the Hill Country defines the end of the coastal plains and the beginning of the Great Plains. Thick growths of low cedars and oaks give the vistas an overall green look, yet close up much of the land is rocky limestone dotted with cactus and prickly pear. From March through summer, wildflowers carpet the hills with bright colors.

Many early settlers here were German, and the towns retain that heritage. Today, artists, photographers, and authors have gravitated here, finding inspiration in the region's scenic beauty and peaceful nature. The state's greatest concentration of wineries is in this region, and abundant orchards yield small but sweet peaches in summer.

A PERFECT DAY IN THE HILL COUNTRY

Visit the Cowboy Artists of America Museum in Kerrville, then head to Fredericksburg to browse through the shops along Main Street and have lunch

FREDERICKSBURG

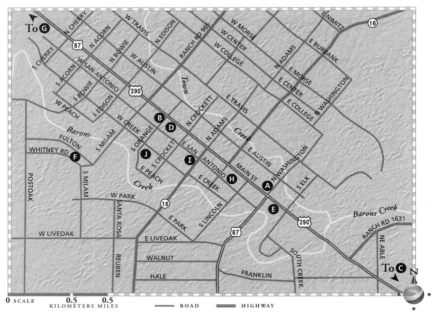

SIGHTS

- **A** Admiral Nimitz Museum and Historical Center
- **B** Pioneer Museum Complex
- **C** Wildseed Farms Market Center

WINERIES

- **D** Fredericksburg Winery

FOOD

- **E** Ernie's Mediterranean Grill
- **F** Fredericksburg Herb Farm
- **G** Hilltop Cafe
- **H** Navajo Grill
- **I** Peach Tree Tea Room

LODGING

- **J** Corner Cottage & Garden Room B&B

at the Peach Tree Tea Room (call ahead for reservations). Tour the Lyndon B. Johnson Ranch and other parts of the historical parks at Stonewall and Johnson City as desired. Dine out at Ernie's Mediterranean Grill where you can enjoy dishes that range from pasta to duck. Overnight at one of the bed-and-breakfasts in Fredericksburg or around Wimberley.

ORIENTATION

Popular for weeklong vacations and weekend getaways, the Hill Country can be explored in a number of ways. Concentrate on one destination at a time—Fredericksburg and Kerrville have numerous things to see and do while Wimberley invites kicking back and relaxing more. You may also want to use one destination as a base for exploring several areas, since most sites in this chapter are within a short drive of each other. A third option is to explore several areas on a scenic drive through the region. (See the Hill Country Back Roads scenic route at end of chapter.)

FREDERICKSBURG/JOHNSON CITY AREA SIGHTSEEING HIGHLIGHTS

Martha Stewart fans will love Fredericksburg, a German country town known for its bed-and-breakfasts, arts-and-crafts shops, and an increasing number of excellent restaurants opened by chefs escaping big-city hassles.

★★★★ LYNDON B. JOHNSON STATE AND NATIONAL HISTORICAL PARKS
U.S. 290, 830/868-7128, www.nps.gov for national park; 830/644-2252, www.tpwd.state.tx.us for state park

In two sites, 14 miles apart, the LBJ parks tell the life story of the late president, illustrating how closely the history of the man and the land were intertwined. At the national park at Johnson City, visitors see the **LBJ Boyhood Home and Johnson Settlement**, which includes his grandfather's log cabin, a living-history farm, and some longhorn cattle. West on U.S. 290, outside Stonewall at the state park, you can begin a bus tour of the **LBJ Ranch**, which will take you across the Pedernales River to see his reconstructed birthplace, a country schoolhouse he attended, the Texas White House (as his ranch home was called), the family cemetery, and his grave. The state park also contains the **Sauer-Beckmann Farm**, a living-history museum re-creating rural farm life in the early 1900s.

Details: *Sites open daily; Stonewall visitors center 8–5, Johnson City Center 8:45–5. Call for tour schedules. (2–3 hours)*

★★★ ADMIRAL NIMITZ MUSEUM AND HISTORICAL CENTER
304 E. Main St., Fredericksburg, 830/997-4379, nimitzm@ktc.com, www.tpwd.state.tx.us

HILL COUNTRY

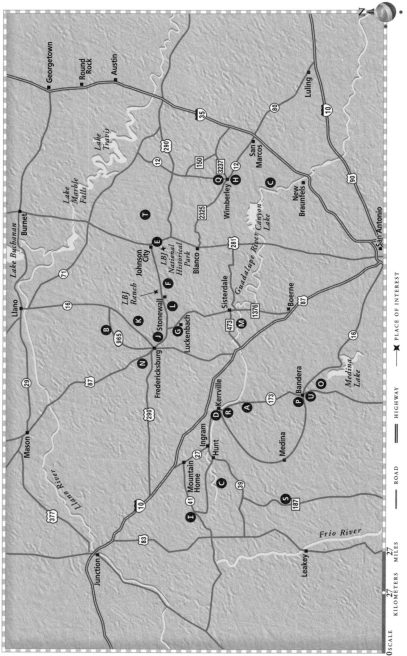

N

Georgetown

Round Rock

Austin

Luling

80

10

35

290

12

150

3237

Q

H

12

San Marcos

New Braunfels

C

90

Lake Travis

Lake Marble Falls

Lake Buchanan

Burnet

2325

T

Guadalupe River Canyon Lake

San Antonio

71

E

Johnson City

LBJ National Historical Park

Blanco

281

Sisterdale

Llano

16

LBJ Ranch

K

F

L

Stonewall

G

Luckenbach

473

M

1376

Boerne

87

B

965

J

Fredericksburg

N

16

29

87

Medina Lake

P

Bandera

O

290

Kerville

D

R

A

173

Mason

Llano River

Ingram

27

Hunt

Medina

10

Mountain Home

41

39

C

S

187

I

377

83

Frio River

Junction

Leakey

O SCALE   27
KILOMETERS   MILES

PLACE OF INTEREST

HIGHWAY

ROAD

On Main Street in Fredericksburg, this complex named for Fleet Admiral Chester A. Nimitz, who was born in this German town, salutes all who served in World War II. The restored Nimitz Steamboat Hotel chronicles early history of the town, the Nimitz family, the career of Admiral Nimitz, and the history of WWII in the Pacific. Other major components are the Plaza of Presidents, honoring 10 who served in WWII; the George Bush Gallery of the Pacific War, a developing exhibition; and the History Walk of the Pacific War, with aircraft, tanks, and guns displayed.

Details: Daily 8–5. $3 adults, $1.50 ages 6–12. (1–2 hours)

★★★ ENCHANTED ROCK STATE NATURAL AREA
On Rte. 965, 18 miles north of Fredericksburg, 915/247-3903, www.tpwd.state.tx.us

This unusual solid-granite mound, 500 feet high, was considered sacred by the Indians and today is revered by rock climbers. It's estimated to be one billion years old. In the last few years, the area has become so popular that at times visitation is limited to protect the environment. Call ahead for information on park regulations.

SIGHTS
Ⓐ Cowboy Artists of America Museum
Ⓑ Enchanted Rock State Natural Area
Ⓒ Floating the rivers
Ⓓ Hill Country Museum
Ⓔ Lyndon B. Johnson National Historical Park
Ⓕ Lyndon B. Johnson State Historical Park
Ⓖ Luckenbach
Ⓗ Wimberley
Ⓘ Y.O. Ranch

WINERIES
Ⓙ Becker Vineyards
Ⓚ Bell Mountain Vineyards

WINERIES *(continued)*
Ⓛ Grape Creek Vineyards
Ⓜ Sister Creek Vineyards

FOOD
Ⓓ Cowboy Steak House
Ⓗ Cypress Creek Café
Ⓓ Cypress Grill
Ⓝ Hilltop Cafe
Ⓓ Joe's Jefferson Street Café
Ⓓ Pampell's Antiques & Soda Fountain

LODGING
Ⓗ Blair House
Ⓝ Das Jager Haus
Ⓞ Flying L Guest Ranch

LODGING *(continued)*
Ⓓ Inn of the Hills River Resort
Ⓟ Mayan Ranch
Ⓗ Mountain View Motel
Ⓘ Y.O. Ranch

CAMPING
Ⓠ Blue Hole Recreation
Ⓓ Guadalupe River RV Resort
Ⓡ Kerrville-Schreiner State Park
Ⓢ Lost Maples State Natural Area
Ⓣ Pedernales Falls State Park
Ⓤ Skyline Ranch RV Park

Note: Items with the same letter are located in the same area.

Details: *Open year-round. $5/person, 13 and older. (30 minutes–2 hours)*

★★★ WINERIES

About a half-dozen wineries, within driving distance of each other, are open to visitors. Some are in historic buildings and retain an Old World feeling about the winemaking. Start at the **Fredericksburg Winery**, 247 W. Main Street, 830/990-8747, which has tours, tastings, and a gift store with all kinds of Texas food products.

Other wineries and vineyards in the area include **Becker Vineyards**, off U.S. 290 at Jenschke Lane 10 miles east of Fredericksburg, 800/946-9463; **Bell Mountain Vineyards**, 14 miles north of Fredericksburg on Route 16, 830/685-3297; **Grape Creek Vineyards**, on U.S. 290, four miles west of Stonewall, 800/950-7392; and **Sister Creek Vineyards**, on Route 1376 at Sisterdale (13 miles north of Boerne), 830/324-6704.

Details: *Call ahead for times and days for tours, tastings, and sales. (2–4 hours)*

★★ PIONEER MUSEUM COMPLEX
309 W. Main St., Fredericksburg, 830/997-2835, gchs@ktc.net, www.ktc.net/gchs

In Fredericksburg, the showpiece of this German village is a furnished eight-room stone home built in 1849 with kitchen and wine cellar. Property of the Gillespie County Historical Society, the complex also includes a blacksmith shop, log cabin, schoolhouse, smokehouse, and Sunday House—as the German farmers called the homes they built for coming to market and church over the weekends.

Details: *Mon–Sat 10–5, Sun 1–5. $3 ages 12 and older, under 12 free. (1 hour)*

★ WILDSEED FARMS MARKET CENTER
100 Legacy Dr., Fredericksburg, 830/990-1393, www.wildseedfarms.com

One of the largest working wildflower farms in the country, this spread on the edge of town has pathways through rows and rows of flowers in varying stages of growth (there's a picking area for bouquet-gathering), picnic areas, and a market center where you can buy seeds and other gifts.

Details: *On U.S. 290 about 7 miles east of Fredericksburg. Daily 9:30–6. Free. (2 hours)*

KERRVILLE AREA SIGHTSEEING HIGHLIGHTS

Located on the Guadalupe River, just off I-10 about an hour northwest of San Antonio, Kerrville is the largest city in the Hill Country, with about 25,000 population. A longtime popular summer resort area, it's an arts center with a ranching heritage.

★★★★ **COWBOY ARTISTS OF AMERICA MUSEUM**
1550 Rte. 173 South, Kerrville, 830/896-2553, webmaster@ caamuseum.com, www.caamuseum.com
From its scenic setting with views of the Hill Country to its unusual vaulted dome ceilings, this museum provides the perfect showcase for portrayals of cowboy and frontier life by living Western artists. Both rotating and permanent exhibits are on display.
Details: *Mon–Sat 9–5, Sun 1–5. $3 adults, $2.50 seniors, $1 ages 6–17. (1 ½ hours)*

★★★★ **Y.O. RANCH**
Off Rte. 41 southwest of Mountain Home, 800/YO-RANCH, gus@yoranch.com, www.yoranch.com
One of the legendary ranches of Texas, dating to the 1800s, the Y.O. sprawls across 40,000 acres where herds of cattle and native and exotic animals roam. On two-hour guided photo safaris, guests see longhorns, cowboys, zebras, giraffes, and antelope, and learn the history of the ranch. Lunch or dinner is included in the price. Do the morning or evening tour in summer; middays are hot. City slickers should ask about the annual Memorial Day weekend trail ride, complete with herding longhorns, eating off a chuck wagon, and bedding down on the range.
Details: *32 miles from Kerrville; tours year-round at 10 a.m., noon, and 4 p.m. Reservations are necessary. (3 hours)*

★★ **HILL COUNTRY MUSEUM**
226 Earl Garrett St., Kerrville, 830/896-8633
This castle-like stone mansion, built in 1879 and now nearly hidden by other buildings, shows the lifestyle of Kerrville's most prominent

settler—Captain Charles A. Schreiner, merchant, rancher, and Texas Ranger.

The museum also houses an eclectic collection, ranging from a mammoth tusk to the exquisite (and very expensive) beaded gowns worn by local socialites who served as duchesses in Fiesta San Antonio celebrations.

Details: *Mon–Sat 10–4:30 (usually closed for lunch). $3 adults, $1.50 ages 6–17. (30 minutes–1 hour)*

OTHER SIGHTSEEING HIGHLIGHTS

★★★★ WIMBERLEY
Chamber of Comerce, 512/847-2201,
www.wimberley-tx.com

This charming little town next to the Blanco River and Cypress Creek has a stop-and-browse collection of shops and galleries around the Village Square, where you will find art, crafts, and antiques. Market Day, the first Saturday of each month April through December, draws vendors from across the state and big crowds of bargain-hunters.

Details: *(1–2 hours)*

★★★ FLOATING THE GUADALUPE AND MEDINA RIVERS
Summer days are meant for canoeing or floating in an inner tube on one of the area's scenic rivers and streams, where rapids add some thrills and spills. Favorite places for tubing are around Hunt on the Guadalupe River and Bandera on the Medina River. Beware: The

rivers can be dangerous in certain places. Equipment can be rented (and advice obtained) from river outfitters.

Details: (2 hours minimum)

★★★ LUCKENBACH
On Rte. 1376 off U.S. 290 (turn at the KOA Campground), 830/997-3224, somebody@luckenbachtexas.com, www.luckenbachtexas.com.

Made famous by a country-western song, Luckenbach is a 10-acre tree-shaded spot off a back road with a couple of historic buildings. Once you find it, buy a Long Neck and poke around the old general store, where you'll likely encounter a few people pickin' guitars and singing in the back room. Mail a postcard from the post office in the store, see if the blacksmith shop is fired up, and check out the dance hall for evening action. That's the extent of the town. And don't go on Wednesdays—town's closed. It's liveliest for Willie Nelson's Fourth of July concert and other special events.

Details: About 10 miles southeast of Fredericksburg. The town is down a small road by South Grape Creek Bridge. (1 hour)

FITNESS AND RECREATION
In downtown Kerrville, **Louise Hays Park** on Thompson Drive, 830/257-7300, fronts the Guadalupe River, which forms a natural—and popular—swimming pool here. At **Riverside Nature Center & Arboretum**, 150 Lemos Street, Kerrville, 830/25-RIVER, a small farm converted into a sanctuary for native plants and wildlife has more than 90 species of Texas trees; it's open daily dawn to dusk.

Enchanted Rock State Natural Area, Route 965 north of Fredericksburg, 915/247-3903, has about five miles of trails and primitive camping. Horse lovers, hikers, backpackers, and all-terrain cyclists should check out **Hill Country State Natural Area**, Route 1077 off Route 173 south of Bandera, 830/796-4413, a former ranch turned equestrian park. It has 36 miles of multiuse trails, swimming, fishing, equestrian campsites, and primitive camping. Horse rentals are available at the many dude ranches in the area.

The **Fredericksburg Herb**

Wildlife Alert! Deer are plentiful in the Hill Country. Stay alert for the animals when you're driving, particularly at night.

Farm, 402 Whitney Street, 830/997-8615, long popular for its herbs and other organic products, now has a day spa for men and women, the Quiet Haus, offering aromatherapeutic massages and skin-care treatments.

FOOD

Beyond Old World German food, local fare includes steaks, barbecue, and New American cuisine. Most prices are in the $10 to $15 range but a few may run higher. Peach orchards and gardens yield yummy produce, often available from roadside stands in season.

Fredericksburg has a growing number of excellent restaurants. A well-established favorite, whose recipes are coveted statewide, is the **Peach Tree Tea Room**, 210 S. Adams Street, 830/997-9527, in a restored 1895 limestone home along with a deli and gift gallery. It's open for breakfast and lunch, and reservations are advised. The **Fredericksburg Herb Farm**, 402 Whitney Street, 830/997-8615, serves freshly prepared foods using herbs and produce from its gardens; it's open for lunch only and reservations are advised. In a contemporary decor, **Ernie's Mediterranean Grill**, 423 E. Main Street, 830/997-7478, branches out from pastas into fresh fish, pork tenderloin, and duck breast, prepared with Italian, French, and Spanish influences. A courtyard with a fountain leads into **Navajo Grill**, 209 E. Main Street, 830/990-8289, where Cajun and Southwestern touches add creative flair to the dishes, such as mashed potatoes with little crawfish. About 10 miles north of town on U.S. 87, an old gas station now houses the **Hilltop Cafe**, 830/997-8922, which draws raves for its regional dishes, often with Greek and Cajun flavors.

In Kerrville, the **Cowboy Steak House**, 416 Main Street, 830/896-5688, has mesquite-grilled meats complemented by a selection of more than 200 wines served in a ranch setting. You'll find an eclectic menu with fresh seafood, chicken-fried steak, and Southern cooking at **Joe's Jefferson Street Café**, 1001 Jefferson Street, 830/257-2929, located in a 100-year-old Victorian home with an outdoor patio. Slightly more upscale, **Cypress Grill**, 433 Water Street, 830/896-5577, a casual bistro in a historic limestone building, often has live music to accompany its dinners, which range from comfort foods to the exotic, such as venison and quail. At **Pampell's Antiques & Soda Fountain**, 701 Water Street, 830/257-8454, you can step up to an old-fashioned soda fountain and order ice-cream drinks.

In Wimberley, **Cypress Creek Café**, on the Village Square, 512/847-2515, is popular for breakfast and vegetarian dishes and is the hot spot with live entertainment on weekend evenings.

LODGING

The area around Fredericksburg has more than 200 bed-and-breakfasts, from country cottages to gingerbread Victorian homes and stone barns. While some are traditional bed-and-breakfasts, with a host/hostess who prepares breakfast in the home, many are guest houses that you have to yourself, where breakfast may be items left for you to prepare, or only tea and coffee, or brought to you by the hostess.

In Fredericksburg, **Gastehaus Schmidt** reservation service, 830/997-5612, gasthaus@ktc.net, www.ktc.net/GSchmidt, profiles more than 100 bed-and-breakfasts and guest houses in a booklet and will help you find the accommodation that meets your needs. It's the largest of four reservation services; others are **Bed & Breakfast of Fredericksburg**, 830/997-4712, **Be My Guest**, 830/997-7227, and **Hill Country Lodging & Reservation Service**, 800/745-3591. All are listed along with many individual motels, bed-and-breakfasts, guest houses, and other accommodations in the visitors guide brochure available from the convention and visitor bureau, 830/997-6523.

Here are a couple of choices in the area: **Das Jager Haus**, about eight miles north of Fredericksburg off U.S. 87, 830/997-5612, is a rustic two-story cabin in the country where you're likely to see deer, turkey, and armadillos. Furnished with antiques and collectibles, it has a living area with fireplace, loft bedroom, sun room with Jacuzzi for two, and a deck. Rates are about $100 a night; coffee/tea provided. The **Corner Cottage & Garden Room B&B**, about three blocks from Main Street in Fredericksburg, 830/997-5612, has two private suites, each with a fireplace and one with a Jacuzzi for two; a full gourmet breakfast is served. Rates start around $85.

In the Kerrville area, families have been gathering for years at **Inn of the Hills River Resort**, 1001 Route 27 West (often called the Junction Highway), 800/292-5690. The resort has four pools, a garden courtyard, playground, and some rooms overlooking the Guadalupe River; rates start at $65. For authentic ranch accommodations, hang your hat at the famed **Y.O. Ranch**, Mountain Home, 800/YO-RANCH, which has rustic (though modernized) cabins and a swimming pool. Rates start at $85 per person, $50 for ages 15 and under, including three meals. The ranch is northwest of Kerrville, off Route 41 outside Mountain Home.

City slickers who want to saddle up and bunk down on a dude ranch can do it around Bandera, which has a dozen or more guest ranches, some working spreads and others upscale resorts. The **Bandera Convention & Visitors Bureau**, 800/364-3833, bandera@hctc.net, www.tourtexas.com/bandera, provides a guide to the guest ranches. Here are a couple: **Flying L Guest**

Ranch, outside Bandera off Route 173 south, 800/292-5134, a resort-ranch with 41 suites, has everything from horseback riding and hayrides to a golf course and swimming. **Mayan Ranch**, on the Medina River outside Bandera off Route 16, 830/796-3312, has cowboy breakfasts and steak frys in addition to dining-room meals, horseback riding, and swimming. Rates are usually $90 to $105 a day per person and include two or three meals.

Wimberley also has a number of bed-and-breakfasts, from luxury to rustic. **Blair House**, 100 Spoke Inn, Wimberley, 800/460-3909, is an elegant, sybaritic retreat with spa services to complement its luxurious rooms in a stone ranch-style home and two separate cottages. All rooms have private baths and TV/VCRs; some have whirlpools and/or open onto porches or decks. Rates are about $135, including a gourmet breakfast and evening dessert and wine. For those on a lower budget, the **Mountain View Motel**, Route 12 south of Wimberley, 512/847-2992, overlooks the Blanco River Valley and offers a swimming pool and nature trail with native plants and even an allosaurus footprint. Rooms start at $55 with continental breakfast. For information on area accommodations, contact **Wimberley Lodging Reservation Service**, 800/460-3909; **Texas Hill Country Retreats**, 800/236-9411; **Country Innkeepers**, 800/230-0805; or **Hill Country Accommodations**, 800/926-5028.

CAMPING

Kerrville-Schreiner State Park, 2385 Bandera Highway (Route 173 south of Kerrville), 830/257-5392, on the Guadalupe River has swimming, fishing, boating, rest rooms with showers, tent camping, and hookups. **Lost Maples State Natural Area**, five miles north of Vanderpool on Route 187 southwest of Kerrville, 830/966-3413, has rugged canyons, clear streams and springs, and beautiful fall foliage, as well as campsites with water and electricity. **Pedernales Falls State Park**, eight miles east of Johnson City on Route 2766, 830/868-7304, is a scenic preserve with waterfalls, wildlife, fishing, swimming, hiking, nature study, and campsites.

Guadalupe River RV Resort, 2605 Route 27, west from Kerrville, 800/582-1916, has two pools, a clubhouse, spa, hookups, and cottages on the river. There are numerous RV parks and campgrounds around Bandera, including several on Medina River and Medina Lake. Among them are **Skyline Ranch RV Park**, west of Bandera on Route 16, 830/796-4958, a Good Sam park by the river. At Wimberley, **Blue Hole Recreation**, about a mile northeast of town off Route 3237, 512/847-9127, has camping, picnic sites and a natural swimming hole on Cypress Creek.

NIGHTLIFE AND SPECIAL EVENTS

Learn to do the Texas two-step and the Cotton-Eyed Joe at dance halls where toe-tappin' country-western music goes until the wee hours, particularly on weekends. You'll find dance halls scattered about the area but particularly along Bandera's Main Street, where there's usually action every night except Monday and Tuesday. Among popular spots in Bandera are the **Silver Dollar**, 308 Main Street, 210/796-8826, and **Cabaret Dance Hall**, 801 Main Street, 210/460-3095. You're usually welcome to bring your own guitar and pick away. In Kerrville, there's live country-western music nightly except Sunday at the **Inn Pub**, in Inn of the Hills Resort, 1001 Route 27 West, 830/895-5000. Outside Fredericksburg, **Luckenbach Dance Hall** frequently has live entertainment; for schedules call 830/997-3224.

Summer brings calf-roping and bull-riding at rodeos, usually twice weekly from Memorial Day weekend through Labor Day weekend at Bandera. For details, call the Bandera County Convention & Visitors Bureau, 800/364-3833.

Plays and musicals are produced under the stars during summer at **Hill Country Arts Foundation Point Theatre**, a 722-seat outdoor amphitheater on the banks of the Guadalupe River at Ingram, about six miles west of Kerrville on Route 27. The center for performing and visual arts also has indoor productions during the year. For a schedule, contact the foundation during weekday business hours, 830/367-5121.

The area hosts numerous festivals. Among the most popular: **Kerrville Folk Festival**, 830/257-3600, with 18 days of musical events starting the Thursday before Memorial Day; **Texas State Arts & Crafts Fair** in Kerrville, 830/896-5711, with the juried work of 200 of the state's best artists and crafts demonstrations, Friday through Monday on Memorial Day weekend. Fredericksburg has more than 50 annual events, including its **Night in Old Fredericksburg Festival** in July, **Oktoberfest** and the **Fredericksburg Food & Wine Fest** in October, and the **Weihnachten in Fredericksburg**, a Christmas market and festival in December. For information, contact the **Fredericksburg Convention & Visitor Bureau**, 830/997-6523. See Wimberley entry (under Other Sightseeing Highlights) for information about its monthly Market Days.

SHOPPING

Arts, crafts, and antiques shops abound in the Hill Country. The small town of Fredericksburg has more than 100 antiques and specialty shops for everything from jewelry to jams, both locally made. Among the options: **Jeep Collins Jewelrymaker**, 148 E. Main Street, has nice designs of handcrafted work (and a workshop open to visitors). The **Fredericksburg Herb Farm**, 241 E. Main Street and 402 Whitney Street, has herbs and spa items, and the **Peach Tree Gift Gallery & Tea Room**, 210 S. Adams Street, has country crafts and collectibles. The **Hill Country Music Shop**, 155 E. Main Street, has guitars, harps, handcrafted dulcimers and other instruments. Among more than a dozen antiques stores, the **Antique Mall of Fredericksburg**, 1102 E. Main Street, has about 30 dealers.

Gallery browsing and antiquing are good in Wimberley and around Kerrville. In Wimberley, **Annette's Country Store** has American country antiques and vintage linens, while **Sable V Fine Art Gallery** has glass sculpture and paintings, and **Teeks Gallery** specializes in art by women; all are located on the town square. **Wimberley Glass Works**, 111 Spoke Hill Drive, has a workshop and gallery, and **Billie Bob's Knob**, 2 miles north on Route 12, has fashions and gifts.

Antique shops are located along Route 27 from Comfort through Kerrville to Hunt, on Routes 16 and 173 around Kerrville, and in Kerrville along the 700 and 800 blocks of Water Street. Among your options are **Water Street Antique Company**, 820 Water Street, and **Old Republic Square** with 10 shops, 219–225 Main Street. Jewelry lovers shouldn't miss the **James Avery Craftsman Shop and Visitor Center**, 3.5 miles north of Kerrville on Harper Road (Route 783), 830/895-1122. The designer's beautiful silver and gold works range from small, affordable charms to expensive master-pieces. The shop is open Monday through Saturday from 9 to 5:30.

Hill Country Back Roads

Nearly any highway or back road in the Hill Country yields scenic views of canyons, hills, and valleys with spring-fed rivers. The area is particularly colorful from spring through summer when wildflowers splash the hills with a changing rainbow of colors.

From Kerrville, go east on Route 27 along the Guadalupe River, take Route 473 to Route 32, and turn southeast. Known as the **Devil's Backbone**, Route 32 dips, climbs, and winds along the edge of the Blanco River Valley. At Route 12, turn north through Wimberley, then head west on U.S. 290 by the Pedernales River and **LBJ Ranch** into Fredericksburg. Take Route 16 back to Kerrville.

Another option from Kerrville: south on Route 173 to Bandera, northwest on Route 16 to Medina, west on Route 337 to Leakey (pronounced LAY-key), north on U.S. 83 to Route 41, northeast to **Mountain Home**, and Route 27 back to Kerrville. Or, from Route 337, turn north at Vanderpool onto Route 187 and go by **Lost Maples State Natural Area** to Route 39, then go northeast to Kerrville.

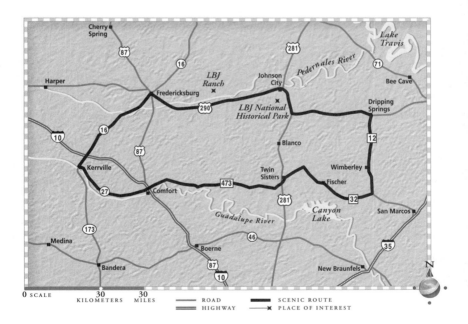

6
NEW BRAUNFELS

For generations, Texas families have packed up their cars and headed to New Braunfels to play in its clear cool rivers each summer. And they return by the thousands in late fall to raise a few steins of beer and dance to oompah music at Wurstfest, the town's annual celebration of its German heritage.

Located in central Texas, about 50 miles southwest of Austin and 30 miles northeast of San Antonio, this recreational playground sits on the tree-shaded Comal and Guadalupe Rivers on the edge of the Hill Country, where green vistas begin to give way to the desert and plains of West Texas. Both rivers are prime floating territory, with some small rapids to add a few thrills and spills.

In 1844 Prince Carl of Solms-Braunfels came to Texas seeking a suitable spot for Germans to settle; in 1845 he founded the town and brought in 6,000 immigrants, many of them artisans, craftsmen, and businessmen. Even today, the charming town of about 30,000 retains a strong German flavor, with fun *biergartens*, traditional *fachwerk* (half timber, half masonry) buildings, and numerous businesses with German names. You're likely to hear more German than just "*Willkommen*" spoken here.

A PERFECT DAY IN NEW BRAUNFELS

Stop by Naegelin's Bakery downtown to pick up fresh *kolaches* (German rolls and pastries with a variety of fillings) and other goodies for breakfast, then

DOWNTOWN NEW BRAUNFELS

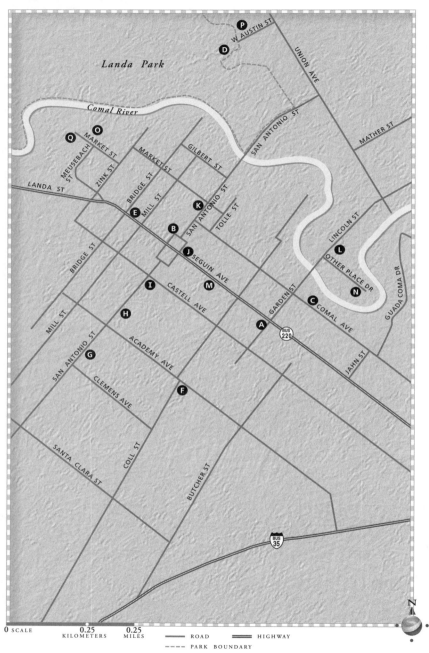

stroll around the nearby Main Plaza and adjacent streets to see historic buildings and visit the Hummel Museum. Spend the afternoon floating on the Comal or Guadalupe River (or at the Schlitterbahn if you want more action), have dinner at the Huisache Grill, and end the day browsing around historic Gruene with a spin on the dance floor at Gruene Hall.

SIGHTSEEING HIGHLIGHTS

★★★★ COMAL AND GUADALUPE RIVERS

Summer is synonymous with tubing on the Comal and Guadalupe Rivers. For the uninitiated, tubing means plopping in an inner tube and floating down the river, preferably towing an ice chest with drinks in another tube. Friends enjoy linking tubes in a chain, each person hooking their toes under the tube in front of them. The Comal River, which flows from the state's largest springs at New Braunfels' **Landa Park**, is only 2.5 miles long before it joins the Guadalupe River in town. There are several access points to the Comal River, some charging $1; tube rentals are widely available. Entering the upper part of the Comal around Ole Mill Stream and floating to the last exit at Union Avenue takes about 2¹/₂ hours; shuttles will return you upstream. For the most part, it's a lazy, gentle float, though there are a few rapids and the popular—and often crowded—Tube Chute around a small dam. Shaded by huge old oak trees, **Landa Park**, off Landa Street northwest of the Main Plaza, 830/608-2160, is a municipal oasis, with swimming pools, golf

---

SIGHTS

Ⓐ Chamber of
    Commerce/Visitors
    Center
Ⓑ Hummel Museum
Ⓒ Lindheimer Home
Ⓓ Schlitterbahn
Ⓔ Sophienburg Archives
Ⓕ Sophienburg Museum
Ⓖ Wagenfuehr Home
    and Buckhorn Barber
    Shop

FOOD

Ⓗ Huisache Grill
Ⓘ Krause's Café
Ⓙ Naegelin's Bakery
Ⓚ Wolfgang's Keller
    Restaurant

LODGING

Ⓛ Camp Warnecke
    Estates
Ⓜ Hotel Faust

LODGING (continued)

Ⓝ The Other Place
Ⓚ Prince Solms Inn
Ⓞ River Run
    Condominiums
Ⓟ Schlitterbahn Resorts

CAMPING

Ⓠ Landa RV Park and
    Campground

Note: Items with the same letter are located in the same area.

---

course, picnic areas, miniature train, and miniature golf, and a lake with paddleboats and glass-bottom boats.

More action awaits tubers, rafters, canoeists, and kayakers in the **Guadalupe River Scenic Area** between Canyon Lake and New Braunfels. You'll shoot some rapids and waterfalls and encounter some potentially dangerous spots on this wider river. Many people float the Guadalupe in larger rafts that carry a half-dozen or so people. A popular put-in point is the first crossing, north of Gruene, though you can get in closer to Canyon Dam about 20 miles upstream. It's wise to use a river outfitter who can provide equipment, advice, and usually shuttle service. Wear life preservers!

Details: Several outfitters are located at Gruene and along the river road toward Canyon Dam. Around $12/day for tubing; $18/day for rafting. (3–8 hours)

★★★★ **HISTORIC GRUENE**
Off N. Loop 337, 830/629-5077, www.gruene.net
To the north along the Guadalupe River, the one-time ghost town of Gruene (pronounced "green") bustles with renewed life. Now a part of New Braunfels, it retains a unique identity as a little country town mixing a German heritage with the flavor of the Old West. The entire community, founded as a cotton-growing area in 1872, is on the National Register of Historic Places. **Gruene Hall**, a honky-tonk saloon and dance hall dating to the late 1800s, still draws a steady crowd (see Nightlife and Special Events). An old cotton gin has become the **Gristmill Restaurant and Bar**, and an 1878 mercantile store is now a general store with a soda fountain, Texas gifts, and walls decorated with nostalgic ads. Other historic buildings house working potters, furniture makers, and specialty shops, with an emphasis on Texas products including area wines. Frequent arts and crafts festivals and market days draw many weekend visitors.

Details: Old Gruene Rd. on northern edge of New Braunfels. (2–3 hours)

★★★★ **HISTORIC NEW BRAUNFELS**
Chamber of Commerce/Visitor Center, 390 S. Seguin St.
830/629-2943, nbcc@nbcham.org, www.nbcham.org
Many of the town's early homes and buildings have been preserved and are in use today. A brief walking tour downtown will take you past original structures, some dating to the mid-1800s and others of varying

Victorian styles from the turn of the century to the 1920s. From the New Braunfels Chamber of Commerce/Visitor Center, or at sights throughout town, pick up a downtown walking tour brochure. A good route: Start at the visitor center and follow Seguin Street to the Main Plaza; circle it, and explore San Antonio Street in both directions. Stop at New Braunfels Coffee on the Main Plaza for refreshments.

Only a few historic homes are open. The **Lindheimer Home**, 491 Comal Street, built in 1852, has many original furnishings and shows the German *fachwerk* construction using native limestone and cedar. Closer to downtown are the **Wagenfuehr Home and Buckhorn Barber Shop**, 521 W. San Antonio Street.

Details: *Homes open Memorial Day–Aug 31 2–5 every day but Wed; rest of year same hours but weekends only. Open daily during Wurstfest. $1.50 adults, 50¢ ages 6–17 for the Lindheimer Home and Wagenfuehr Home and Buckhorn Barber Shop. (2 hours)*

★★★★ SCHLITTERBAHN
305 W. Austin St., 830/625-2351, fun@schlitterbahn.com, www.schlitterbahn.com

With water, water everywhere, from tyke-safe playgrounds to

SCHLITTERBAHN

Schlitterbahn

NEW BRAUNFELS

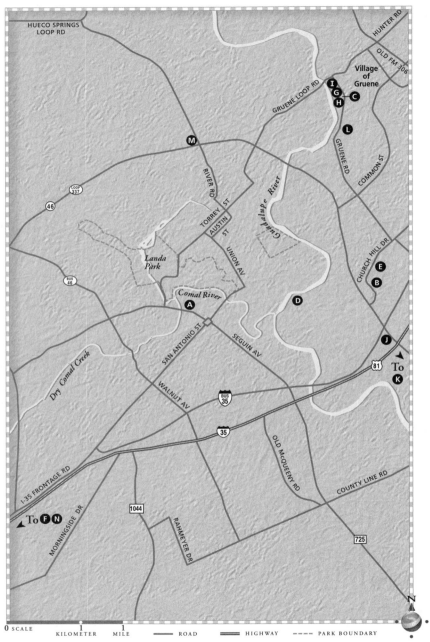

teenage-thriller tube chutes and uphill water coasters, this 65-acre amusement park is one "cool dude" and is repeatedly voted tops by amusement-park fans. In keeping with the town's German heritage, the park was named Schlitterbahn, meaning "slippery road," and its landmark 60-foot castle tower replicates a guard tower at the Solms Castle in Braunfels, Germany. The park has six "Wet Worlds" and 40 attractions, including water slides, lazy streams, and raging rivers. An innovator in park rides, it has three uphill water roller coasters, including a six-story, 1,000-foot-long "Master Blaster," said to be the tallest and steepest in the world. Children's life jackets are provided free. Note: The park gets quite crowded some summer days. Be sure to take sunscreen.

Details: Mid-May–mid-Aug daily 10–6; late Apr–mid-May and mid-Aug–mid-Sep weekends 10–6, hours sometimes extended to 8. $23.99 ages 12 and up, $19.99 ages 3–11, under 3 free; midday admission and multiday passes at reduced prices. One price covers all attractions. (4–6 hours)

★★★ HUMMEL MUSEUM
199 Main Plaza, 800/456-4866
http://bigmac.bullcreek.austin.tx.us/hummel/index.htm
You don't have to be a collector of these fetching little figurines to enjoy this museum, which nicely showcases the original art of Sister M. I. Hummel, the German nun whose paintings of children inspired the making of the statuettes. The collection includes more than 300 works of art, displayed on a rotating basis, plus Hummel figurines. The art belongs to a family in Switzerland and was brought here by

SIGHTS
Ⓐ Comal River
Ⓑ Conservation Plaza
Ⓒ Gruene Hall
Ⓓ Guadalupe River
Ⓔ Museum of Handmade Furniture
Ⓕ Natural Bridge Caverns

FOOD
Ⓖ Gristmill Restaurant and Bar
Ⓗ Gruene Mansion Inn
Ⓘ Guadalupe Smoked Meat Co.
Ⓙ New Braunfels Smokehouse
Ⓚ Oma's Haus Restaurant

LODGING
Ⓛ Gruene Country Homestead Inn
Ⓗ Gruene Mansion Inn
Ⓜ Oak Hill Estate

CAMPING
Ⓝ Hill Country RV Resort

Note: Items with the same letter are located in the same area.

New Braunfels resident Sieglinde Schoen Smith, whose family lived near the convent where Sister Hummel worked. As a child, she was a model for some of Sister Hummel's paintings.

Details: Mon–Sat 10– 5, Sun noon–5. $5 adults, $4.50 seniors, $3 students, under 5 free. (1–1 1/2 hours)

★★★ MUSEUM OF HANDMADE FURNITURE
1370 Church Hill Dr., 830/629-6504

This unique museum houses more than 75 original pieces of hand-crafted furniture from the mid-1800s and a collection of home accessories in Breustedt Haus, a historic landmark built in 1858. Tours also include a furnished log cabin and a barn with workshop.

Details: Jan–Feb and Sep–Oct Sat and Sun 1–4; Mar–May Wed–Sun 1–4; Jun–Aug Tue–Sat 10–4, Sun 1–4; during Wurstfest daily 10–4; closed mid-Nov–Dec. $5 adults, $4 seniors, $1 ages 6–12. (1 hour)

★★★ NATURAL BRIDGE CAVERNS
26495 Natural Bridge Caverns Rd., 210/651-6101, nabrcavern@aol.com, www.naturalbridgetexas.com /caverns

When the summer temperatures soar, retreat to this underground wonderland where it's always about 70 degrees (and damp). Designated a U.S. Natural Landmark, the caverns, about 17 miles southwest of New Braunfels, extend like a maze for about a mile. A paved walkway (wear comfortable, nonslippery shoes) leads visitors past colorful formations of stalactites and stalagmites in underground chambers sometimes as large as a football field. The cave is named for the natural limestone bridge at the entrance.

Details: From New Braunfels, take I-35 south, then go northwest on Hwy. 3009; Memorial Day–Labor Day daily 9–6, rest of year daily 9–4, with tours leaving about every 30 minutes. $9 adults, $8 seniors, $6 ages 4–12. (2 hours)

★★ CONSERVATION PLAZA
1300 Church Hill Dr., 830/629-2943

On the north edge of town, off Loop 337 west of I-35, an 1850s German village has been created with historic buildings brought from the area. They include a farmhouse and barn, cabinetry shop, school, music studio, and a restored two-story home with period furnishings. The plaza is owned by the New Braunfels Conservation Society.

Details: Tue–Fri 10–3, Sat and Sun 2–5. $2 adults, 50¢ ages 6–17. (1 hour)

★ **SOPHIENBURG MUSEUM & ARCHIVES**
401 W. Coll St. (museum), and 200 N. Seguin St. (archives), 830/629-1900, gertxhst@sat.net, www.nbtx.com/ sophienburg
Through pictures, maps, and artifacts, the museum chronicles the history of German settlers in the area. The archives include an extensive collection of records dating back to the early settlers.
Details: Museum: Mon–Sat 10–5, Sun 1–5; archives: Mon–Fri 10–4. Museum: $1.50 adults, 50¢ students; archives: $2.50 adults, $1 students. (1 hour)

FITNESS AND RECREATION
Canyon Lake, about 20 miles north of New Braunfels, is a scenic sailing, boating, swimming, skiing, and fishing escape, its blue water extending like fingers into steep canyons. Formed by a dam on the Guadalupe River, the lake yields good catches of catfish and bass, while the Guadalupe River below has trout. **Canyon Lake Marina**, 830/935-4333, has services at Canyon Park on the north side of the lake, and **Cranes Mill Marina**, 830/899-7718, is on the south side at Cranes Mill Park. The **Corps of Engineers**, 830/964-3341, has seven parks around the shoreline. For more information, call the **Canyon Lake Chamber of Commerce**, 800/528-2104.

FOOD
German foods—sausages, sauerbraten, Wiener schnitzel—and smoked meats have always been top choices here, but you'll also find Texas fare such as chicken-fried steak and New American cuisine. Prices are amazingly low, with most dinners running less than $12.
    The Santa Fe–style **Huisache Grill**, 303 W. San Antonio Street, 830/620-9001, is a pleasant retreat serving excellent New American cooking complemented with a nice wine list (including by-the-glass choices). Its chicken tortilla soup is slightly spicy and, as it should be, filled with goodies, including avocados. The popular grilled pork tenderloin comes charbroiled with a rum-apple sauce on the side and fresh grilled vegetables. For the most upscale night out, **Wolfgang's Keller Restaurant** in the historic Prince Solms Inn, 295 E. San Antonio Street, 800/625-9169, is the place, serving continental cuisine in an

elegant, slightly formal setting. It has German specialties such as *rouladen*, a variety of schnitzel choices and wursts, grilled fish, and steaks, with entrées costing $14 to $20.

Traditional family favorites for German dishes (American home cooking also served) are **Oma's Haus Restaurant**, 541 Highway 46, (just east of I-35), 830/625-3280, and **Krause's Café**, 148 S. Castell Street, 830/625-7581.

Feast on barbecued beef brisket and sausage and all kinds of smoked meats at **New Braunfels Smokehouse**, 140 Highway 46 South (just west of I-35), 830/625-2416, which has indoor and outdoor dining. Amid trees overlooking the Guadalupe River in Gruene, barbecue lovers will find good baby-back ribs, brisket, sausage, and chicken, plus all the side dishes, at the **Guadalupe Smoked Meat Co.**, 1299 Gruene Road, 830/629-6121.

Also in Gruene, the **Gristmill Restaurant and Bar**, 1287 Gruene Road, 830/625-0684, located in a restored cotton gin, provides a fun evening and a variety of fare from barbecue and Tex-Mex to grilled fish and steaks. Eat inside or outside under the trees overlooking the Guadalupe River. For those who want a more elegant setting and upscale dining, nearby is **Gruene Mansion Inn**, 1275 Gruene Road, 830/620-0760.

Don't miss one of the town's specialties—German bakeries, which turn out fresh *kolaches*, pastries, and breads daily. Stop by **Naegelin's Bakery**, 129 S. Seguin Avenue, 830/625-5722, the state's oldest, in business since 1868.

LODGING

From historic hotels to elegant bed-and-breakfasts, condominiums, and rustic cabins, New Braunfels meets a variety of vacationers' needs in lodging. Many places have lower rates during the week than on weekends and offer off-season bargains in winter.

Two charming older hotels are located downtown. A small garden with a fountain welcomes guests to the **Hotel Faust**, 240 S. Seguin Street, 830/625-7791, where a 1929 Model A Ford sits in the large lobby. The 62-room hotel, built in 1929, is furnished in styles from that period. Starting rates are $39 to $69. A historic landmark dating to 1898, **Prince Solms Inn**, 295 E. San Antonio Street, 800/625-9169, has a warm, romantic ambiance with antique furnishings. The eight rooms and two suites are individually decorated; rates start around $80 including breakfast.

Schlitterbahn Resorts, 305 W. Austin Street, 830/625-2351, has a variety of accommodations, including cottages, motel rooms, apartments, and condos at various sites on the grounds of its extensive water park. Many of the lodgings have kitchenettes, and easy access to the water park and Comal

---

River is an added benefit. Rates start at about $60. **River Run
Condominiums**, 500 N. Market Street, 830/629-0077, has 63 one- and
two-bedroom fully furnished accommodations amid trees along the upper
part of the Comal River; rates are $65 to $165. Lower on the Comal, **The
Other Place**, 385 Other Place Drive, 830/625-5114, has family-friendly cabins amid tree-shaded grounds, starting at $100.

You can get information and make reservations at approximately 120 condos, cottages and homes in the area through the **New Braunfels Resort
Accommodations**, 405 S. Seguin Street, 800/990-4FUN, resort@nbtx.com,
www.newbraunfels.com/resort. Among its selections: **Camp Warnecke
Estates**, 371 W. Lincoln Street, by the Comal, has fully furnished condos with
one to three bedrooms at rates of $145 to $225.

Among the many bed-and-breakfasts, **Gruene Country Homestead
Inn**, 832 Gruene Road, 800/238-5534, puts guests into historic buildings that
date to the 1840s and are decorated with antiques and country furnishings.
Most rooms have porches; rates start at $95, including breakfast. A Texas
Historic Landmark and once a cotton plantation, **Gruene Mansion Inn**,
1275 Gruene Road, 830/629-2641, sits by the Guadalupe River, offering
cottages and rooms in Victorian rustic 1870s style. Rates start at $85, with
breakfast optional at an extra $5 per person. On 10 acres of ranch land at the
edge of town, **Oak Hill Estate**, 1355 River Road, 800/774-3170, provides
an elegant retreat in a 6,000-square-foot home and a separate rock cottage.
Three guest rooms each have private baths and access the veranda, while the
cottage has two bedrooms. Rates start at $60 including full breakfast.

For information on bed-and-breakfasts in the area, check the **New
Braunfels Bed & Breakfast Association** Web site, www.texasbedand
breakfast.com or call the **Greater New Braunfels Chamber of
Commerce**, 800/572-2626 or 830/625-2385, which offers a brochure describing a number of bed-and-breakfasts.

CAMPING

Hill Country RV Resort, 131 Ruekle Road, 830/625-1919, has more than 200 sites with hookups, activity buildings, an indoor pool, sauna, hot tub, convenience store, and more. **Landa RV Park and Campground**, 565 N. Market Street, 800/281-1219, has about 100 sites, from tent camping to full hookups, close to the Comal River. Other camping is available at nearby Canyon Lake.

NIGHTLIFE AND SPECIAL EVENTS

Kick up your heels at the state's oldest beer hall and dance spot, **Gruene Hall**, 1281 Gruene Road, 830/606-1281, on the north edge of New Braunfels. This large, open-air hall and outdoor garden has been a watering hole since the late 1870s and in the last 20 years has drawn such big-name entertainers as George Strait, Lyle Lovett, and Jerry Jeff Walker. It's a genuine historic honky-tonk that looks like it ought to be in movies—and indeed has served as the setting for commercials. It's open daily, usually from 11 a.m. to 9 p.m., until midnight or later Thursday through Saturday, with live music most evenings in summer and on weekends the rest of the year, and also special concerts.

The strong German heritage of the New Braunfels area is apparent in its numerous *biergartens*, where the customers tap their feet to oompah music and dance the polka. Following the European tradition, children are welcome, and you'll often see parents and grandparents teaching little tykes how to dance. Among the lively spots are **Bavarian Village Restaurant and Biergarten**, 212 W. Austin Street, 830/625-0815, and **Oma's Haus Restaurant and Biergarten**, 541 Highway 46 (just east of I-35), 830/625-3280.

New Braunfels also joins in the German tradition of saluting the sausage (accompanied by a good deal of beer) each fall at a **Wurstfest** celebration, 800/221-4369, that draws more than 150,000 merrymakers from all over the country and abroad. The 10-day event takes place in the huge Wursthalle and Marketplatz at Landa Park, with live entertainment, polka dancing, and food, beverage, and souvenir booths. Revelers dance until the wee hours. Wurstfest always starts the Friday before the first Monday in November.

SHOPPING

Bargain-hunters can shop until they drop in this area, which has one of the state's largest concentrations of outlet stores. The **New Braunfels Factory**

Stores, on I-35 at Exit 188, 88/SHOP-333, has about 30 shops including such brand names as Bass, Van Heusen, Easy Spirit, and West Point Pepperell linens. About 16 miles northeast, San Marcos has two major centers, **Prime Outlets**, 3939 I-35, 800/628-9465, and **Tanger Outlet Center**, 4015 I-35, 800/408-8424; both are at Exit 200. Among about 115 shops at Prime Outlets are such brands as Anne Klein, Ann Taylor, Carole Little, Dana Buchman, Donna Karan, and Coach leather goods. Among about 50 shops at Tanger Outlet Center are such names as Liz Claiborne, Disney, Nautica, and Tommy Hilfiger.

River Road

Buy some fresh bread, meats, and cheeses from a smokehouse, pick up a vintage bottle from Texas Wines in Gruene, and head off for a picnic along one of the state's prettiest short drives—north from New Braunfels off Loop 337. Called the **River Road**, it twists and turns with the Guadalupe River for about 15 miles to Sattler, just below Canyon Dam.

The emerald river, with occasional churning rapids, flows through narrow valleys at times, then beneath limestone bluffs. Cypress trees hang over the banks. The road crosses the river four times on low bridges and often winds through a cathedral of trees. From riverside picnic areas, you can watch a parade of people rafting, canoeing, and tubing down the river. Anglers cast for rainbow trout and other catches. In the early morning or late evening, you may see deer enjoying the scenery with you.

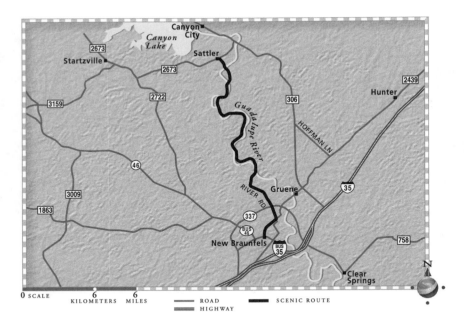

7
SAN ANTONIO

In San Antonio, Spanish, Mexican, and early Texan history blend into one fun city with character, gusto, and foreign intrigue. With nearly 300 years as a cultural crossroads, the city has a colorful past and takes every opportunity to celebrate it.

Located in south-central Texas, the city was founded in 1718 when the Spanish built a series of missions here, including one now known as the Alamo. It was etched in history in 1836 when a small band of Texans lost their lives trying to defend it against a Mexican army of thousands. The Alamo still stands, now smack-dab in the middle of the city, dwarfed by twentieth-century buildings.

Downtown San Antonio retains an Old World feeling, with narrow streets, plazas, and Spanish architecture blending with modern skyscrapers. The heart of the city is the River Walk, a European-style promenade below street level winding about three miles along the San Antonio River. Lush landscaping and night lighting give the River Walk a romantic air, enhanced by Venetian-style taxis cruising the river.

The eighth-largest U.S. city (with a population of 1.06 million) and one of the nation's most popular vacation destinations, San Antonio mixes the past with such crowd-pleasing present-day attractions as Sea World and Six Flags Fiesta Texas.

¡Olé!

A PERFECT DAY IN SAN ANTONIO

Start on the Mission Trail, visiting Mission San José and Mission Concepción. Head to Brackenridge Park to experience the hands-on Witte Museum, then go downtown to the Institute of Texan Cultures. End your formal touring with the Alamo, then relax on a boat ride through downtown on the San Antonio River. Afterward stroll along the River Walk and choose from among its many restaurants for dinner. Families might prefer to visit the Alamo, River Walk, and Witte Museum and then go to Sea World or Six Flags Fiesta Texas for the late afternoon and evening.

ORIENTATION

Many of the attractions are in the downtown area, some within walking distance of each other and others easily accessible by the city's VIA motorized streetcars, reproductions of old ones that once served San Antonio. When touring the Alamo and HemisFair areas, Market Square, and the King William District, use the streetcars, which run on four tourist routes. The fare is 50¢; call VIA, 210/362-2020, for information. Downtown streets are narrow and winding, and parking is a problem; so it's wise to use the transit system to get from one area to another.

While bus routes or trolley tours do serve other sights, it's useful to have a car. Several sights are slightly northeast of downtown, around Brackenridge Park. The Mission Trail goes southeast from downtown, and a 12-mile hike-and-bike trail is being developed to link the Alamo downtown with the other missions.

DOWNTOWN AREA SIGHTSEEING HIGHLIGHTS

★★★★ THE ALAMO
300 Alamo Plaza, 210/225-1391, www.TheAlamo.org
The state's best-known landmark, the Alamo is considered the cradle of Texas liberty. Originally called Mission San Antonio de Valero, it was the first of five missions established here by the Spaniards starting in 1718. It was renamed and fortified by the Mexicans, then put into the history books in 1836 when 189 Texas patriots—including the legendary Davy Crockett—fought to their deaths for the freedom of Texas against an army of 4,000 Mexican troops. "Remember the Alamo" became a battle cry six weeks later as a group of ragtag Texans surprised and defeated the Mexican army outside Houston.

The small but striking Texas shrine in the midst of downtown has a chapel, a museum, and a documentary film.

The battle of the Alamo comes to life at two nearby theaters. Across from the Alamo, the **Texas Adventure**, 307 Alamo Plaza, 210/227-8224, www.tx-adventure.com, uses 3-D ghosts to tell the story of the battle in a 30-minute special-effects film. At the **Rivercenter Mall IMAX Theatre**, 849 E. Commerce Street, 210/225-6517, www.imax-sa.com, the 13-day siege comes to life in an award-winning docudrama on the six-story screen.

Details: Alamo: Memorial Day–Labor Day Mon–Sat 9–6:30, Sun 10–6:30; rest of year until 5:30. Donation requested. Texas Adventure: Sun–Thu 10–5, Fri and Sat 10–8. $7.50 adults, $5.90 seniors, $4.50 ages 3–11. IMAX Theatre: shows six times daily, call for schedule. $7.25 adults, $6.75 seniors, $4.75 ages 3–11 (1 1/2–2 hours)

★★★★ INSTITUTE OF TEXAN CULTURES
801 S. Bowie St., 210/458-2300,
www.texancultures.utsa.edu

Located in HemisFair Park, this museum looks more at the people than the events that shaped the state, exploring the customs and lifestyles of more than two dozen ethnic groups who've played a role in history here. Check out the history and faces of Texas on a colorful multimedia show in the dome. While at the park, you can take glass elevators to the top of the 750-foot-high **Tower of the Americas**, 210/207-8615, for panoramic views.

Details: Museum: Tue–Sun 9–5. $4 adults, $2 seniors, ages 3–12, and students with identification. Tower: daily 8 a.m.–11 p.m. Elevator fees $3 adults, $2 seniors, $1 ages 4–11. (2 hours)

★★★★ RIVER WALK

San Antonio Convention & Visitors Bureau, 800/447-3372

Officially the Paseo del Rio, this urban renewal project along the San Antonio River has reenergized the city and become the focal point of downtown. The pedestrian path is about 20 feet below street level, accessed by numerous flights of stairs, and winds for about three miles along both banks of the river. Old cypress and oak trees shade the cobblestone and flagstone walkways, and lush foliage lends a garden atmosphere. Quiet Venetian-style river taxis putter along the jade-green river, carrying sightseers and diners; ticket booths for the river cruises are located along the walk. Sidewalk

SAN ANTONIO

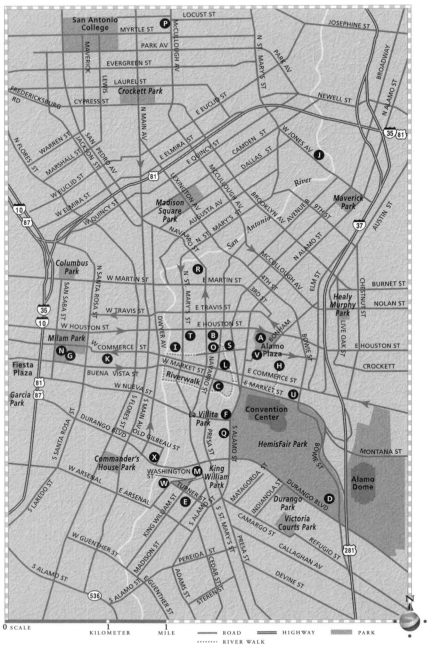

Crockett Park

San Antonio College

Madison Square Park

Columbus Park

Maverick Park

Healy Murphy Park

Milam Park

Fiesta Plaza

Garcia Park

Riverwalk

Alamo Plaza

La Villita Park

Convention Center

HemisFair Park

Commander's House Park

King William Park

Durango Park

Victoria Courts Park

Alamo Dome

0 SCALE   1 KILOMETER   1 MILE   — ROAD   ▬ HIGHWAY   ▮ PARK

········ RIVER WALK

N

cafés, art galleries, boutiques, shops, nightclubs, and hotels line the promenade, which is particularly fun—and romantic—at night, with lighting in the trees.

Also on the River Walk, **Arneson River Theatre**, 210/207-8610, with seats on one side of the river and a stage on the other, has numerous outdoor shows, and the river is the site of several seasonal parades.

Details: (1 hour minimum)

★★★ LA VILLITA
S. Alamo and Nueva Sts., 210/207-8610
The site of the city's original settlement that developed around the mission now called the Alamo, this restored "Little Village" bordering the river downtown has become a charming arts-and-crafts center. Within the adobe houses are working artists' studios, shops, restaurants, and a historic exhibit.

Details: Across from the Convention Center. Area accessible any time; shops open daily 10–6. Free. (1–2 hours)

★★★ MARKET SQUARE
515 W. Commerce St., 210/207-8600
Step into Mexico at this colorful market area, busy from dawn until late at night. Like a village, it includes a large farmers' market, popular Mexican restaurants, a bakery, art galleries, boutiques, a plaza for

---

SIGHTS
- **A** Alamo
- **B** Buckhorn Saloon & Museums
- **C** Hertzberg Circus Museum
- **D** Institute of Texan Cultures
- **E** King William District
- **F** La Villita
- **G** Market Square
- **H** Rivercenter Mall IMAX Theatre
- **I** River Walk
- **J** San Antonio Museum of Art
- **K** Spanish Governor's Palace

FOOD
- **L** Boudro's, A Texas Bistro
- **M** El Mirador

FOOD (continued)
- **N** Mi Tierra Café and Bakery
- **O** Paesano's
- **P** Restaurant Biga

LODGING
- **Q** Fairmount
- **R** Havana Riverwalk Inn
- **S** Hyatt Regency
- **T** La Mansion del Rio
- **U** Marriott River Walk
- **V** Menger Hotel
- **W** Ogé House
- **X** Riverwalk Inn

promenading and people-watching, and El Mercado, a market with several dozen vendors selling handicrafts and souvenirs from Latin America. It's acceptable to bargain for a lower price at El Mercado. Festival events frequently add to the action.

Details: *Located near I-35 at the west end of downtown between Commerce and Dolorosa Sts. Most shops open Jun–Aug 10–8, Sep–May 10–6, but restaurants are open longer hours. (1 hour minimum)*

★★★ SPANISH GOVERNOR'S PALACE
105 Plaza de Armas, 210/224-0601

A National Historic Landmark, this adobe structure dating back to 1749 served as the seat of the Spanish government in Texas from the mid-1700s into the early 1800s. It has carved doors, low beamed ceilings, a lovely interior patio with a fountain, and several rooms with period furnishings.

Details: *On Military Plaza, between City Hall and Market Square. Mon–Sat 9–5, Sun 10–5. $1 adults, 50¢ under age 14. (45 minutes)*

★★ BUCKHORN SALOON & MUSEUMS
318 E. Houston St., 210/270-9465,
www.buckhornsaloon.com

You can step back into San Antonio's frontier days at this turn-of-the-century saloon where a collection of mounted animal horns grew into a museum with 3,500 specimens of everything from grizzlies to game fish. The new site includes Old West entertainment.

Details: *Daily 9:30–5. $9.95 adults, $7.95 ages 6–11. (1–2 hours)*

★★ KING WILLIAM DISTRICT
San Antonio Conservation Society, 107 King William St., 210/224-6163

With its Victorian homes, this historic neighborhood settled by Germans presents a totally different architectural dimension to the city. It's centered around King William Street south of downtown. Take a walking tour and visit the **Steves Homestead Museum**, 509 King William Street, 210/225-5924, and **Guenther House**, 205 E. Guenther, 210/227-1061, a museum, restaurant, and store.

Details: *(1–2 hours)*

★ HERTZBERG CIRCUS MUSEUM
210 Market St., 210/207-7810

Big Top fans will applaud the Hertzberg, which chronicles the history of "The Greatest Show on Earth." More than 20,000 items are in the collection, including antique posters, a miniature circus, and Tom Thumb's carriage.

Details: *Mon–Sat 10–5 and Jun–Aug additionally Sun 1–5. $2.50 adults, $2 seniors, $1 ages 3–12. (1 hour)*

GREATER SAN ANTONIO SIGHTSEEING HIGHLIGHTS

★★★★ BRACKENRIDGE PARK/SAN ANTONIO ZOOLOGICAL GARDENS AND AQUARIUM
Park: 2800 block of Broadway, 210/736-9534; Zoo/Aquarium: 3903 N. St. Mary's St., 210/734-7183, www.sazoo-aq.org

About two miles north of downtown, this large park is a delightful oasis with many attractions, the star being the San Antonio Zoo. But it also has a carousel with antique horses, paddleboats for cruising the San Antonio River, a miniature railroad, a cable-car Skyride, and the beautiful Japanese Tea Gardens, where pebbled paths lead over rustic stone bridges and placid pools. Ranked among the top zoos in the country and home to more than 3,000 animals, the San Antonio Zoo is a crowd-pleaser with natural-habitat settings, including sections with African and Australian animals. Ask about riding an elephant or a camel.

Details: *Park: Open daily, rides usually operate Mon–Fri 10–5, Sat and Sun 10–6. Park free, varying fees for rides; call for specifics. Zoo/Aquarium: Memorial Day–Labor Day daily 9–8 (ticket sales stop at 6); rest of year until 6 (5 for ticket sales). $6 adults, $4 ages 3–11. (2–4 hours)*

★★★★ MCNAY ART MUSEUM
6000 N. New Braunfels St., 210/824-5368, www.mcnayart.org

The museum focuses on nineteenth- and twentieth-century art, displaying works by such masters as Matisse, Picasso, van Gogh, Cézanne, and O'Keeffe in the Mediterranean-style home of the late Marion Koogler McNay, an art patron. It also has Indian arts and crafts and beautifully landscaped grounds.

Details: *Tue–Sat 10–5, Sun noon–5. Donation requested. (2 hours)*

GREATER SAN ANTONIO

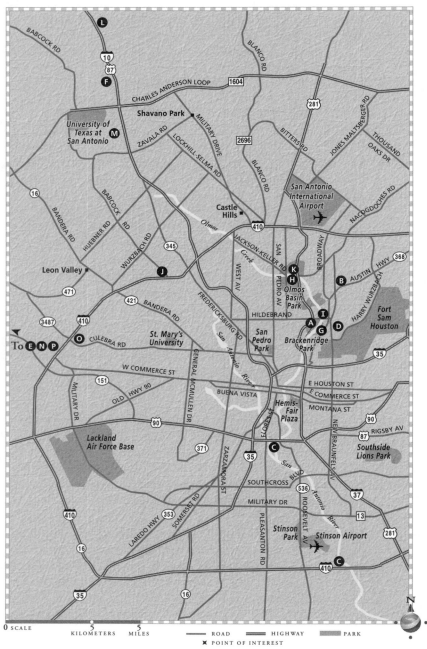

BABCOCK RD

L

10
87
F

BLANCO RD

CHARLES ANDERSON LOOP · 1604

281

Shavano Park

MILITARY DRIVE

University of
Texas at
San Antonio **M**

ZAVALA RD

LOCKHILL-SELMA RD

2696

BITTERS RD

JONES MALTSBERGER RD

THOUSAND
OAKS DR

16

BANDERA RD

HUEBNER RD

BABCOCK RD

WURZBACH RD

345

San Antonio
International
Airport

NACOGDOCHES RD

Castle
Hills

Olmos

410

Creek

JACKSON-KELLER RD

Leon Valley

471

J

421

BANDERA RD

WEST AV

PEDRO AV

SAN

BROADWAY

AUSTIN HWY

368

K
H
B

3487

410

FREDERICKSBURG RD

HILDEBRAND

Olmos
Basin
Park

HARRY WURZBACH

Fort
Sam
Houston

To **E N P**

O

CULEBRA RD

St. Mary's
University

San Antonio River

GENERAL MCMULLEN DR

San
Pedro
Park

A
I
G
D

Brackenridge
Park

35

W COMMERCE ST

151

OLD HWY 90

BUENA VISTA

FLORES ST

E HOUSTON ST
E COMMERCE ST
MONTANA ST

90

MILITARY DR

90

Hemis-
Fair
Plaza

NEW BRAUNFELS AV

RIGSBY AV

87

Lackland
Air Force Base

371

35

C

San
Antonio River

Southside
Lions Park

ZARZAMORA ST

SOUTHCROSS BLVD

536

37

MILITARY DR

ROOSEVELT AV

13

410

LAREDO HWY

353

SOMERSET RD

PLEASANTON RD

Stinson
Park

Stinson Airport

281

16

C

410

35

16

N

0 SCALE   5   5
       KILOMETERS   MILES

━━━ ROAD   ═══ HIGHWAY   � PARK

✕ POINT OF INTEREST

★★★★ **MISSION TRAIL**
**6701 San José Dr. (Visitors Center), 210/534-8833 or
210/932-1001, www.nps.gov**
Four missions built in the early 1700s by the Spaniards, all still active
parishes, are now part of the San Antonio Missions National
Historical Park. More than places of worship, these compounds were
educational, work, and social centers. Today, the missions illustrate
the different roles they played during eighteenth-century life.

Mission San José, 6701 San José Drive at Mission Road, a fully
restored compound called the Queen of Missions, is known for its
beautiful carvings. **Mission Concepción**, 807 Mission Road, is considered one of the oldest unrestored stone churches in the country.
Farther out, **Mission San Juan**, 9101 Graf Road, and **Mission
Espada**, 10040 Espada Road, have small chapels, and the latter has
an aqueduct. While the Alamo was one of the original missions, it is
separate from this trail.

Details: Daily 9–5. Donation requested. (1 ½–2 hours)

★★★★ **WITTE MUSEUM**
**3801 Broadway, 210/357-1900, witte@wittemuseum.org,
www.wittemuseum.org**
This eclectic museum turns history and science into a fun, hands-on
learning experience. At the Witte Museum explore a four-level science treehouse, decipher ancient rock art, walk through a thorny
Texas landscape, and meet some "vanished Texans"—dinosaurs who
once roamed the area.

*Details: Next to Brackenridge Park, Memorial Day–Labor Day
Mon–Sat 10–6 (Tue until 9), Sun noon–6; rest of year until 5 (Tue 'til*

SIGHTS
Ⓐ Brackenridge Park/San
Antonio Zoologicial
Gardens and Aquarium
Ⓑ McNay Art Museum
Ⓒ Mission Trail
Ⓓ San Antonio Botanical
Gardens and Lucile
Halsell Conservatory
Ⓔ SeaWorld of Texas
Ⓕ Six Flags Fiesta Texas
Ⓖ Witte Museum

FOOD
Ⓗ Alamo Quarry Market
Ⓘ La Calesa
Ⓙ Massimo Ristorante
Italiano
Ⓚ Paesano's
Ⓛ Rudy's Country Store
& Bar-B-Q

LODGING
Ⓜ Hampton Inn Fiesta
Park
Ⓝ Hyatt Regency Hill
Country Resort
Ⓞ La Quinta Ingram Park

CAMPING
Ⓟ Admiralty RV Resort

9). $5.95 adults, $4.95 seniors, $3.95 ages 4–11; free Tue 3–9 p.m. (2–3 hours)

★★★ SAN ANTONIO BOTANICAL GARDENS AND LUCILE HALSELL CONSERVATORY
555 Funston Pl., 210/207-3255, www.sabot.org
Besides having formal gardens, this 33-acre oasis offers a Walk Through Texas trail that shows native flora and architecture of the diverse regions of the state. At the conservatory, a tunnel leads 16 feet below ground to various ecosystems thriving under glass pyramids. The site is wheelchair accessible and offers a touch-and-smell garden for the visually impaired.

Details: Mar–Oct daily 9–6, Jun–Aug Thu until 9; Nov–Feb daily 8–5. $4 adults, $2 seniors, $1 ages 3–12. (1½–2 hours)

★★★ SAN ANTONIO MUSEUM OF ART
200 W. Jones Ave., 210/978-8100, www.samuseum.org
Housed in the castle-like old Lone Star Brewery, a National Historic Landmark, the museum showcases art of the Americas, from pre-Columbian to twentieth-century and including sculpture, folk art, photography, and decorative arts. A new $11 million wing houses the Nelson A. Rockefeller Center for Latin American Art, considered the premier collection of Latin works spanning nearly 3,000 years.

Details: Tue 10–9, Wed–Sat 10–5, Sun noon–5. $4 adults, $2 seniors and students with identification, $1.75 ages 4–11, free Tue 3–9. (1½–2 hours)

★★★ SEA WORLD OF TEXAS
Ellison Dr. and Westover Hills Blvd., 210/523-3611, www.seaworld.com
Everyone loves Shamu the whale, one of the stars at this popular water park, which has more than 25 attractions, including rides and performances by whales, dolphins, sea lions, otters, and walruses. Come face to face with a shark, see 200 polar penguins, and touch a dolphin. Test your nerves on the Steel Eel and Great White roller coasters, then cool off in a wet and wild ride on the Rio Loco.

Details: Off Rte. 151, about 16 miles northwest of downtown. Mid-May–mid-Aug daily 10–6, 8, or 10; mid-Aug–Oct and Apr–mid-May weekends 10–6 or later; open some weekdays Apr–mid-May and daily in mid-Mar, call for details. $31.95 adults, $21.95 ages 3–11. (4–6 hours)

★★★ **SIX FLAGS FIESTA TEXAS**
I-10 West at La Cantera Pkwy. 800/473-4378,
www.sixflags.com
A family theme park that celebrates the many cultures of Texas, this home of Bugs Bunny and his Looney Tunes friends entertains with thrill rides, a water park, and live shows. Polka in the German section; join in a fiesta at the Hispanic village; and hop on the rides such as the Rattler, one of the world's tallest wooden roller coasters, and Joker's Revenge, which catapults you in a 360-degree loop, corkscrew turns, and a spiral—all backward!

Details: Mar–late May and mid-Aug–Nov weekends 10–8 or 10; late May–mid-Aug daily 10–10 $33 for those 48 inches and taller, $22.50 under 48 inches and seniors, under age 2 free; $5 parking per car. (4–6 hours)

FITNESS AND RECREATION

Brackenridge Park, 2800 Broadway, 210/207-8480 or 210/736-9534, has horseback riding, golfing, bike trails, and picnic areas, as well as other attractions. **HemisFair Park**, 200 S. Alamo Street, 210/207-8572, site of the 1968 World's Fair, has a water park where visitors can stroll through 12 acres of landscaped grounds with fountains. The park also has a large children's playground. On the northwestern edge of the city, the **Friedrich Wilderness Park**, 21395 Milsa Road off I-10 West, 210/698-1057, has five miles of hiking trails in hilly, wooded terrain, considered a bird-watchers' haven. The free park is normally open daily, except Monday, from dawn to dusk.

The city has professional sports, most notably the **San Antonio Spurs** basketball team, 210/554-7700, which plays in the Alamodome downtown. **Retama Park**, 210/651-7000, on the northeast edge of the city, offers pari-mutuel horse racing. The area also has about three dozen golf courses, including a number of outstanding public courses such as **La Cantera Golf Club**, 800/446-5387, and the **Quarry Golf Club**, 800/347-7759. For a golfing guide, contact the **San Antonio Convention & Visitors Bureau**, 800/447-3372.

FOOD

Mexican food—fajitas and enchiladas as well as regional specialties from Mexico—reigns supreme here. Order up a margarita or *cerveza* (beer), some nachos or *ceviche* (marinated fish with fresh salsa), and work your way to *bunuelos* (cinnamon-sugar pastries) for dessert. Barbecue also commands a great following. Restaurant browsing is popular along the River Walk, where many eateries post menus. Except for the more upscale, most dining-out runs less than $20 here, and some Mexican restaurants will be even less.

La Calesa, 2103 E. Hildebrand Avenue, 210/822-4475, serves authentic Mexican cuisine, including specialties from the Yucatán region, in a small cottage. **El Mirador**, 722 S. St. Mary's Street, 210/225-9444, combines Southwestern and traditional Mexican cuisine, presenting such specialties as *moles*, the dishes with hints of chocolate in the sauce.

At Market Square, strolling mariachis and Christmas decorations add color to the bustling family scene at **Mi Tierra Café & Bakery**, 218 Produce Row, 210/225-1262, a 24-hour eatery long popular for late-night, early-morning breakfast as well as lunch and dinner. It's touristy, but fun and a good place to watch Hispanic family celebrations.

Northern Italian dishes are the focus at **Paesano's**, 555 E. Basse Street, 210/828-5191, and on the River Walk, 111 W. Crockett Street, Suite 101, 210/227-2782; a favorite is the shrimp Paesano cooked in lemon-butter-garlic sauce. In a historic building on the River Walk, **Boudro's, A Texas Bistro**, 421 E. Commerce Street, 210/224-8484, blends Southwestern and New American, with a few Cajun items. Its salmon tacos are favorites. Tuscan influences show in the upscale **Massimo Ristorante Italiano**, 4263 NW Loop 410 at Babcock, 210/342-8556, which has tasty seafood along with lightly sauced Italian dishes.

From the starter of crusty sourdough bread to the desserts, top-of-the-line **Restaurant Biga**, 206 E. Locust Street, 210/225-0722, delivers a fine-dining experience with superbly seasoned/sauced items on a changing menu of New American cooking served in an old mansion.

Among many barbecue spots, **Rudy's Country Store & Bar-B-Q**, 24152 I-10 West at Leon Springs, 210/698-0418, is a fun excursion with slow-cooked meats served indoors and outdoors.

A number of restaurants have opened in the newly developed **Alamo Quarry Market**, U.S. 281 north at Basse Road, 210/225-1000, a former quarry and cement plant turned into an upscale shopping-entertainment center.

LODGING

San Antonio has some delightful, renovated historic hotels in the downtown area, big-name lodgings along the River Walk, Victorian bed-and-breakfasts and a luxury resort on the edge of the city. Numerous chain motels are available to fit any budget.

Downtown, the Spanish-style **La Mansion del Rio**, 112 College Street, 800/292-7300, built around a restored nineteenth-century building, has some rooms with balconies overlooking the San Antonio River. Rates run about $240 but promotions can lower that to about $100. Opposite the Alamo, the **Menger Hotel**, 204 Alamo Plaza, 800/345-9285, exudes Texas history, dating back to the mid-1800s with historic and newer lobbies, a courtyard, and a pool. Rooms start at about $120. The newest boutique hotel is **Havana Riverwalk Inn**, 1015 Navarro Street, 888/224-2008, in a renovated Mediterranean-style historic building on a quieter section of the river. It takes a 1920s Havana theme from its original name, offering 27 individually decorated rooms starting at $110, with breakfast. Another small historic hotel, located by La Villita, is the **Fairmount**, 401 S. Alamo Street, 210/224-8800, one of the Wyndham-Grand Heritage group, with 37 elegantly decorated rooms with sitting areas and marble baths. Rates run about $200 but ask about promotions.

Newer hotels downtown fronting the River Walk include the **Hyatt Regency**, 123 Losoya Street, 800/233-1234, with rooms from $270 or $159 weekends (sometimes as low as $95 on promotions); and **Marriott River Walk**, 711 E. River Walk, 800/648-4462, with rooms from $229, or $169 on weekend two-for-breakfast specials and sometimes below $100 on seasonal promotions.

The city offers a dozen or more bed-and-breakfasts, most on the edge of downtown and in the neighboring historic King William District. The most unusual is the **Riverwalk Inn**, 329 Old Guilbeau Street, 800/254-4440. It's easy to imagine yourself back in the frontier days at this collection of 1840s log cabins with front porches overlooking the river and downtown. Its 11 guest rooms are decorated with quilts and early Texas furnishings and each has a private bath. Rates start around $100, including a generous continental breakfast. On weekends, "Davy Crockett" and other living-history storytellers often show up to talk about life here in 1836. Adjoining the River Walk, the elegant **Ogé House**, 209 Washington Street, 800/242-2770, is a meticulously restored 1850s antebellum mansion with verandas, fireplaces, formal dining room and grand staircase. Its 10 guest suites and rooms are furnished with antiques and have private baths. Rates start at about $110, including full breakfast. For other bed-and-breakfasts, contact the B&B Hosts of San Antonio and South Texas, 800/356-1605.

San Antonio has numerous economy and midpriced chain motels and hotels, many of them around Loop 410 where it crosses interstate highways and U.S. 281, which passes the airport. Among the options: Convenient to Sea World, **La Quinta Ingram Park**, 7134 NW Loop 410, 210/680-8883, has a pool and rooms starting at $65 with breakfast. In the Six Flags Fiesta Texas area west on I-10, **Hampton Inn Fiesta Park**, 11010 I-10 West, 210/561-9058, has a pool and rooms from $69, including continental breakfast.

West of the city is one of the state's premier lodgings, **Hyatt Regency Hill Country Resort**, 9800 Hyatt Resort Drive (off Route 151 near Sea World), 800/233-1234, with limestone buildings, ranch-style furnishings, a river for tubing, golf course, and other amenities. Rates start at $275, but you may find promotions for around $115.

CAMPING
On the western edge of the city, convenient to Sea World, **Admiralty RV Resort**, 1485 Ellison Drive, 800/999-7872, earns high campground ratings for its 240 sites with full hookups, a heated pool, Jacuzzi for adults, playground, club room, and other amenities, including a free shuttle to Sea World. For other options, see listings in the chapter about New Braunfels, which is about 35 miles northeast of San Antonio on I-35.

NIGHTLIFE AND SPECIAL EVENTS
Much of the city's nighttime action centers around the River Walk. Options range from quiet pubs to the **Hard Rock Café**, 111 W. Crockett Street, 210/224-7625, and **Planet Hollywood**, 245 E. Commerce Street, 210/212-7827. On the eastern edge of downtown, near HemisFair Park and the Alamodome, a new entertainment district called **Sunset Station** is developing in the St. Paul Square National Historic District on Commerce Street. A live music pavilion, dance hall, rock 'n' roll club and piano bar are among the options. A former cement plant with landmark smokestacks has been turned into a festive retail-entertainment center known as **Alamo Quarry Market**, U.S. 281 north at Basse Road, 210/225-1000. With parts of the original structure integrated into the design, the market has upscale shops, restaurants, bookstores, theaters, and clubs.

Outdoor performances are scheduled at **Arneson River Theatre**, on the River Walk, 210/207-8610. Other venues include **Majestic Performing Arts Center**, 212 E. Houston Street, 210/226-3333, which includes two elegant restored theaters, the Majestic and the Empire, for San Antonio Symphony concerts and touring shows; and **Guadalupe Cultural Arts Center**, 1301 Guadalupe Street, 210/271-9070, site of live theater, musical concerts, and other events.

San Antonio loves to party, so you'll find celebrations year-round. Among the most notable are the **San Antonio Stock Show and Rodeo** in early

February, 210/225-5851; **Fiesta San Antonio**, in mid-April 10 days of parades, special events, concerts, and elegant balls celebrating Texas' independence and cultural diversity, 210/227-5191; **Texas Folklife Festival**, a four-day celebration in late July and early August, 210/458-2300; and **Diez y Seis de Septiembre**, a mid-September celebration of Mexican independence from Spain, 210/223-3151. There are also Christmas events along the River Walk illuminated by 70,000 lights strung on trees and bridges. Events include **Las Posadas**, a re-creation of a sixteenth-century nativity pageant, held in mid-December, 210/224-6163.

SHOPPING

Besides traditional shopping malls and Western wear stores, San Antonio entices shoppers with excellent choices of arts and crafts, particularly Southwestern and Latin American work. In addition to stores along the River Walk, in hotels, and along streets downtown, **La Villita**, 210/207-8610, Alamo and Nueva Streets, houses a collection of shops where weavers, potters, painters, and jewelry-makers work and sell their crafts in historic buildings. At La Villita, **Nueva Street Gallery**, 210/229-9810, has contemporary art by Texans; and **River Art Group Gallery**, 210/226-8752, features changing displays of fine art and crafts by local and regional artists. **Art Inc. Gallery of Fine Art**, 800/225-0278, presents emerging local artists. Other shops carry fashion and rugs from Mexico, Guatemala and Peru.

West of downtown, **Market Square**, between Commerce and Dolorosa Streets, 210/207-8600, has art galleries and a Mexican market of 35 small shops filled with pottery, clothes, jewelry, trinkets and other items from Latin America and elsewhere. At Market Square, **Galeria Ortiz**, 102 Concho

Street, 210/225-0731, one of the oldest galleries in the city, sells outstanding Southwestern art, jewelry, and pottery.

For more information on the many galleries, request a **San Antonio Art Gallery Association Gallery Guide** from the city visitors bureau, 800/447-3372.

Hill Country Loop

San Antonio lies on the edge of the **Texas Hill Country**—*considered by many the most scenic area of the state. Its rolling terrain is dotted with dark green cedar and oaks, gradually giving way to cactus and prickly pear. Clear rivers run beneath limestone cliffs and canyons, and views seem to stretch forever under a huge sky. The following scenic drive can be a one- or two-day trip or the beginning leg of an extended vacation. From San Antonio, follow U.S. 90 west to **Castroville** and take time to explore this charming historic town settled by Alsatians in 1844. Continue on U.S. 90 to **Uvalde**, turn north on U.S. 83 skirting the **Frio River**, then east on Route 337 to Vanderpool and north on Route 187. Turn northeast on Route 39 into **Kerrville**, a good spot to spend the night. Follow Route 16 south through **Bandera**, then Route 46 east to Boerne, and I-10 back into San Antonio. Antiquing fans will find lots of good browsing along this route.*

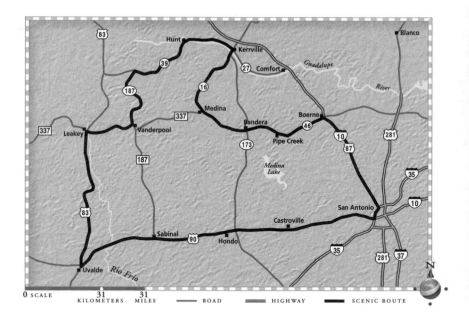

8
CORPUS CHRISTI
BAY AREA

A little more than halfway down the Texas shoreline the land arcs southward, forming the Coastal Bend, one of the state's prime vacation destinations. Slender barrier islands with beautiful beaches stretch for more than 100 miles along the Gulf of Mexico, and the South Texas mesquite brushland blends into marshland to create a habitat rich in wildlife.

Corpus Christi, which traces its history to the days when Spanish galleons sailed in and out of its protected bay, is the state's prettiest city by the sea. Modern freighters sail into the port within sight of life-size replicas of Columbus's fabled *Niña*, *Pinta*, and *Santa Maria* permanently on exhibit here, and windsurfers skim across the bay waters.

Beyond the bay, Mustang and Padre barrier islands beckon anglers and sun-worshippers. While hotels and condos dot the coastline of Mustang Island, most of Padre is a national seashore of virgin beach. At the upper tip of Mustang Island, Port Aransas (or Port A, as it's called) is a funky fishing village. Anglers come here looking for trophy game fish, and families come to cast in the surf and build castles in the sand. A little farther up the coast, Rockport is an artists' colony.

The entire area is a bird-watchers' haven, considered one of the top birding spots in the country. The endangered whooping cranes winter in this area, and visitors can see these majestic birds in special boat tours from Rockport.

CORPUS CHRISTI

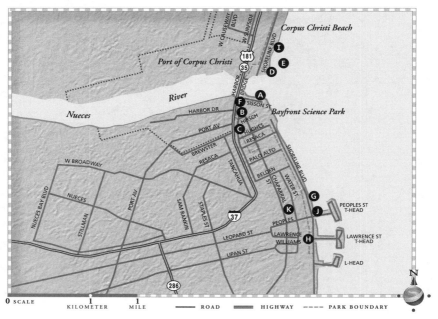

SIGHTS

A Art Museum of South Texas
B Asian Cultures Museum
C Heritage Park
D Texas State Aquarium
E USS *Lexington* Museum on the Bay
F World of Discovery: Columbus Ships/Corpus Christi Museum of Science & History

FOOD

G Republic of Texas Bar & Grill
H Water Street Oyster Bar and Seafood Company

LODGING

I Best Western Sandy Shores Beach Hotel
G Omni Bayfront Hotel
J Omni Marina Hotel
K Ramada Inn Bayfront

Note: Items with the same letter are located in the same area.

A PERFECT DAY IN CORPUS CHRISTI

In Corpus Christi, explore the huge aircraft carrier USS *Lexington*, learn about marine life in the Gulf of Mexico at the Texas State Aquarium, and see the replicas of Columbus' fleet, the *Niña*, *Pinta*, and *Santa Maria*. Then pack up swimsuits, snacks, and drinks and head across the causeway to the beach on Padre Island or Mustang Island.

DOWNTOWN CORPUS CHRISTI SIGHTSEEING HIGHLIGHTS

The major sights are clustered around Bayfront Arts and Science Park, on a point at the north end of downtown next to the ship channel leading to the port. Some sights are on the downtown side of the channel and others are on the north side, along Corpus Christi Beach. You can cross the channel on Harbor Bridge, which offers great views of the area, or in summer take the Water Taxi, 361/289-2600, which runs back and forth across the ship channel.

★★★★ **TEXAS STATE AQUARIUM**
2710 N. Shoreline Blvd. at Corpus Christi Beach
800/477-GULF
Go deep beneath the sea, wander through colorful coral gardens, and nose up to a shark at this small but outstanding aquarium that focuses on the rich marine life native to the Gulf of Mexico and the Caribbean Sea. More than 250 sea life species range from tiny, brilliant angelfish to large stingrays. River otters put on a playful show in the "Otter Space" exhibit, and the alligator marsh has an albino named Eve.

> **Details:** *Memorial Day–Labor Day Mon–Sat 9–6, Sun 10–6; rest of year until 5. $8.75 adults, $6.75 seniors and ages 12–17, $5 ages 4–11. (2 hours)*

★★★★ **USS *LEXINGTON* MUSEUM ON THE BAY**
2914 N. Shoreline Blvd. off Corpus Christi Beach,
800/LADY-LEX, ladylex@usslexington.com,
www.usslexington.com
Fondly called "the Lex" and known as the Blue Ghost during its World War II service in the Pacific, this giant naval aircraft carrier welcomes visitors to inspect it stem to stern. Explore the hangar deck, the flight deck, and the admiral's quarters. In addition to pictorial exhibits describing life on the ship, there are vintage airplanes

aboard. Via a simulator, you can fly a jet fighter yourself or take a helicopter ride from the deck (extra fees apply). Wear nonslippery shoes and be prepared to navigate narrow passages and steep stairs.

Details: *Daily 9–5, sometimes later in summer. $9 adults, $7 seniors, $4 ages 4–12. (2 hours)*

★★★★ **WORLD OF DISCOVERY: CHRISTOPHER COLUMBUS SHIPS/CORPUS CHRISTI MUSEUM OF SCIENCE & HISTORY**
1900 N. Chaparral St., 361/883-2862
Columbus' voyages to the New World with the *Niña*, *Pinta*, and *Santa Maria* come alive here as visitors board life-size replicas of the wooden ships and learn about sailing in the fifteenth century. Visitors can explore the tiny *Pinta* and *Santa Maria*, which seem like toy ships compared to the big freighters passing nearby. Sailing schools are offered on the *Niña*, which also tours. The story of the original fleet is told in an exhibit and video in the adjacent Museum of Science & History, which also houses a Smithsonian Institution exhibit commemorating the 500th anniversary of Columbus' voyages to the New World. The museum also has an award-winning shipwreck exhibit, with treasures from a ship lost in this area in 1554.

Details: *Memorial Day–Labor Day Mon–Sat 10–6, Sun noon–6; rest of year until 5. $8 adults, $6.50 seniors, $7 ages 13–17, $4 ages 4–12; fees cover both the museum and ships. (1 1/2–2 hours)*

★★★ **BAYFRONT/HARBOR**
Corpus Christi's focal point is its beautiful bay, which can be enjoyed by foot, car, and boat. A two-mile-long **seawall** extends from the Bayfront Arts and Science Park to the marina area, offering a wide sidewalk for strolling, jogging, and skating. Along the way, *miradores del mar*, small pavilion-like overlooks, provide resting spots to take in the view; one of the *miradores* has a statue dedicated to the late Tejano star Selena, who was from Corpus Christi. Extending from Shoreline Boulevard in the downtown area, **Ocean Drive** follows the bayfront for seven miles, passing stately homes overlooking the waterfront. From the Peoples Street T-Head marina, **Capt. Clark's Flagship Tours**, 361/884-8306, runs narrated cruises of the bay, providing skyline and harbor views augmented with history. Sunset cruises are particularly popular and usually include music on weekends. From Ingleside, on the north side of Corpus Christi Bay,

Dolphin Connection, 361/882-4126, takes visitors on guided boat trips to see dolphins playing in the bay; hours vary and trips depend on dolphin activity, so call for information.

Details: (1–3 hours)

★★ BAYFRONT ARTS AND SCIENCE PARK

A scenic spot by the ship channel where ocean freighters come and go under the 250-foot-high Harbor Bridge, the bayfront park is home to a number of attractions besides the Columbus ships and adjacent museum. The park's centerpiece is the **Watergarden**, with 150 jet fountains that are lit at night. Overlooking the Watergarden, the modern **Art Museum of South Texas**, 1902 N. Shoreline Boulevard, 361/884-3844, is as eye-catching outside as the pictures displayed inside. Adjoining the plaza, **Heritage Park**, 1581 N. Chaparral Street, 361/883-0639, has a collection of restored turn-of-the-twentieth-century homes; and the **Asian Cultures Museum**, 1809 N. Chaparral Street, 361/882-2641, showcases legends and lifestyles of the Orient.

Details: Art Museum: Tue–Sat 10–5, Sun 1–5. $3 adults, $2 seniors and ages 13–18, $1 ages 2–12. Heritage Park: Mon–Thu 10–5, Fri and Sat 9–2. Free; guided tours: $3 adults, $2 seniors, $1 children. Asian Cultures Museum: Tue–Sat 10–5. $4 adults, $3.50 seniors, $2.50 ages 6–15. (1–2 hours)

OTHER SIGHTSEEING HIGHLIGHTS

★★★★ BEACHES

The longest, most beautiful beaches in Texas stretch for more than 130 miles along the barrier islands across from Corpus Christi Bay, Mustang and Padre Islands on the Gulf of Mexico. Windsurfing, sailing, swimming, fishing, and other water sports are popular. The surf is usually gentle, though you can sometimes catch larger waves. Much of this stretch of seashore is virgin beach on Padre Island. While a large number of hotels and condos have been built on Mustang Island, the development is mainly low- or mid-rise and there's still open space.

A causeway leads from the city to the islands. Visitors can access the beaches and accommodations along Mustang Island from various points off Route 361, the only road down the island. Padre has a limited number of accommodations within a few miles of the causeway, then Park Road 22 leads into **Padre Island National Seashore**, 361/949-8068, www.nps.gov, a 66-mile strip of undeveloped land with flat beaches and sand dunes. The paved road ends at the park visitor center, which has a nature trail, restrooms, showers, and a store. Beyond there, two-wheel-drive vehicles can go the first five miles, then only four-wheel-drive vehicles are permitted. Camping is allowed on both Mustang and Padre Islands. Admission to Padre Island National Seashore is $10 per vehicle, granting access for seven days.

Beware: While you're playing on the beach, watch for vehicles; they're allowed to drive on many stretches of the shore.

Uninhabited **San Jose Island**, across the channel from Port Aransas on the northern tip of Mustang Island, offers day visitors a Robinson Crusoe experience—shelling, swimming, fishing, and bird-watching on quiet beaches. Boats run frequently each day from the harborfront, and it's only a 15-minute ride, but there are no facilities on San Jose. For San Jose Island boat trips, contact Woody's Sports Center, 114 W. Cotter Avenue, Port Aransas, 361/749-5252.

Details: (half–full day)

★★★★ BIRD-WATCHING

One of the top birding areas of the country, this region of Texas boasts roseate spoonbills, herons, pelicans, hummingbirds, whooping cranes, egrets, flycatchers, warblers, osprey, and hundreds more—in all, about 500 documented species of land birds and waterfowl. Some birds are here year-round, others spend certain seasons here, and some fly over on migratory journeys. Even if you're not a birder, pack your binoculars to take advantage of the extensive sighting opportunities. Keep watch at the beach or as you drive along the bayfront, or go to areas identified as good birding spots.

In Corpus Christi, the **Hans A. Suter Wildlife Park**, located at Oso Bay, Ennis Joslin and Nile Streets, 361/884-7275, has a viewing tower, boardwalk, and hiking trails. The Corpus Christi Area Convention and Visitors Bureau, 800/678-OCEAN, publishes a flyer listing sources of information about birding. The **Port Aransas Birding Center**, on Ross Avenue off Cut-Off Road near the water treatment plant, has a boardwalk viewing area and guided birding tours Wednesday at 10:30 a.m. (weather permitting). For more information about the Port Aransas Birding Center call the Port Aransas-Mustang Island Convention and Visitors Bureau at 800/45-

COAST. The Texas Parks & Wildlife Department, 800/792-1112, and the Texas Department of Transportation publish a large, beautifully illustrated, fold-out map, *The Great Texas Coastal Birding Trail*, detailing birding sites and specific directions along the central Texas coast. Maps are available from the state parks department and usually at Texas Travel Information Centers, located at major highway entry points into the state.

Details:. *(1–3 hours per site)*

★★★ FISHING

For decades, anglers from all over the country have come to Port Aransas to cast in the surrounding waters for mackerel, pompano, kingfish, grouper, flounder, speckled trout, and trophy sailfish and marlin. There's fishing in the bay and surf, off piers, and far out in the deep blue sea. Numerous charter boats operate from Corpus Christi, Port Aransas, and Rockport.

Details: *For information, including a list of charter operators and fishing piers, contact the Corpus Christi Area Convention and Visitors Bureau, 800/678-OCEAN; and the Port Aransas-Mustang Island Convention & Visitors Bureau, 800/45-COAST. (half–full day)*

ROCKPORT-FULTON AREA SIGHTSEEING HIGHLIGHTS

Northeast of Corpus Christi about 40 miles, Rockport and its neighbor Fulton face Aransas Bay and the Intracoastal Waterway. Huge old live oak trees, many gnarled by the wind, augment palms. On the Great Texas Coastal Birding Trail, the area draws thousands of migrating fowl from fall through spring.

★★★★ ARANSAS NATIONAL WILDLIFE REFUGE
About 35 miles northeast of Rockport via Rtes. 35, then 774 and 2040, Austwell, 361/286-3559, www.fws.gov

Home to an estimated 300 species of birds, plus deer, javelinas, alligators, and other wildlife, this large refuge northeast of Rockport attracts its biggest crowds for the endangered whooping cranes, which migrate here each winter. A 16-mile paved road, hiking trails, and an observation tower allow good wildlife viewing. A visitors center offers information and a video about the whoopers. To see the greatest concentration of birds, including whoopers, come between November and March in early morning and late evening.

CORPUS CHRISTI BAY AREA

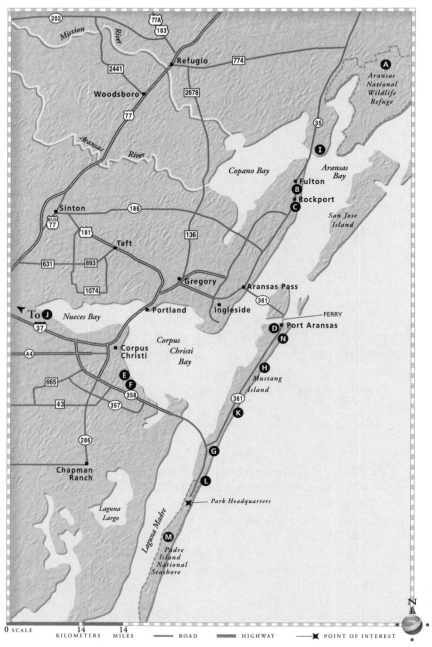

202
77A
183
Mission River
Refugio
774
2441
Woodsboro
2678
77
Aransas River
Aransas National Wildlife Refuge
A
35
I
Copano Bay
Aransas Bay
Fulton
B
Rockport
C
Sinton
188
BUS 77
181
Taft
136
San Jose Island
631
893
1074
Gregory
Aransas Pass
361
To J
Nueces Bay
Portland
Ingleside
FERRY
37
D
Port Aransas
44
Corpus Christi
Corpus Christi Bay
N
665
E
F
H
43
358
Mustang Island
357
361
K
286
G
Chapman Ranch
L
Laguna Largo
Park Headquarters
Laguna Madre
M
Padre Island National Seashore
N

0 SCALE 14 KILOMETERS 14 MILES —— ROAD === HIGHWAY —★ POINT OF INTEREST

Details: Refuge open daily dawn–dusk; center open daily 8:30–4:30. $5/vehicle. (1–2 hours)

★★★★ WHOOPING CRANE TOURS

An excellent way to see waterfowl, including the whoopers, is via a boat tour. A major operator in Rockport is **Captain Ted's Whooping Crane Tours**, 800/338-4551, which runs trips November 1 to May 1. Tours cover 60 miles of wetlands in a glassed-in birding boat. Whooper-spotting is the focus until April, then the trips concentrate on 12 rookery islands.

Details: Tours go daily except Tue in season. $33/person, no one under 12 admitted. Check at Rockport Yacht Basin and Sandollar Marina for a choice of operators. (3 hours)

★★★ FULTON MANSION STATE HISTORICAL PARK
317 Fulton Beach Rd., 361/729-0386, www.tpwd.state.tx.us
Overlooking Aransas Bay, this restored four-story French Empire-style home of a cattle baron was quite extravagant for its time, built in 1876 with such modern amenities as hot and cold running water, a heating/ventilation system, and gas lighting.

Details: Wed–Sun with tours hourly 9–3 (except at noon). $4 adults, $2 students, under age 6 free. (45 minutes)

SIGHTS
Ⓐ Aransas National Wildlife Refuge
Ⓑ Fulton Mansion State Historical Park
Ⓒ Texas Maritime Museum
Ⓒ Whooping Crane Tour

FOOD
Ⓓ Beulah's at Tarpon Inn
Ⓑ Charlotte Plummer's Seafare
Ⓔ Marco's
Ⓓ Trout Street Bar & Grill

FOOD (continued)
Ⓒ Valenari's Italian Restaurant
Ⓕ Yardarm Restaurant

LODGING
Ⓖ Holiday Inn Gulf Beach SunSpree Resort
Ⓒ Hoopes' House
Ⓒ Hummingbird Lodge and Education Center
Ⓖ Island House Condominiums
Ⓗ Port Royal Ocean Resort Condominiums

CAMPING
Ⓞ Goose Island State Park
Ⓓ Island RV Resort and Campground
Ⓙ Lake Corpus Christi State Park
Ⓚ Mustang Island State Park
Ⓛ Padre Balli Park
Ⓜ Padre Island National Seashore
Ⓝ Pioneer RV Resort

Note: Items with the same letter are located in the same area.

★★ TEXAS MARITIME MUSEUM
Navigation Circle, Rockport, 361/729-1271
Next to the Rockport Harbor, this museum chronicles the state's seafaring heritage, from the days of pirates to offshore oil rigs.
    Details: *Tue–Sat 10–4, Sun 1–4. $4 adults, $2 ages 4–12. (1 hour)*

FITNESS AND RECREATION
From walkers to windsurfers, everyone flocks to the waterfront. The seawall along Shoreline Drive fronting Corpus Christi Bay attracts joggers, strollers, bikers, and those who simply want to sit and enjoy the scenic overlooks.

Wind surfing is especially good on Corpus Christi Bay and in the Gulf. **J.P. Luby Surf Park**, Route 361 at Zahn Road on Mustang Island, 361/991-RIDE, rents horses for riding on the beach.

Padre Island National Seashore, 361/949-8068, has a two-mile paved Grasslands Nature Trail showcasing native plants and flowers, and the beachfront yields sand dollars and shells. **Corpus Christi Botanical Gardens**, 8545 S. Staples, 361/852-2100, also has a nature trail and is a good birding site.

FOOD
Oysters, shrimp, red snapper, and other seafood invite indulgences here. Most restaurants are casual, particularly those on Padre and Mustang Islands, and prices usually run $10 to $20 for dinner, though a few are more expensive.

In downtown Corpus Christi, **Water Street Oyster Bar and Seafood Company**, 309 N. Water Street, 361/882-8683, has an extensive menu and daily specials of seafood served plain and simple or with tempting sauces that add regional flavor. The lively restaurant is next to Water Street Market, a collection of restored buildings that house interesting shops around a courtyard. Another favorite spot, **Yardarm Restaurant**, 4310 Ocean Drive, 361/855-8157, serves good seafood in a nautical setting with great views of Corpus Christi Bay. Good steaks and panoramic views of the city and bay draw diners to the upscale **Republic of Texas Bar & Grill**, 900 N. Shoreline Boulevard in the Omni Bayfront Hotel, 361/887-1600, where meals may run $20 to $30. For a change of pace from seafood, go for northern Italian food at **Marco's**, 3812 S. Alameda Street, 361/853-2000.

In Port Aransas, on the harbor, **Trout Street Bar & Grill**, 104 W. Cotter Street, 361/749-6936, adds Cajun touches to many of its dishes—and

---

FREE RIDES

It's a free boat ride from Aransas Pass on the mainland to Port Aransas on the northern tip of Mustang Island. Ferries run 24 hours a day, the ride lasts about 10 minutes, and you often see dolphins playing in the water. Port Aransas gives visitors another free ride— on its city trolley, which normally runs 10 a.m. to 5 p.m.

---

is known for its tequila shrimp. A longtime favorite, **Beulah's at Tarpon Inn**, 200 E. Cotter Street, 361/749-4888, offers upscale (but still casual) dining inside or outside on the veranda of the historic Tarpon Inn.

In the Rockport-Fulton area, **Charlotte Plummer's Seafare**, 202 N. Fulton Beach Road, 361/729-1185, has casual indoor and outdoor dining overlooking Aransas Bay. While the emphasis is on fresh seafood, there also are char-grilled steaks and other items. **Valenari's Italian Restaurant**, 105 N. Austin Street, Rockport, 361/727-0717, has candlelight dining featuring pastas and changing specials, which include such items as fresh seafood and Gorgonzola-stuffed tenderloin. The bistro often has live music.

Since the area is so popular with snowbirds, many restaurants offer senior specials. Also, check about winter days of operation; some restaurants may close for several weeks or be open only the latter half of the week.

LODGING

From harborside hotels in Corpus Christi to beachfront hotels, condos, and cottages, there's lodging here to suit a variety of budgets. In Corpus Christi, **Best Western Sandy Shores Beach Hotel**, 3200 Surfside, 800/242-5814, is a 250-room hotel on the beach near the aquarium and other attractions; it has three restaurants. In the marina area, Omni has two properties, each mid-rise hotels with balconies overlooking the bay: **Omni Bayfront Hotel**, 900 N. Shoreline Boulevard, and **Omni Marina Hotel**, 707 N. Shoreline Boulevard; call 800/THE-OMNI for either. **Ramada Inn Bayfront**, 601 N. Water Street, 800/688-0334, has rooms with balconies and is close to the marina. Rates for these start at $60 to $80, but may be higher in summer.

On North Padre Island, **Holiday Inn Gulf Beach SunSpree Resort**, 15202 Windward Drive, 888/949-8041, is a full-service beachfront hotel with

KINGSVILLE

About 50 miles southwest of Corpus Christi, the fabled **King Ranch**—one of the largest and oldest working ranches in the world—sprawls across 825,000 acres in four counties. Founded in 1853 and considered the birthplace of American ranching, King Ranch originated the Santa Gertrudis breed of cattle and registered the first American quarter horse. The **Ranch Visitors Center**, on Route 141 at Santa Gertrudis, 361/592-8055, shows a video detailing the history of the area and offers several different types of ranch tours, including nature and bird-watching trips.

The gateway to the ranch is Kingsville, which has several noteworthy sights. **King Ranch Museum**, 405 N. Sixth Street, 361/595-1881, introduces visitors to the ranch and the family who developed it, tracing its history through pictures and an exhibit of vintage coaches, saddles, and other memorabilia. Stop by **King Ranch Saddle Shop**, 201 E. Kleberg Street, 800/282-KING, to look at leather goods produced under the ranch brand. Also in town, the **John E. Conner Museum, Texas A&M University–Kingsville** campus, 361/593-2819, showcases the area's multicultural history and displays more than 250 mounted North American game trophies.

150 rooms, two pools, outdoor bar and waterfront restaurant. Rates start around $60 in winter, $120 in summer. **Island House Condominiums**, 15340 Leeward Drive, 800/333-8806, has one- to three-bedroom units starting at $70 in winter, $100 in summer.

On Mustang Island, the beachfront **Port Royal Ocean Resort Condominiums**, 6317 Route 361, 800/242-1034, has one- to three-bedroom units built around a 500-foot tiered swimming lagoon with cabana bars. Rates start around $100 in winter, $185 in summer; ask about discounts.

There are numerous condos and resorts on Mustang and Padre Islands. To find one that suits your needs, check with a rental company. Among companies handling resort rentals are **Wes-Tex Management Company** in Port Aransas, 800/221-1447; and **MG Management Condominium Rentals** in Port Aransas, 800/248-1095.

In the Rockport-Fulton area, **Hoopes' House**, 417 N. Broadway, Rockport, 361/729-8424 or 800/528-7782, a restored 1890s Victorian home on the National Register of Historic Places with a gazebo, pool, and hot tub, has eight guest rooms with private baths. Each guest room is complemented with bathrobes and hair dryers; rates start at $110 with full breakfast. Nature-oriented travelers should check out the **Hummingbird Lodge and Education Center**, 5652 FM Road 1781, Rockport, 888/827-7555 or 800/528-7782, which sits on Copano Bay under a canopy of old oak trees. Its 72-foot porch has feeders that attract 300 to 500 hummingbirds in September, and there's also good birding at other times. The center also does nature and boat tours. Eight guest rooms decorated in antiques and Mexican furnishings have private baths; rates are $70 and breakfast is available at an additional charge.

Both the **Corpus Christi Convention & Visitors Department**, 800/678-OCEAN, and the **Port Aransas–Mustang Island Convention & Visitors Bureau**, 800/45-COAST, offer visitor guides and brochures that include accommodations information.

CAMPING

Campers will find a larger than normal selection of sites in this area, both in Corpus Christi and on the beaches. **Lake Corpus Christi State Park**, six miles south of Mathis on Park Road 25 off Route 359, 361/547-2635 or 512/389-8900 for reservations, offers 350 acres on the lake with campsites, rest rooms, and showers.

On North Padre Island, **Padre Balli Park**, Park Road 22, 361/949-8121, has 66 sites with water and electricity and covered picnic areas. Beach camping is permitted on **Padre Island National Seashore**, 361/949-8068; the visitors center has rest rooms with showers and a convenience store. **Mustang Island State Park**, Route 361, 361/749-5246 or 512/389-8900 for reservations, has 48 campsites with electricity and water, and beach camping. On Mustang Island just south of Port Aransas, **Pioneer RV Resort**, Route 361, 361/749-6248, has more than 200 full hookups, a pool, bathhouse, laundry, store, and other amenities. In Port Aransas, **Island RV Resort and Campground**, 700 Sixth Street, 361/749-5600, is a Good Sam park with 199 spaces near beaches and a birding center. It has a pool, bathhouse, recreation hall, and laundry. North of Rockport-Fulton and not far from the Aransas National Wildlife Refuge, **Goose Island State Park**, 361/729-2858 or 512/389-8900 for reservations, has 102 sites in wooded and beachfront areas with nature trails and a boat ramp.

NIGHTLIFE AND SPECIAL EVENTS

At the Corpus Christi Marina, catch the Wednesday evening **sailboat races** at 5:30 and dine at one of the marina restaurants. The marina hosts a number of special events, so check locally for activities when you're there. Sunset cruises also leave from the marina. Check with **Captain Clark's Flagship**, 361/884-8306, for boat options, including a large paddle wheeler. Across the causeway, on North Padre Island, toast the sunset over Laguna Madre at rustic but fun **Frenchy's Crabhouse**, off Park Road 22, 361/949-8201. In Port Aransas, check along the harborfront—particularly on Cotter Avenue—for places with live music.

In Corpus Christi, **Harbor Playhouse**, 1 Bayfront Park, 361/888-7469, the state's oldest continually performing community theater, has frequent productions. The bayfront **Cole Park**, 1526 Ocean Drive, 361/884-7275, has an outdoor concert series in summer.

Numerous fun events celebrate the seafaring heritage of the area. Of note: The **Annual Buccaneer Days**, 361/882-3242, in late April/early May recalls the colorful pirate history of Corpus Christi. The **Annual U.S. Open Windsurfing Regatta**, 361/985-1555, draws windsurfers and spectators from across the country to Corpus Christi Bay in mid- to late May. The **Annual Rockport Art Festival**, 361/729-6445, showcases works of local and regional artists over the July 4 holiday in Rockport. In mid-September, the **Annual Bayfest & Folklife Celebration**, 361/887-0868, brings food, games, arts and crafts, and entertainment along the waterfront in Corpus Christi.

In Aransas Pass, the **Annual Shrimporee**, 800/633-3028, in mid-September treats participants to fresh seafood and live entertainment. In early December, the **Annual Harbor Lights Festival & Boat Parade**, 361/985-1555, in Corpus Christi includes a colorful parade of boats at the marina and lighting of a 75-foot Christmas tree. At nearby Kingsville, a **Ranch Hand Breakfast** at the King Ranch, 800/333-5032, in mid-November kicks off holiday celebrations in the area.

9

RIO GRANDE VALLEY
AND SOUTH TEXAS

At a latitude similar to South Florida, the southern part of Texas looks and feels like the tropics—spiced with salsa. Tall palm trees, lush gardens with vivid bougainvillea, and miles of citrus groves define the Rio Grande Valley, which Texans refer to simply as the Valley.

Off the mainland, resort hotels and condos line the lower tip of South Padre Island, a sliver of land with the Gulf at its front door and a beautiful bay called Laguna Madre at its back.

To all this, add the foreign flair of Mexico with its colorful markets, lively music, and fun restaurants, easily accessible from the Texas towns strung along the Rio Grande. Heavy traffic in both directions has created bicultural, bilingual communities on both sides of the river.

The Rio Grande Valley encompasses McAllen, Harlingen, Brownsville, and South Padre Island, where there's lively action on and off the water. One of the nation's fastest-growing areas, the Valley is popular year-round, drawing not only summer visitors but also thousands of "winter Texans"—northerners who come south each year to escape their cold climes. Considered one of the top 10 birding sites in the country, the Valley is a major migratory "rest stop" and home to many tropical birds not seen elsewhere in the States.

About 100 miles above the Valley, the city of Laredo is a bustling international trade center with strong Spanish and Mexican influences.

RIO GRANDE VALLEY/SOUTH TEXAS

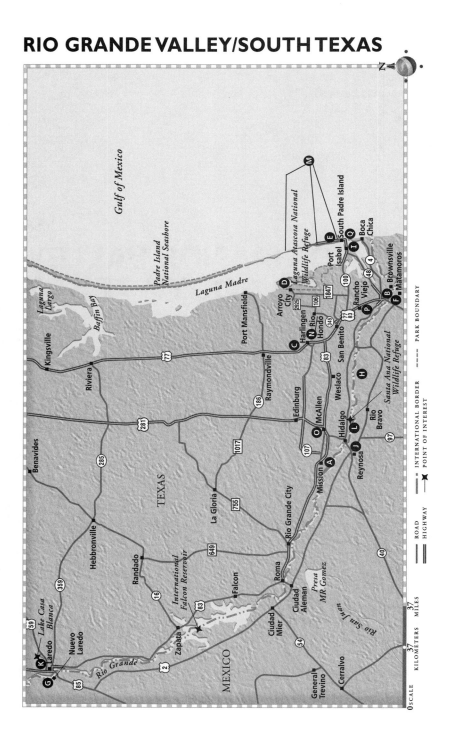

A PERFECT DAY IN THE RIO GRANDE VALLEY AND SOUTH TEXAS

Head out early to spot birds and other wildlife at one of the national refuges, either Laguna Atascosa north of Brownsville or Santa Ana south of McAllen. Then play in the Gulf and relax on the beach at South Padre Island. Plan an afternoon visit to the Gladys Porter Zoo in Brownsville, then cross the border into Matamoros or Reynosa for a more lively evening of dining and shopping, or to slightly quieter Nuevo Progreso.

SIGHTSEEING HIGHLIGHTS

★★★★ GLADYS PORTER ZOO
500 Ringgold St., Brownsville, 956/546-2177 (recording) or 956/546-7187, www.gpz.org

With more than 250 species of tropical plants, this attraction is a

SIGHTS
- **A** Bentsen-Rio Grande Valley State Park
- **B** Confederate Air Force/Rio Grande Valley Wing
- **B** Gladys Porter Zoo
- **C** Iwo Jima Memorial and Museum
- **D** Laguna Atascosa National Wildlife Refuge
- **E** Laguna Madre Nature Trail
- **F** Matamoros
- **G** Nuevo Laredo
- **H** Nuevo Progreso
- **I** Port Isabel Lighthouse State Historic Site
- **J** Reynosa
- **B** Sabal Palm Audubon Center and Sanctuary
- **K** San Augustin Plaza

SIGHTS (continued)
- **L** Santa Ana/Lower Rio Grande National Wildlife Refuge
- **E** Sea Turtle, Inc.
- **M** South Padre Island's Beaches
- **N** Texas Air Museum

FOOD
- **E** 202 Bayside Bar & Grill
- **K** Cotulla Style Pit Bar-B-Q
- **G** El Dorado
- **O** España
- **J** La Mansion del Prado
- **F** Las Dos Republicas
- **O** Santa Fe Steak House
- **E** Scampi's Restaurant & Bar
- **K** Tack Room
- **G** Victoria's

LODGING
- **E** Brown Pelican Inn
- **O** Doubletree Club Hotel
- **B** Holiday Inn Fort Brown Resort
- **E** Holiday Inn Sunspree Resort
- **K** La Posada Hotel & Suites
- **E** Radisson Resort South Padre Island
- **P** Rancho Viejo Resort
- **E** Sheraton Fiesta South Padre Island Beach Resort

CAMPING
- **A** Bentsen-Rio Grande Valley State Park
- **Q** Isla Blanca Park
- **K** Lake Casa Blanca International State Park

Note: Items with the same letter are located in the same area.

botanical wonderland as well as an outstanding small zoo focused on preserving rare and endangered plants and animals. Moats and streams, rather than cages, form boundaries for the animals, who live in open habitats simulating their natural environments. More than 1,500 specimens are grouped by geographic regions.

Details: *Memorial Day–Labor Day daily 9–6:30; rest of year until 5. $6 adults, $4.75 seniors, $3 ages 2–13. (1–2 hours)*

★★★★ SOUTH PADRE ISLAND'S BEACHES

For a resort atmosphere, South Padre Island is the premier beach destination in Texas. The Gulf, which tends to be tea-colored off Texas, frequently turns deep blue and turquoise here, its gentle surf and wide beaches attracting sun and sand lovers of all ages. Teenagers and college kids (who flock here in great numbers in March and April) love skimming across the water on banana boats and Jet Skis™ or scrambling over the sand in dune buggies. Visitors get a bird's-eye view of the area while parasailing, and horseback riders splash through the surf at sunset.

A beautiful bridge-causeway, with great views of the water and resort strip, crosses Laguna Madre (bay) from Port Isabel. The bridge leads visitors to the small town of South Padre Island, on the southern tip of the narrow 34-mile barrier island of the same name.

Incorporated only in 1973, the town stretches north about five miles, offering numerous mid-rise hotels and condos fronting the Gulf. The island's main paved road, Padre Boulevard, continues another 15 miles, providing access to nearly 30 miles of undeveloped beaches where driving on the sand is allowed. While all kinds of water sports and beach equipment are available for rent in front of the resorts, there are no concessions and no services on the undeveloped shoreline.

Catch the Wave on South Padre Island—it's the free trolley that provides transportation from 7 a.m. to 7 p.m.

Details: *South Padre Island Convention & Visitors Bureau, 800/ SOPADRE, info@sopadre.com, www.sopadre.com. (half-day minimum)*

★★★ CONFEDERATE AIR FORCE/RIO GRANDE VALLEY WING

Brownsville International Airport, Brownsville, 956/541-8585, www.avdigest.com/caf/caf.html

This museum has a collection of working WWII planes, artifacts, and memorabilia and does reenactments of 1940s air battles.

Details: Mon–Sat 9–4. $5 adults, $4 seniors, $3 ages 12–18. (1 hour)

★★★ IWO JIMA MEMORIAL AND MUSEUM
320 Iwo Jima Blvd., Harlingen, 956/412-2207
www.mma-tx.org
Yes, it's the real thing: the original working model for the famous statue at Arlington National Cemetery, depicting the raising of the U.S. flag at Iwo Jima during WWII. Across the street from the 100-foot statue, a museum pays tribute to those who fought in the battle.

Details: Adjacent to Harlingen International Airport and the Marine Military Academy campus. Museum: Mon–Sat 10–4, Sun 1–4. Donation requested. (30 minutes)

★★★ TEXAS AIR MUSEUM
Rio Hondo, Rte. 106, 956/748-2112, rowflyer@aol.com
This small museum at Texas Dusting Service has U.S., German, and Russian aircraft from WWII through the Vietnam conflict.

Details: One mile east of Rio Hondo. Daily 9–4. $4 adults, $2 ages 12–16, $1 age 11 and under. (1 hour)

★★ PORT ISABEL LIGHTHOUSE STATE HISTORIC SITE
Port Isabel, 956/943-1172, www.tpwd.state.tx.us
This landmark at the west end of the causeway leading to South Padre Island was built in 1853. It's normally open for visitors to climb to the top but has been undergoing restoration and may be closed. Check with the visitors center of the Port Isabel Chamber of Commerce, 800/527-6102, in the adjacent lighthouse-keeper's cottage for the latest information about going inside the lighthouse.

Details: Wed–Sun 10–4. $2 adults, $1 ages 6–12. (1 hour)

★★ SAN AUGUSTIN PLAZA
Zaragosa and San Bernardo Sts., Laredo
In the heart of Laredo, this historic area portrays the Spanish colonial heritage of the city. The St. Augustin Church, established in 1767, dates to 1872, and the Republic of the Rio Grande Museum, 956/727-3480, tells the story of the short-lived nation formed by the Laredo area and adjoining states in Mexico in 1839.

Details: Museum: Tue–Sat 9–4, Sun 1–4. Donation requested. (30 mintues–1 hour)

★★ SEA TURTLE, INC.
5805 Gulf Blvd., South Padre Island, 956/761-2544

This organization carries on the conservation work of the local heroine known as the Turtle Lady, who usually opens her home twice weekly to show and talk about endangered sea turtles.

Details: Tue and Sat at 10 a.m., but call to confirm. $2 donation requested. (30 minutes–1 hour)

WILDLIFE REFUGES/BIRDING SIGHTSEEING HIGHLIGHTS

On the Great Texas Coastal Birding Trail and continental flyways, the Valley, particularly along the Rio Grande and around Brownsville, has a number of national wildlife refuges and sanctuaries visited by or home to more than 400 species of birds. Information about bird-watching in the Valley also is available from the Brownsville Convention & Visitors Bureau, 800/626-2639, visitinfo@brownsville.org, www.brownsville.org.

★★★★ LAGUNA ATASCOSA NATIONAL WILDLIFE REFUGE
Rio Hondo, 956/748-3607, www.fws.gov

About 20 miles north of Brownsville, the refuge borders Laguna Madre and affords resting spots for hundreds of migrating birds, including the red-headed duck (which winters here), snow geese, sandhill cranes, white-tailed hawks, and scores more. It's also home to ocelots, mountain lions, and javelinas.

Details: Off Route 106 about 20 miles east of Rio Hondo. Daily sunrise–sunset; visitors center open Dec–Apr daily 10–4; May–Nov variable days 10–4, call for schedule. $2/vehicle. (1–3 hours)

★★★★ SANTA ANA/LOWER RIO GRANDE NATIONAL WILDLIFE REFUGE
Alamo, 956/787-3079, www.fws.gov

This subtropical woodland of native brushy growth and inland lakes provides a haven for numerous birds, waterfowl, and animals. Along the banks of the Rio Grande about 10 miles southeast of McAllen, the refuge offers prime bird-watching, particularly during the winter. Among the feathered visitors: chachalaca, green kingfisher, and least grebe. Visitors can see the wildlife on hiking trails and from photo blinds; cars are allowed to drive through only on Tuesdays and Wednesdays. Tram tours run in the winter.

Details: Off U.S. 281 slightly east of Route 907; open daily dawn–dusk, visitors center open Nov–Apr daily 9–4:30; May–Oct Mon–Fri 8:30–4. Tram tours late Nov–Apr Thu–Mon several times a day. Free to refuge, tram tours $3 adults, $1 ages 12 and under. (1–3 hours)

★★★ BENTSEN–RIO GRANDE VALLEY STATE PARK
Mission, 956/585-1107, www.tpwd.state.tx.us
This park along the Rio Grande has hiking and nature trails from which birders often spot rare species. Camping, hiking, and fishing are available.

Details: About 6 miles southwest of Mission, via U.S. 83 and Route 2062; open sunrise–10 p.m., park office open daily 8–5. $2/person ages 13 and older. (1–2 hours)

★★★ SABAL PALM AUDUBON CENTER AND SANCTUARY
Brownsville, 956/541-8034, www.audubon.org
A native palm jungle like much of the area once was, this forest is rich in tropical plants and wildlife. Look for green jays, buff-bellied hummingbirds, and tropical parulas as you wander its trails.

Details: About six miles southeast of Brownsville on Rte. 1419; open daily dawn–dusk; visitors center: Oct–May Tue–Sun 9–5; Jun–Sep Sat–Sun 9–5. $3 adults, $2 college students, $1 ages 6–18. (1–2 hours)

★★ LAGUNA MADRE NATURE TRAIL
7355 Padre Blvd., South Padre Island, 800/SOPADRE, info@sopadre.com, www.sopadre.com
A 1,500-foot boardwalk takes visitors across four acres of wetlands, which attract many species of birds and other wildlife. Signs help identify species likely to be seen in the area.

Details: By the convention center at the north end of town, open 24 hours. Free. (half day)

MEXICO'S BORDER TOWNS
From Laredo to Brownsville, a number of large cities and villages across the Rio Grande in Mexico are accessible via bridges, offering fun international excursions. Shop for handicrafts—pottery, rugs, silver, brass, onyx, and leather goods—and

MARIACHIS PUT ON A SHOW IN LAREDO

Texas Department of Transportation

enjoy Tex-Mex and Mexican cuisine. Many people also cross the border to get bargains in prescription drugs at Mexican *farmacías*. No paperwork is required to cross the border for the day but do carry proof of citizenship, such as voter registration—and take a doctor's prescription for drugs—in case you're stopped upon return. Your best bet is to leave your car on the U.S. side and walk across one of the bridges; parking is available near the bridges.

Major destinations are **Matamoros**, across from Brownsville; **Reynosa**, across from McAllen; and **Nuevo Laredo**, sister city to Laredo. South of Weslaco and Progreso, Route 1015 leads into **Nuevo Progreso**, a smaller Mexican town with a new market and good shopping. In these towns, shops, restaurants, and *farmacías* line the main and adjacent streets as you exit the bridges. Traditional Mexican markets usually are nearby, and you may find a handicraft center with a selection of top-quality items from around the country. Most merchants take U.S. dollars, and bargaining is customary.

Visitors centers in the Valley and at Laredo can provide information and regulations for crossing into Mexico: **Brownsville Convention & Visitors Bureau**, 800/626-2639, visitinfo@brownsville.org, www.brownsville.org; **Laredo Convention & Visitors Bureau**, 800/361-3360, lcvb@icsi.net, www.visitlaredo.com.

FITNESS AND RECREATION

Beyond all the beach and water sports, there's excellent fishing from piers, the shore, and boats in both Laguna Madre and the Gulf of Mexico. Cast for flounder, trout, redfish, tuna, sailfish, and marlin. In deep-sea fishing, the area holds a number of state records for such catches as blue marlin, mako shark, tarpon, and wahoo. Guided bay fishing usually runs $15 a person for four hours (morning or afternoon trips available), and offshore trips last all day and run $50 to $60 a person; fishing equipment is usually provided. Among operators are **Captain Murphy's Charters** at Sea Ranch Marina, 956/761-2764, and **Jim's Pier** (marina), 956/761-2865, both on South Padre Island.

Windsurfers skim across the waters on **Laguna Madre**, at Boca Chica below the tip of South Padre, and at several other spots. Because of its mild winter climate, the area allows year-round golfing. The largest selection of courses is in the Brownsville-Harlingen area. There's a notable 18-hole public course at the **Valley Inn & Country Club**, Farm Road 802 off U.S. 77/83, 956/548-9199; and guests staying at Rancho Viejo resort may play the two private 18-hole courses at **Rancho Viejo Country Club**, about 10 miles north of Brownsville on U.S. 77, 800/531-7400.

Hunters come from across the country for the white-tailed deer and white-wing dove seasons in the Valley and across the border in Mexico.

For more information, contact the **Brownsville Convention & Visitors Bureau**, 800/626-2639, visitinfo@brownsville.org., www.brownsville.org, and the **South Padre Visitors Center**, 800/SOPADRE, info@sopadre. com, www.sopadre.com.

FOOD

The large shrimping fleet along the coast assures a bounty of fresh seafood, often prepared with a bit of Mexican spice. Tex-Mex fare, specialties of interior Mexico, and game, mainly quail, are popular, too. Dress usually is casual, particularly on South Padre Island. A few upscale spots will be dressier. Most restaurants are moderately priced, ranging around $15 to $20.

On South Padre Island, bayside **Scampi's Restaurant & Bar**, 206 W. Aries Street, 956/761-1755, is a quiet, more upscale gathering spot for watching sunsets and enjoying a feast of shrimp in all sizes and flavorings—from garlicky to the restaurant's signature peanut-butter shrimp with a tinge of ginger. The **202 Bayside Bar & Grill**, 202 W. Whiting Street, 956/761-8481, adds new spice to South Texas with a blending of Pacific Rim touches, including fiery Thai items.

In McAllen, **España**, 701 N. Main Street, 956/618-5242, located in an old home, lives up to its name by serving Spanish and other Mediterranean-style foods, including the classic paella with a variety of seafood, chicken, and sausage cooked with rice and flavored with saffron. Saltillo tile floors and Mexican folk art accent the **Santa Fe Steak House**, 1918 S. 10th Street, 956/630-2331, where the menu emphasizes steaks but also offers fresh fish.

Across the border, popular dining options include **La Mansion del Prado** at P.J. Mendez and Emilio Portes Gil Streets in Reynosa; and **Las Dos Republicas**, on Abasolo Street opposite Juárez Market in Matamoros.

In Laredo, for that special night out, the **Tack Room** in La Posada Hotel & Suites, 1000 Zaragosa Street, 956/722-1701, provides fine dining in an elegant atmosphere. Tasty breakfast tacos, Mexican specialties, and barbecue at low prices beckon crowds to **Cotulla Style Pit Bar-B-Q**, 4502 McPherson Street, 965/724-5747, which closes by 6 p.m. or earlier. Across the border in Nuevo Laredo, both **Victoria's** (at Matamoros Street) and **El Dorado** (Belden and Ocampo Streets) have specialties from interior Mexico.

LODGING

Accommodations range from midrise condos and hotels fronting the Gulf of Mexico on South Padre Island to resorts with lush tropical gardens and hacienda-style inns by the Rio Grande. Winter is low season, summer high, and rates are usually lower on weekdays.

South Padre Island has the greatest concentration and choice of places to stay. Many properties offer both hotel rooms and condos. **Radisson Resort South Padre Island**, 500 Padre Boulevard, 800/292-7704, has rooms and two-bedroom condos on the beachfront, water sports, pools, and entertainment. Rates start at $95 winter, $150 summer. **Holiday Inn Sunspree Resort**, 100 Padre Boulevard, 800/531-7405, also on the Gulf, offers rooms, suites, and two-bedroom condos with tennis, pools, and a recreation program in summer. Its rates start at about $70 winter, $120 summer. **Sheraton Fiesta South Padre Island Beach Resort**, 310 Padre Boulevard, 800/672-4747, has a huge pool, swim-up *palapa* bar, beachside bar and grill, and rooms and condos starting at $80 in winter and $149 summer; ask about special promotions. **Brown Pelican Inn**, 207 W. Aries Boulevard, 956/761-2722, overlooking Laguna Madre, has eight rooms furnished with antiques; all have private baths and most have access to the second-floor porch. Rates are $70 to $120, including continental breakfast.

Numerous rental agencies can assist in finding condos, and there are several reservation services. Among the largest companies are **Service 24**, 800/828-4287, and **Padre Island Rentals/Island Reservation Service**, 800/926-6926. The *South Padre Island Visitors Guide*, available from the convention and visitors bureau, 800/SOPADRE, lists rental agencies, condos, hotels, and motels.

In Brownsville, **Holiday Inn Fort Brown Resort**, 1900 E. Elizabeth Street, 800/HOLIDAY, is set in a tropical garden near the international bridge between the United States and Mexico; its rooms start at around $80. About 10 miles north of Brownsville, the **Rancho Viejo Resort**, on U.S. 77 at Rancho Viejo, 800/531-7400, offers rooms and Spanish-style villas by two golf courses along wandering waterways, starting at about $100. In McAllen, the **Doubletree Club Hotel**, 101 N. Main Street, 800/222-8733, is a historic Spanish colonial–style lodging with part of the property dating to 1918; rooms start at about $60, including full breakfast and evening cocktails.

In Laredo, **La Posada Hotel & Suites**, 1000 Zaragosa Street, 800/444-2099, is the city's premier lodging, a nineteenth-century Spanish colonial convent with tropical courtyards. Located next to the Rio Grande, it offers two pools, several restaurants, a fitness center, and easy access to Mexico. Rates start at about $90.

CAMPING

Since McAllen, Harlingen, Brownsville, and South Padre Island are prime destinations in winter for northerners escaping the cold, the area has an abundance of RV sites—in fact, more than 500 parks, two-thirds of them around McAllen. Many campgrounds offer a lively social schedule of pot-luck dinners and other activities. For listings of area parks, contact the **Texas Recreational Vehicle Association**, P.O. Box 308, Los Fresnos, Texas 78566; the convention and visitors bureaus of Brownsville and McAllen; and the chamber of commerce in Harlingen.

For those who like to be close to the beach, **Isla Blanca Park**, 956/761-5493, at the southern tip of South Padre Island, has one of the largest campgrounds, along with jetty fishing, a marina, grocery store, laundry, rest rooms and showers, barbecue grills, and picnic areas. Near Mission outside McAllen, **Bentsen–Rio Grande Valley State Park**, 956/585-1107, sits by the river and is known for its excellent bird-watching. It has hiking trails, a nature trail, boat ramp, rest rooms and showers, and RV hookups.

On the edge of Laredo, **Lake Casa Blanca International State Park**, 956/725-3826, has campsites, a boat ramp, fishing facilities, and more.

NIGHTLIFE AND SPECIAL EVENTS

The greatest number of options for nighttime entertainment are on South Padre Island; in Laredo; and across the border at Matamoros and Nuevo Laredo, Mexico.

At South Padre, crowds gather to dine and dance under the stars at **Louie's Backyard**, 2305 Laguna Boulevard, 956/761-6406. **Coconuts**, 2301 Laguna Boulevard, 956/761-4218, is a thatched-roof tropical escape on the bayside; and **Wahoo Saloon**, 201 W. Pike Street, 956/761-5344, is a good place to pop down oysters and listen to blues. Another popular spot is **Wanna-Wanna Beach Bar & Grill** on the Gulf at the Island Inn, 5100 Gulf Boulevard, 956/761-7688.

Walk across the border for a foreign-flavored evening at Matamoros, opposite Brownsville; Reynosa, opposite McAllen; and Nuevo Laredo, twin city to Laredo. Within a short distance of the international bridges you'll find numerous restaurants, often with live music and lounges.

In Matamoros, a big name is **Garcia's**, 82 Calle Alvaro Obregon, which has not only dining, cocktails, and live entertainment but also shopping. In Nuevo Laredo, **El Dorado** at Belden and Ocampo Streets and **Señor Frog's** on Ocampo Street are popular. Beware: All three cities on the Mexico side of the Rio Grande are large, and you should take the same personal safety precautions you would in any metropolitan area, particularly at night.

McAllen has its own brand of entertainment—square dancing. It's known as the square-dance capital of the world, and you can swing to lively calls nearly every day of the week, particularly during winter. Check locally about dance sites. The city also has a symphony, touring Broadway productions, and a number of clubs with live music.

In special events, the **Texas Citrus Fiesta**, 956/585-9724, celebrates the area's big industry each January in Mission; and the **Texas Square Dance Jamboree**, 956/682-2871, draws thousands to McAllen in early February. Spring break brings tens of thousands to South Padre Island during March and April, and **Pirate Days** at South Padre in mid-October recounts the early history of the coast. For information, contact the convention and visitors bureau, 800/SOPADRE. In Brownsville, **Charro Days Fiesta**, 956/542-4245, celebrates the area's multicultural heritage in February. Laredo goes all out with a 10-day international fiesta for **George Washington's Birthday**, 956/722-0589, in mid-February. It also has a **Borderfest** the first weekend in July. Both Laredos have **Fiestas Patrias** in mid-September. Contact the **Laredo Convention & Visitors Bureau**, 800/361-3360, for information.

10
WEST TEXAS/BIG BEND

Vast and rugged, West Texas confirms one popular image of the state yet dispels another myth. West of the Pecos River, for miles and miles, you'll see expanses of sky cupping arid land with only scrubby growth. The region is part of the Chihuahua Desert, where spindly cactuses often afford the only shade. A roadrunner darting across the highway may be the only sign of life a driver sees for 40 or 50 miles.

Yet this desert stretching from the Rio Grande northwestward to the New Mexico border is punctuated with peaks soaring above 8,000 feet—not your normal image of Texas. Indeed, West Texas has several mountain ranges and 90 peaks more than a mile high.

Midland and Odessa, oil communities only 20 miles apart, serve as a gateway to this area's biggest attraction, Big Bend National Park on the Rio Grande. Adjacent to the park is Terlingua, a funky ghost town. If the area around Marfa looks vaguely familiar—the way you always thought Texas would look—that's because the film *Giant*, with James Dean, Elizabeth Taylor, and Rock Hudson, was shot here. At the center of this region are the scenic Davis Mountains and Fort Davis, a small town with one of the Southwest's best-preserved frontier forts.

Caution: The distance between towns with services can sometimes be 50 miles or more, so keep your eye on the gas gauge and always travel with drinking water.

WEST TEXAS/BIG BEND

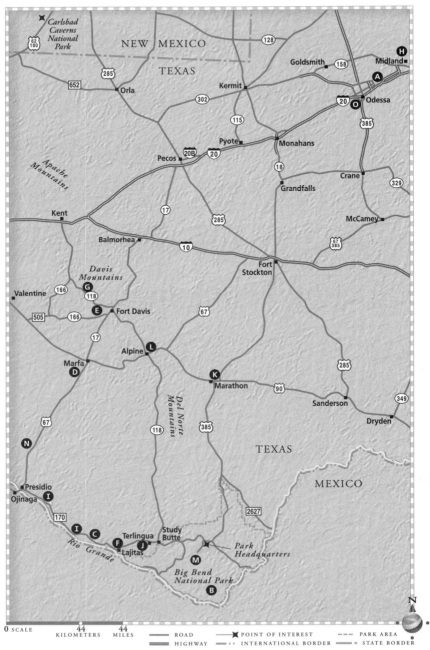

Carlsbad Caverns National Park

NEW MEXICO

TEXAS

128

Goldsmith

158

Midland

H

A

62
180

285

652

Orla

Kermit

302

O

20

Odessa

385

115

Pyote

Monahans

Apache
Mountains

Pecos

20B

20

18

Grandfalls

Crane

329

Kent

17

285

McCamey

67
385

Balmorhea

10

Davis
Mountains

G

118

Fort
Stockton

Valentine

166

E

Fort Davis

67

505

166

285

17

Alpine

L

Marfa

D

K

Marathon

90

Sanderson

349

Del Norte
Mountains

285

Dryden

118

385

TEXAS

N

MEXICO

Presidio

I

Ojinaga

2627

170

I

C

Terlingua

F

Study
Butte

Park
Headquarters

Lajitas

J

M

Rio Grande

Big Bend
National Park

B

N

0 SCALE	44	44		
	KILOMETERS	MILES	ROAD	POINT OF INTEREST	PARK AREA
			HIGHWAY	INTERNATIONAL BORDER	STATE BORDER

A PERFECT DAY IN WEST TEXAS/BIG BEND

Spend Friday night at Fort Davis, joining the star party at McDonald Observatory in the evening. Visit Fort Davis National Historic Site the next morning, then take Route 17, U.S. 67, and Route 170 (the scenic River Road) to Big Bend National Park. Make reservations ahead to spend the night at Chisos Mountains Lodge. Plan to spend a second day in the park.

BIG BEND REGION SIGHTSEEING HIGHLIGHTS

★★★★ BIG BEND NATIONAL PARK

915/477-2251 (information), 915/477-2291 (lodging), BIBEInformation@nps.gov, www.nps.gov/bibe

Where the Rio Grande makes a big U-turn, the river, the desert, and the mountains combine in a vast wilderness ranging in altitude from 1,850 feet to 7,835 feet. Mostly Chihuahua Desert, the terrain supports more than 1,100 types of plants, from scrubby-looking cactuses that burst forth in color in spring and after rainfall, to junipers, piñon pines, and even aspens and maples in the mountains. Jackrabbits, roadrunners, javelinas, mountain lions, and more than 430 bird species inhabit the park, which encompasses more than

---

SIGHTS

- **A** American Airpower Heritage Museum and Confederate Air Force
- **B** Big Bend National Park
- **C** Big Bend Ranch State Park
- **D** Chinati Foundation
- **E** Davis Mountains State Park
- **F** Lajitas
- **G** McDonald Observatory
- **H** Permian Basin Petroleum Museum
- **I** River Road
- **J** Terlingua

FOOD

- **F** Badlands Restaurant
- **K** Café Cenizo
- **L** Reata
- **J** Starlight Theatre
- **H** Venezia
- **O** Wild Scallion

LODGING

- **M** Chisos Mountains Lodge
- **N** Cibolo Creek Ranch
- **K** Gage Hotel
- **E** Indian Lodge

LODGING (continued)

- **F** Lajitas on the Rio Grande
- **O** Mellie Van Horn's Historic Inn

CAMPING

- **B** Big Bend National Park
- **C** Big Bend Ranch State Park
- **E** Davis Mountains State Park
- **F** Lajitas on the Rio Grande
- **A** Midessa KOA
- **H** Midland RV Park

Note: Items with the same letter are located in the same area.

800,000 acres. This is no drive-through-on-the-way-somewhere-else park—the closest entrance is 40 miles south of U.S. 90 and it's another 30 miles to the park headquarters. While the park's rugged beauty can be appreciated from a car window, allow time to explore some of the many hiking opportunities—from short, easy walks to rugged overnight treks. Floating on the Rio Grande gives a different perspective of the land, taking visitors through narrow, steep canyons.

For a minimum visit, plan to stop at the **Panther Junction Visitor Center**, drive to **Chisos Basin** (the winding road climbs 2,000 feet in six miles), and take the **Ross Maxwell Scenic Drive** to **Santa Elena Canyon**. There are limited overnight accommodations in the park—advance reservations are a must at the lodge—and in adjacent Study Butte and Lajitas. In the area, Alpine has the most lodging possibilities.

Details: *Access park via U.S. 385 from Marathon (70 miles), Rte. 118 from Alpine (108 miles), or U.S. 67 and River Rd. 170 from Marfa (156 miles). Open year-round. $10/vehicle, permit good seven days. (2 or more days)*

★★★★ RIVER ROAD/LAJITAS/TERLINGUA
800/944-9907 (information), info@lajitas.com,
www.lajitas.com, www.visitbigbend.com

Known as El Camino del Rio, the River Road (Route 170) skirts the Rio Grande between Presidio and Lajitas, offering the most spectacular gateway to Big Bend and one of the most scenic drives in the country. The flat valley around Presidio turns into rugged, wild terrain, with mountains rising on both the Texas and Mexico sides of the river. Numerous dips in the road are marked with flash-flood warnings—sudden downpours can turn these dry areas into raging streams. The route winds through canyons, becoming quite steep (15 percent grade) at times. This is open-range country, so watch for horses and cattle straying onto the road. There are no services on the 50-mile stretch.

Built on the site of an old army post, Lajitas looks like a movie set with its **Badlands Hotel and Saloon**, Old West storefronts along a boardwalk (truly wooden boards), and hitching posts where you may see a horse along with the ubiquitous Suburbans that Texans love. Saunter over to the **Lajitas Trading Post**, an old general store whose resident goat likes to guzzle beer.

From Lajitas, Route 170 continues eastward to **Big Bend National Park**, taking you by the tiny community of Terlingua, which rouses from slumber each November for a chili Olympics of worldwide fame. Once a mining boomtown, Terlingua is now more a state of mind than a town; but look for a "Ghost Town" sign and drive up the hill. You'll find some life at a couple of restored buildings, including a good gift shop called the **Terlingua Trading Co.**, a couple of river outfitters, and the **Starlight Theatre**, a restaurant. Take time to enjoy the drop-dead view of the distant desert mountain range from the boardwalk/porch.

Details: (1 1/2–2 hours)

★★★ **BIG BEND RANCH STATE PARK**
Off Rte. 170, 915/229-3416, www.tpwd.state.tx.us
For those who want to get into really primitive back country, this 287,000-acre wilderness just west of Lajitas offers rugged mountains and canyons where few have trekked. You must get a permit to enter the park, which offers camping, hiking, rafting, canoeing, and fishing. To park headquarters, it's a 1 1/2-hour drive on a gravel road, but the less adventurous can take a daylong bus trip to explore the remote territory. **The Barton Warnock Environmental Education Center**, east of Lajitas, 915/424-3327, is an entry station that provides background on the region and has trails through its desert garden. It is open daily from 8 to 5.

Details: Entrance stations across from Fort Leaton ruins on Rte. 170 near Presidio and at Barton Warnock Environmental Education Center. $6 adults, $4 under age 12. Bus tours offered the first and third Sat each month for $60/person; reserve through the Texas Parks and Wildlife Department, 512/389-8900. (6 hours–full day)

A "HOT" SPOT
Without even trying, Presidio is a "hot" spot—the town that often makes news on the daily weather report as having the highest temperature in the nation. The dry, dusty town anchors one end of the scenic River Road along the Rio Grande.

FORT DAVIS/DAVIS MOUNTAINS SIGHTSEEING HIGHLIGHTS

★★★★ DAVIS MOUNTAINS STATE PARK
Hwy. 118, 915/426-3337, www.tpwd.state.tx.us
Popular for its Indian Lodge resort and campsites, this state park has good hiking and a don't-miss scenic drive that winds up a mountain to sweeping panoramic views southward of the Chihuahua Desert punctuated with mountain ranges. There are two lookout points, which are good picnic spots.

Details: About four miles northwest of the town of Fort Davis on Hwy. 118. Open year-round. $3/person, seniors and under 13 free. (1–2 hours)

★★★★ FORT DAVIS
Hwys. 17 and 118, 800/524-3015, ftdavis@overland.net, www.fortdavis.com
With nary a streetlight or a stop sign, you could zip through this little gem of a town, but put on the brakes and use it as a base for exploring the Davis Mountains area on the way to or from Big Bend. In town, browse along Main Street, which has excellent gift shops and galleries in its old buildings, a drugstore with soda fountain, and the historic Hotel Limpia, dating to 1912. A couple of blocks off Main Street are two museums worth a visit, depending on your interests, but their hours are irregular. The **Overland Trail Museum**, three blocks west of Main Street near the fort, 915/426-3904, open April through November, chronicles early days on the frontier through its collection of memorabilia in a pioneer home; and the **Neill Doll Museum**, seven blocks west of the courthouse, 915/426-3969, showcases a collection of more than 300 dolls and toys from the early 1800s in a turn-of-the-century house decorated in antiques.

Details: (1–3 hours)

★★★★ FORT DAVIS NATIONAL HISTORIC SITE
Fort Davis, 915/426-3224, www.nps.gov/foda
From the 1850s, Fort Davis was a key military post and is now one of the best-preserved frontier forts in the Southwest. In the 1870s and 1880s, several African American regiments, known as Buffalo Soldiers, served here in the fight against Apache Indians. Scenically situated at the mouth of a canyon along the old **San Antonio–El Paso**

FORT DAVIS

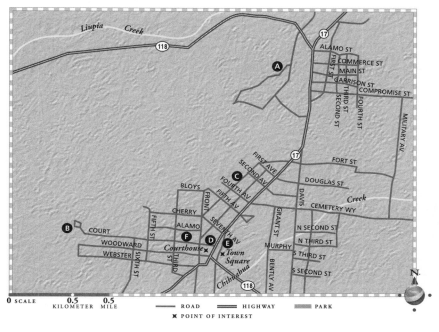

SIGHTS

Ⓐ Fort Davis National
Historic Site
Ⓑ Neill Doll Musuem
Ⓒ Overland Trail Museum

FOOD

Ⓓ The Drugstore
Ⓔ Hotel Limpia Dining
Room

LODGING

Ⓔ Hotel Limpia
Ⓕ Veranda

Note: Items with the same letter are located in the same place.

Overland Trail, the fort still has more than two dozen of its 50 original structures, including an impressive Officers Row of stone homes and a line of barracks flanking a large parade ground. Listen and you'll hear bugles and hoofbeat recordings that echo across the fort several times daily. Hike up the hill from the parking lot for a great scenic overlook of the fort and the plains stretching east. A video at the visitors center tells the history of the fort, and several buildings have

CIRCLING THE SIGHTS

Most sights in this area can be covered on a scenic circle trip from Midland-Odessa. Follow I-20 west, U.S. 385 south to Marathon, U.S. 90 west to Alpine, and Highway 118 to Big Bend National Park. Return via Highway 170 to Presidio, U.S. 67 to Marfa, then Highways 17, 166, and 118 to Fort Davis. Take Highway 17, I-10 east to Fort Stockton, Highway 18 to Monahans, and I-20 back to Midland-Odessa.

been furnished and are open for self-guided tours. From Memorial Day to Labor Day, costumed interpreters present demonstrations and talk about life at the fort.

Details: *On the north end of town, near intersection of Routes 118 and 17. Memorial Day–Labor Day daily 8–6; rest of year until 5. $2/person or $4/vehicle, under age 16 free. (1–1½ hours)*

★★★★ MCDONALD OBSERVATORY
Rte. 118, 915/426-3640, frankc@astro.as.utexas.edu, www.as.utexas.edu/mcdonald

Considered one of the world's major astronomy research sites, this University of Texas facility crowns 6,800-foot Mount Locke, its huge white domes visible for miles across the Davis Mountains. Day or night, the sweeping view of the West Texas mountain terrain from the facility is worth the drive itself. The visitors center offers an introduction to the facility, astronomy exhibits, a video, and gift shop. Twice daily, the public has a chance to view the sun through a specially filtered telescope at the visitors center. The center provides an informative brochure for a self-guided walking/driving tour, which ends at the dome that houses the 107-inch telescope used to help NASA's space missions among other projects. (Beware: There's a climb to see the telescope.) Guided tours (fee charged) provide more background about the facility and explanations of the telescopes, including the new Hobby-Eberly Telescope with a 432-inch mirror—the largest in North America and one of the largest in the world. Because the West Texas air is so clear and the location so distant from any city lights, the stargazing is spectacular. The observatory hosts public star parties three nights each week (see Nightlife section). Caution: Remember that the altitude here is about 7,000 feet.

Details: *16 miles northwest of Fort Davis on Rte. 118. Visitors center open daily 9–5 and for star-gazing parties Tue, Fri, and Sat evenings at sunset; solar viewing daily 11 and 3:30 weather permitting; guided tours at 11:30 and 2 (also daily at 9:30 in Mar, Jun, Jul, and Aug). Donation requested; tours $3 adults, $2 ages 6–12, or $8 families; star parties $3 adults, $2 ages 6–12, or $8/family. (1–3 hours)*

OTHER SIGHTSEEING HIGHLIGHTS

★★★ AMERICAN AIRPOWER HERITAGE MUSEUM AND CONFEDERATE AIR FORCE

9600 Wright Dr., Midland, 915/563-1000, aahm-info@ avdigest.com, www.avdigest.com/aahm/aahm.html

Dedicated to rescuing, restoring, and preserving vintage military aircraft, the Confederate Air Force (CAF) at Midland International Airport has more than 130 WWII planes in flying condition. The exhibit of U.S., British, German, and Japanese planes changes frequently, with about 20 on display at one time. Among the collection are a B-17 Flying Fortress and a Messerschmitt; flying demonstrations are given. Through interactive exhibits, the museum details air battles of WWII, including a walk through D-Day.

Details: *By the Midland Airport. Mon–Sat 9–5, Sun noon–5. $6 adults, $5 seniors and ages 13–18, $4 ages 6–12. (1–2 hours)*

★★★ CHINATI FOUNDATION

U.S. 67, Marfa, 915/729-4362, www.chinati.org

An old army post on the edge of Marfa provides the unusual setting for a permanent collection of large works of art by contemporary artists, among them Donald Judd, who created the foundation.

Details: *Off U.S. 67 about a half-mile south of Marfa. Thu–Sat 1–5 or by appointment. Donation requested. (1 hour)*

★★★ PERMIAN BASIN PETROLEUM MUSEUM

1500 I-20 W., Midland, 915/683-4403, www.petroleummuseum.org

Located in one of the world's biggest oil-producing areas, this museum tells the story of black gold in a way the average person can understand and enjoy. The museum takes visitors deep into a Permian-period sea to learn about the formation of oil, through a 1920s boomtown, and onto an old rig to experience a well blowout. **Details:** *Mon–Sat 9–5, Sun 2–5. $4 adults, $3 seniors, $2 ages 6–12. (1 1/2 hours)*

FITNESS AND RECREATION

Rafting the Rio Grande takes you into remote back country through spectacular canyons with sheer cliffs rising 1,500 feet above the river. Outfitters operating mainly from the Study Butte/Terlingua area and Lajitas do trips of varying lengths. Even the shorter trips take most of the day, counting transportation to put-in sites on the river. Overnight trips are popular, allowing leisurely time on the river with camping at riverside beaches. And dinner isn't canned beans—wilderness chefs cook hearty meals with fresh ingredients. The Rio Grande is fairly gentle here, though there are some rapids. Guided trips cost about $90 to $100 a day.

Major outfitters include **Far Flung Adventures**, 800/359-4138 in Terlingua; **Rio Grande Adventures**, 800/343-1640, and **Texas River Expeditions**, 800/839-7238, both in Study Butte; and **Big Bend River Tours**, 800/545-4240, at Lajitas. Several outfitters do specialized overnight trips, with themes such as stargazing, photography, wine tasting, and gourmet dining.

FOOD

Despite the remoteness, visitors will find some excellent restaurants in the Big Bend/Davis Mountains area, but reservations are advisable since most are small. Dress is casual.

At Terlingua, **Starlight Theatre**, 915/371-2326, serves excellent steaks in a cowboy-casual setting with fantastic mountain views through the front door. Meals are usually less than $15 but credit cards are not accepted. In Lajitas, the **Badlands Restaurant**, 800/944-9907, serves "Lajitas fajitas" and other Tex-Mex and American selections in a casual setting at inexpensive to moderate prices. In Marathon, beside the historic Gage hotel on U.S. 90, **Café Cenizo**, 800/884-GAGE, serves Mexican specialties and Southwestern dishes in a ranch-type setting with a courtyard and fountain. In Alpine, **Reata**, 203 N. Fifth Street, 915/837-9232, has upscale "cowboy" cuisine—few ranch hands ate this good—with hot biscuits for starters and excellent steaks. Named for the ranch in the film *Giant*, Reata is located in an old house decorated with memorabilia from the '50s movie, which was shot here. Prices are moderate to moderately expensive at these two restaurants.

In Fort Davis, the top spot to eat is **Hotel Limpia Dining Room**, on Highway 17/Main Street, 915/426-3241, with moderately priced choices ranging from pasta to steak (with Southwestern touches on many dishes). **The Drugstore**, also on Main Street, 915/426-3118, is an inexpensive favorite for breakfast, lunch, and its old-fashioned soda-fountain drinks.

In Midland, the upscale **Wild Scallion**, 4400 N. Midland Drive, 915/520-5455, serves freshly prepared contemporary American cuisine in a villa-type setting at moderately expensive prices. **Venezia**, 2101 W. Wadley Avenue, 915/687-0900, concentrates on northern Italian cuisine emphasizing seafood and offers patio dining at moderate prices.

LODGING

At Big Bend National Park, the only accommodations are at **Chisos Mountains Lodge**, at Chisos Basin, 915/477-2291, which has rooms and cottages with spectacular views of the mountains, a dining room, and gift shop. Rates start at about $75; rooms book up early. Bed down on the Western frontier at **Lajitas on the Rio Grande**, Highway 170 west of Big Bend, 800/944-9907, which has Old West–style hotel and motel accommodations (with such modern amenities as a swimming pool), plus condos and homes; rates start at $75.

A gateway to Big Bend, Marathon is hardly more than a wide spot on U.S. 90, but its historic **Gage** hotel, 800/884-GAGE, on U.S. 90, invites stopping to enjoy rocking chairs on the front porch with views of the distant mountains. Indian, Mexican, and old ranch decor and furnishings blend in this 1927 hotel, built by a cattle baron, and in the new Los Portales addition around a courtyard. Rates start at $85 with private bath.

In Fort Davis, **Hotel Limpia**, Highway 17/Main Street, 800/662-5517, has rooms in five historic buildings, the most prominent being the original hotel built on the town square in 1912. The pink limestone building boasts a veranda with rocking chairs, a parlor, and airy rooms, many furnished with antiques and all with private baths. Rates start at $69. The **Veranda**, a historic adobe inn built in 1883, on Court Avenue about two blocks from the town square, has 10 rooms that start at $70, including breakfast. About four miles outside Fort Davis on Route 118, in the Davis Mountains State Park, the white, pueblo-style **Indian Lodge**, 915/426-3254, has an older section dating to the 1930s with thick adobe walls, open beams with cane ceilings, and handcrafted furnishings; rates start at $55 and rooms book quickly for the entire year.

The most remote and probably most luxurious lodging is **Cibolo Creek Ranch**, 915/ 229-3737, outside Shafter, between Marfa and Presidio on U.S. 67, where 1850s adobe forts have been turned into guest rooms furnished with Spanish and Mexican antiques. The historic ranch of more than 25,000 acres offers hiking, swimming, fishing, and horseback riding. Rates start at $250, including meals, prepared by the resident chef using many ingredients grown on the ranch.

In Odessa, **Mellie Van Horn's Historic Inn**, 903 N. Sam Houston Street, 915/337-3000, a 1930s boarding house, has 16 rooms with private baths, with rates starting at $79, including breakfast. Numerous chain motels are available in the Midland-Odessa area.

The Big Bend Area Travel Association publishes a guide to the area, listing various kinds of accommodations. For information, contact the **Alpine Chamber of Commerce**, 800/561-3735.

CAMPING

Big Bend National Park has first-come, first-served campgrounds at Chisos Basin and Rio Grande Village, where there's also an RV park. Primitive camping in the back country is allowed with a permit (free) obtained at the Panther Junction Visitor Center. For information, call park concessions, 915/477-2291; for the RV park, call 915/477-2293. Campgrounds are frequently filled; call ahead at the numbers above or the park headquarters, 915/477-2251. **Lajitas on the Rio Grande**, 915/424-3471, has an RV park and draws numerous "snowbirds" escaping cold northern winters. **Big Bend Ranch State Park**, outside Lajitas on Route 170, 915/229-3416, or 512/389-8900 for reservations, allows primitive camping only. There are RV parks and campgrounds in Alpine, Marathon, Marfa, and the Terlingua area.

Outside Fort Davis, **Davis Mountains State Park**, 915/426-3337 or 512/389-8900 for reservations, has tent camping and hookups, rest rooms, and showers in a scenic setting. Frequently there are evening programs.

Midland RV Park, 2134 S. Midland Drive, 915/697-0801, offers hookups (with phone plug-ins), shaded areas, rest rooms and showers, a recreation hall, and laundry. **Midessa KOA**, 500 S. Route 1290, 915/563-2368, between Midland and Odessa, provides cabins as well as hookups, a convenience store, rest rooms and showers, a pool, and more.

NIGHTLIFE AND SPECIAL EVENTS

The stars, indeed, are big and bright out here, and you'll never get better views than at **McDonald Observatory** star parties every Tuesday, Friday, and

Saturday starting at sunset. Observatory staff point out constellations and assist viewing of planets and other celestial objects through large telescopes. The parties are fun for the whole family. Bring binoculars and a sweater (or coat in winter); at nearly 7,000 feet, it's cool at night. Meet at the visitors center; see McDonald Observatory sightseeing entry for details.

Outside Marfa, people gather in their cars and stare at the sky in search of the mysterious **Marfa Lights**, which often appear on the horizon to the southwest. You'll find the viewing site about nine miles east of town on U.S. 90. Sightings of the lights have been reported for more than a century.

In the Big Bend area, the partially restored ghost town of Terlingua livens up at night at **Starlight Theatre**, 915/371-2326, a restaurant-bar with frequent live entertainment; to find it, follow "Ghost Town" signs leading off Highway 170 west of Study Butte. At Lajitas, about 15 miles beyond Terlingua on Highway 170, mosey into the **Badlands Saloon** at the Lajitas on the Rio Grande Resort, 800/944-9907, where there's usually live entertainment and dancing. In Fort Davis, locals gather at the historic **Sutlers Club** in Hotel Limpia, Highway 17/Main Street, 915/426-3241.

Among special events, crowds come yearly for the **World Championship Chili Cookoff** in Terlingua in November. For information, contact **Far Flung Adventures**, 800/359-4138. **Marfa Lights Festival** is held Labor Day weekend; for information, contact the Marfa Chamber of Commerce, 800/650-9696. Alpine hosts an annual **Cowboy Poetry Gathering** each March; for information, contact the Alpine Chamber of Commerce, 800/561-3735. The **Odessa Shakespeare Festival**, 915/332-1586, brings live performances of the Bard's work April through September to the Globe of the Great Southwest, a replica of Shakespeare's Globe Theatre. In late September/early October at the Midland International Airport, the Confederate Air Force hosts its annual **CAF AirSho**, 915/563-1000, reenacting WWII air battles with its squadron of vintage planes.

Davis Mountains

To savor the desert mountain scenery, pack a lunch and follow a 74-mile loop through the Davis Mountains, which range from golden hills to jagged peaks. From Route 17 south of Fort Davis, take Route 166, which winds west and north past mountains rising to elevations of more than 8,000 feet. Vineyards cover some lower slopes, and piñon and ponderosa pines dot higher elevations. Turn south on Route 118, which climbs into the mountains, twists through canyons, and passes the **McDonald Observatory** (see Sightseeing Highlights) and **Davis Mountains State Park** on the way back to Fort Davis. Detour into the state park and circle up its steep scenic drive for a grand view—hardly changed from the days when wagon trains and stagecoaches rolled west through here. There are several picnic sites along this route, including sites at the state park.

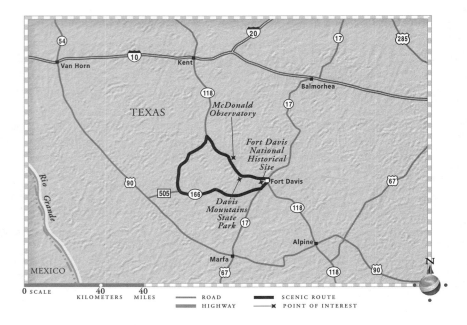

11
EL PASO

Two nations and two states come together in El Paso, creating a unique multi-national city spectacularly situated where the tip of the Rocky Mountains knifes into the Chihuahua Desert. El Paso's population of 600,000 combines with that of Juárez, Mexico (1.7 million), across the Rio Grande, to make a sprawling metropolitan complex that's popular for its year-round sunny climate.

While proudly Texan, the city shares strong similarities in lifestyles, cuisine, and terrain with its western neighbors and Mexico. The city is closer to Albuquerque, Tucson, and Chihuahua City, Mexico, than it is to any major city in Texas. It's even on mountain time (like New Mexico) rather than central time (like most of Texas).

Named for a pass leading north through the mountains, El Paso boasts a rich history, including the arrival of Spanish conquistadors in 1598. The city claims to be the first site of a Thanksgiving between new settlers and Native Americans, predating the celebrated Plymouth feast by 23 years. Its missions date to the 1680s and are considered the oldest in continuous service in the United States.

Beyond its own sights, El Paso often acts as a base for touring southern New Mexico's attractions and as a gateway for exploring the Big Bend–Guadalupe and Davis Mountains region of West Texas.

Remember to protect yourself against the strong sun here and be sure to carry water when outside, particularly in the summer.

A PERFECT DAY IN EL PASO

Take the Mission Trail, visiting Socorro and Ysleta Missions, the Presidio Chapel at San Elizario, and the Tigua Cultural Center. Tour the Museum of Art, then take the Border Jumper Trolley into Juárez for a couple of hours. Have dinner in El Paso or out at Cattleman's Steakhouse at Indian Cliffs Ranch and finish the evening with a drive along scenic Rim Road to see the night lights of El Paso and Juárez.

ORIENTATION

Sightseeing is scattered enough that it's wise to have a car. The Mission Trail and many Western-wear stores are on the southeastern edge of the city, and scenic drives are to the north. Several sights are in the downtown area, which is adjacent to the Rio Grande and Juárez across the river. For touring downtown and Juárez, park the car (at the Civic Center, Santa Fe and San Francisco Streets, 915/534-0600) and walk to sights or use the Sun Metro Trolley, 915/533-3333, which serves downtown hotels, businesses, and nearby sights such as the Magoffin Homestead. The trolley costs 25¢ a trip. To visit Juárez, use the convenient Border Jumper Trolley, 800/259-6284, from the Civic Center or taxis from the area. The Juárez trolley runs during the day only. During the summer the trolley company sometimes operates tours to the missions also. (See details about the trolley in the Juárez Sightseeing Highlight entry.)

When visiting Juárez, note that Mexico also uses the dollar sign, but there it symbolizes pesos. If you're not sure of a price, always ask if it's pesos. While most merchants welcome dollars, most prices are stated in Mexican pesos unless "U.S." is designated.

SIGHTSEEING HIGHLIGHTS

★★★★ EL PASO MUSEUM OF ART
One Arts Festival Plaza, 915/532-1707
In a new contemporary building downtown, this museum is widely known for its multimillion-dollar Kress collection of European masterpieces from the 1300s to the 1700s, including paintings and sculptures from the Venetian, Florentine, and Spanish schools of art. The museum also has twentieth-century American paintings with emphasis on Impressionists, nineteenth-century Mexican colonial works, and 10 to 12 changing exhibits a year. Across from the Civic Center, the

museum overlooks a plaza with reflecting pool, water wall, trees, and an area for outdoor cultural events.

Details: *Tue, Wed, Fri, Sat 9–6, Thu 9–9, Sun noon–5. Donation requested. (1–1 1/2 hours)*

★★★★ JUÁREZ
www.citi-guide.com

One of Mexico's largest cities, Juárez bustles with activity and commerce between the two nations, with cars and trucks jamming the four bridges that cross the Rio Grande, which separates the two cities. For the tourist who is a U.S. citizen, the city offers a chance to visit a foreign country without a passport or even any paperwork if you don't buy more than $400 in merchandise. Mexican arts and crafts, leather goods, pottery, curios, and sterling silver (be sure it has the .925 mark) are good buys, and many people cross the border to buy prescription drugs at much lower prices than in the States. If you're buying drugs, carry your prescription in case you're questioned by border authorities upon your return.

Tourists can visit Juárez on their own, take a tour, or hop aboard the El Paso–Juárez trolley noted below. Many visitors simply walk across the bridge at the foot of Santa Fe Street in El Paso. It feeds into Juárez Avenue, which is lined with drugstores, shops, restaurants, and bars. Wander along Juárez Avenue to 16th of September Avenue, less than a mile, where you will find the City Market, a lively scene of vendors hawking pottery, souvenirs, blankets, clothes, jewelry, and nearly everything else you can imagine. A couple of blocks west you will find the region's oldest building, Our Lady of Guadalupe mission, dating to 1668 and still an active parish. It's adjacent to the 19th-century Juárez Cathedral. Nearby is the Cuauhtemoc Market, where you will encounter more Juárez residents than tourists. Juárez also has bullfights, rodeos, and greyhound racing. Taxis are plentiful along Juárez Avenue; remember to set a price before getting into the cab.

Operating only in daytime, the **El Paso–Juárez Border Jumper Trolley**, www.huntel.com/~intelex/trolley.htm, leaves every hour on the hour from downtown El Paso at the Civic Center and makes several stops in Juárez. Guides explain the route and give other helpful tips about crossing the border. You can get off at any stop and reboard a later trolley. Among its stops are Chihuahua Charlie's bar and grill and the City Market.

GREATER EL PASO

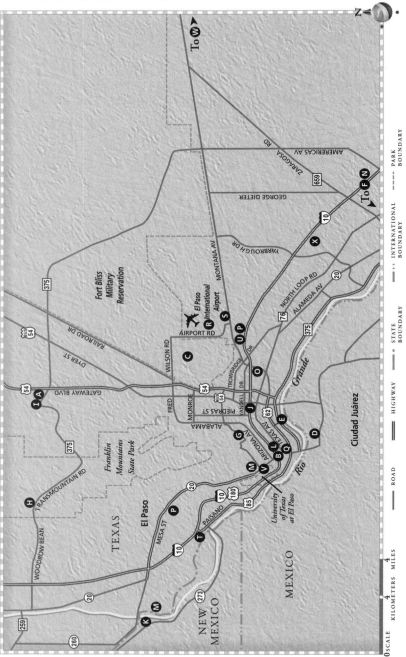

Details: El Paso–Juárez Trolley, One Civic Center Plaza (Santa Fe and San Francisco Sts.), 800/259-6284. Operates May–Oct daily 10–5; rest of year until 4. Fare: $11 adults, $8.50 ages 4–12. (3–5 hours)

★★★★ MISSION TRAIL
El Paso Mission Trail Association, One Civic Center Plaza, 915/534-0677 or 800/351-6024, www.missiontrail.com

Southeast of the city, two beautiful small missions—the oldest active missions in the United States—attest to the area's early Spanish and Indian heritage. With flooding, the Rio Grande has changed course over the years, leaving these treasures on U.S. soil rather than south of the river where they were originally built. Even today, though, the area feels much like Mexico. Both missions were founded about 1682 when the Pueblo Revolt sent Spanish and Indian refugees fleeing from northern New Mexico. The intimate **Socorro Mission**, a prime example of Spanish architecture combined with Indian handicraft and skill, has thick adobe walls and a ceiling of traditional *vigas* (huge beams) and *latillas* (small branches laid horizontally over the beams), with painted Indian designs still visible on the wood. This building dates to around 1840, with the *vigas* and other parts thought to be salvaged from previous structures that had flooded. **Ysleta Mission** was founded for the Tigua Indians, one of two surviving tribes in

SIGHTS
- **A** Border Patrol Museum
- **B** El Paso Museum of Art
- **C** Fort Bliss museums
- **D** Juarez
- **E** Magoffin Home State Historical Park
- **F** Mission Trail
- **G** Rim Road
- **F** Tigua Cultural Center
- **H** Transmountain Road
- **I** Wilderness Park Museum

FOOD
- **J** Bill Parks Bar-B-Que
- **K** Billy Crews
- **L** Café Central
- **M** Casa Jurado
- **N** Cattleman's Steakhouse at Indian Cliffs Ranch
- **D** Chihuahua Charlie's
- **D** Florida
- **O** Forti's Mexican Elder
- **P** Jaxon's

LODGING
- **Q** Camino Real Hotel
- **R** El Paso Airport Hilton
- **S** El Paso Marriott
- **T** Holiday Inn Sunland Park
- **U** Quality Inn
- **V** Sunset Heights Bed & Breakfast Inn

CAMPING
- **W** Hueco Tanks State Historical Park
- **X** Roadrunner RV Campground and Service Center

Note: Items with the same letter are located in the same area.

Texas today. The present church, with its beautiful altar, was built in 1851, and its landmark silver dome bell tower was added later. Beyond the Socorro Mission, the trail also includes the **Presidio Chapel** at San Elizario, built in 1789.

Details: Missions are about 10 miles from downtown on I-10 East. Exit at Zaragosa Rd. and follow signs to the first mission, Ysleta, about two miles down Zaragosa at Old Pueblo Rd. Missions open daily, usually from about 8–5; guide usually at Socorro Fri–Sun mornings. Free. (1–1 1/2 hours)

★★★★ RIM ROAD

From the valley floor at 3,762 feet, the Franklin Mountains rise to more than 7,000 feet, forming a wedge between west and east El Paso. Just north of downtown, Rim Road climbs and twists its way across the lower edge of the range, passing some of the city's prettiest homes and canyons on its way to turnouts with 180-degree views of the region. Make the drive shortly before sunset and watch the valley light up.

Details: From downtown, take Mesa St. north, then turn right on Rim Rd. (watch for "Scenic Drive" signs). From the east, take Piedras St. (30 minutes)

★★★★ TIGUA CULTURAL CENTER
305 Yaya Ln. at Socorro Rd., 915/859-5287

On the mission trail a short distance from Ysleta Mission, the cultural center allows a closer look at Tigua Indian history and culture. You'll find a museum with ancient artifacts, shops with working artisans and their crafts, dance performances, an Indian bread bakery, and a café serving pueblo and Tex-Mex foods.

Details: Tue–Sun 8–5; with dances Sat and Sun, usually at 11, 1, and 3. Free. (1 hour)

★★★★ TRANSMOUNTAIN ROAD/MUSEUMS
Transmountain Rd., Loop 375

On the northern outskirts of the city, one of the highest roads in the state, the four-lane Loop 375, climbs through canyons and over a mile-high pass blasted through sheer rock. Known as the Transmountain Road, it affords a close-up look at desert terrain as well as sweeping views westward from the top. The drive itself takes only about 20 minutes, but allow time for two stops near the eastern end of the road. The one-of-a-kind **Border Patrol Museum** depicts the patrol's adventures in protecting U.S. borders with exhibits of the many modes of transportation used, from canoes to dune buggies to helicopters. A short walk away, **Wilderness Park Museum** traces human adaptation to the Southwestern desert from the time mammoths roamed the land to the pueblo dwellers. It also showcases an excellent collection of pottery, jewelry, baskets, and other artifacts from Mexican and Native American cultures. Outside, a mile-long nature trail wanders through desert exhibits with great views.

Details: Transmountain Rd. connects U.S. 54 on the east to I-10 on the west. Border Patrol Museum: 4315 Transmountain Rd., 915/759-6060; Wilderness Park Museum: 2000 Transmountain Rd., 915/755-4332. Both museums open Tue–Sun 9–5. Donations requested. (2 1/2 hours)

★★★ MAGOFFIN HOME STATE HISTORICAL PARK
1120 Magoffin St., 915/533-5147, www.tpwd.state.tx.us

This adobe hacienda, built in 1875 by settler Joseph Magoffin, was the social and political center of Magoffinsville, as the community was known in the early days of Anglo settlement before it took the valley name of El Paso. Its many original furnishings include unique Victorian-style chairs with Mexican eagle and horseshoe designs carved into the dark wood.

Details: Daily 9–4. $2 adults, $1 students. (30 minutes)

★★ FORT BLISS MUSEUMS
915/568-4518

From the 1850s, Fort Bliss has played an integral role in the development of the El Paso area. It has grown from a site for troops protecting settlers moving west to the largest air defense center in the Western world today. The **Fort Bliss Museum** re-creates the adobe quarters and lifestyle of the original Magoffinsville post in the 1850s.

A block south of the old fort, the **Air Defense/Artillery Museum** has indoor displays tracing the development of defense systems and outdoor exhibits of missiles.

Details: Both museums at Fort Bliss, adjacent to the El Paso airport, on Pleasanton Rd. (follow "Welcome Center" signs). Daily 9–4:30. Donation requested. (1–1 1/2 hours)

FITNESS AND RECREATION

Explore the surrounding Chihuahua Desert by car, foot, or mountain bike from the 10-mile Transmountain Road through **Franklin Mountains State Park**, 915/566-6441, on the northern outskirts of the city. The state park has picnic sites and nature paths, plus mountain biking and equestrian trails and a few primitive camping sites. The entrance fee is $2 per person for ages 13 and older; extra fees apply to some activities. There's no fee to drive or bike the Transmountain Road.

Rock climbers and rock-art enthusiasts should explore **Hueco Tanks State Historical Park**, 915/857-1135, about 30 miles east on U.S. 62/180, where unusual rock formations rise from the desert floor. Natural water holes (*huecos*) formed here, making it an oasis for humans and animals over the centuries. Ancient Indians left pictographs, many still well preserved.

Golfers consider the **Painted Dunes Desert Golf Course**, 12000 McCombs Street, 915/821-2122, one of the country's top municipal courses.

FOOD

The city's close relationship with Mexico influences much of the cuisine, but there's more than enchiladas here—you will find excellent steaks, American bistros, and Italian cooking, besides Tex-Mex, New Mexican, and south-of-the-border specialties. Dress tends to be casual in most restaurants.

Popular **Casa Jurado**, 226 Cincinnati Street, 915/532-6429, and 4772 Doniphan Street, 915/833-1151, has enchiladas and flautas along with interior Mexico specialties such as chicken *mole* and fish prepared Veracruz style. In a white stucco building with balconies, **Forti's Mexican Elder**, 321 Chelsea Street, 915/772-0066, is a longtime favorite for its romantic setting and good Tex-Mex fare. Prices are inexpensive to moderate.

Jaxon's puts a Southwestern touch to many of its grilled dishes (and has a decadently delicious adobe mud pie for chocolate lovers), served in a Santa Fe–style setting at 4799 N. Mesa Street, 915/544-1188, and a ranch setting at 1135 Airway Boulevard, 915/778-9696. The latter site also is a microbrewery. At both places, take time to look at the pictures of old El Paso. Prices are moderate.

Downtown, a baby grand piano and clubby bistro atmosphere set a romantic mood for top-of-the-line **Café Central**, 109 N. Oregon, 915/545-2233. Its changing, eclectic menu presents such choices as quail, halibut, and salmon with creative sauces, butters, and salsas. On the west side, the **Bistro**, 7500 N. Mesa Street, Suite 212, 915/584-5757, has seafood, pasta, weekly specials, and 24 wines by the glass. Both are moderate to moderately expensive.

For barbecue, **Bill Parks Bar-B-Que**, 3130 Gateway East (I-10 near Piedras Street), 915/542-0960, wins accolades for its meats.

Steak lovers have two renowned choices. For an elegant evening at one of the top steak houses in the country, choose **Billy Crews**, 1200 Country Club Road, 505/589-2071, just across the river in Santa Theresa, New Mexico, but considered part of El Paso. It offers custom-cut steaks and 1,300 wine selections. For casual dining in the desert, drive out to **Cattleman's Steakhouse at Indian Cliffs Ranch**, 915/544-3200, about 35 miles southeast of the city. It's a fun family place with cattle and deer, a playground, and other attractions—even hayrides on Sunday afternoon. The steaks are good (and there are other grill choices) and the sunsets are usually awesome. Go east on I-10 to the Fabens exit, then north to the ranch; it's open for dinner only (usually from around 5) and from noon on Sunday. Prices for Cattleman's and Billy Crews are moderate to moderately expensive.

In Juárez, for a lively, fun time head to **Chihuahua Charlie's**, 2525 de la Republica, a sister restaurant to the popular Carlos 'n' Charlie's places at Mexican beach resorts. For a quieter evening, the **Florida**, 412 Juárez Avenue, about four blocks from the Santa Fe Bridge crossing, is a longtime favorite for fine dining at reasonable prices.

LODGING

The city has a wide selection of reasonably priced lodging, with rates usually lowest on weekends. Many lodgings are toward the eastern part of the city, particularly around the airport/Airway Boulevard/I-10 area.

A landmark since its opening in 1912, **Camino Real Hotel**, 101 S. El Paso Street, 800/722-6466, stands out with its modern facade on the skyline and wows guests inside with its Old World lobby. In the heart of downtown, the 360-room renovated historic property with a new, 17-story tower boasts a large Tiffany dome and beautiful gold leaf in the original two-story lobby that's now a bar. Rooms normally are about $100, but weekend specials lower the rate.

Toward the east, **El Paso Airport Hilton**, 2027 Airway Boulevard, 800/742-7248, has a tropical courtyard with a large swimming pool, separate 207-foot Texas Twister water slide, cabana snack bar, and two restaurants. Many accommodations are two-room suites. Rates start at $105 weekdays, $69 weekends with continental breakfast. Nearby, the **El Paso Marriott**, 1600 Airway Bouelvard, 800/228-9290, has rooms from about $125, or weekend specials for $69 with full breakfast. **Quality Inn**, 6201 Gateway West, (I-10 East at Geronimo exit), 800/221-2222, has more than 300 rooms, a pool, and restaurant set on 10 landscaped acres; rates start at $48.

NEW MEXICO

When in El Paso, many visitors include sightseeing in nearby New Mexico. The historic village of **La Mesilla**, about 40 miles away on I-10 West, has a charming Mexican–Old West plaza ringed with adobe buildings that now house interesting shops and cafés. **White Sands National Monument**, a 10-mile stretch of huge dunes, is only 80 miles northeast, and the cool alpine retreat of **Cloudcroft** sits high in the **Sacramento Mountains** about 85 miles northeast.

On the west side, **Holiday Inn Sunland Park**, 900 Sunland Park Drive (at I-10), 800/HOLIDAY, has an outdoor pool with a bar, a full-service restaurant and lounge, and it's close to the Sunland Park Race Track. Its rates start at $64, which includes breakfast.

In a historic district just north of downtown, **Sunset Heights Bed & Breakfast Inn**, 717 W. Yandell Avenue, 800/767-8513, is a turn-of-the-century mansion with beautiful views of the valley and mountains. It has four rooms with private baths, starting at $75 including gourmet multicourse breakfast.

Rates may be higher during special events, particularly around the Sun Bowl football game during the holidays.

CAMPING

About 25 miles east on U.S. 62/180, **Hueco Tanks State Historical Park**, 915/857-1135, or 512/389-8900 for reservations, offers 20 sites for RVs and tent camping. On the eastern edge of the city, **Roadrunner RV Campground and Service Center**, 1212 Lafayette Drive, 915/598-4469, has 120 shaded hookups, a pool, grocery, and other facilities. It's located off I-10 and Yarbrough Drive.

NIGHTLIFE AND SPECIAL EVENTS

Old Kern Place, around Cincinnati and Mesa Streets, just east of the University of Texas at El Paso, draws crowds in the evenings at its cafés, galleries, pubs, bars, and coffeehouses. Among the options: **Ardovinos**, 206 Cincinnati Street, 915/532-9483, offers wine and pizzas that win raves; and

Dolce Vita Coffee Bar, 105 Cincinnati Street, 915/533-8482, has light food, pastries and imaginative coffee drinks. Downtown, the **Dome Bar** with its Tiffany glass dome in the historic Camino Real Hotel lobby, 101 S. El Paso Street, 800/769-4300, is the place to see and be seen.

Try your luck at **Speaking Rock Entertainment Center**, 122 S. Old Pueblo Road, 915/860-7777, a casino with card games, slots, and bingo. It's owned by the Tigua Indian Tribe and located near the Ysleta Mission southeast of El Paso (Zaragosa exit off I-10 East).

Across the border, Juárez pulsates with life at night along busy Juárez Avenue at the south end of Santa Fe Street Bridge, though the crowd tends to be young-adult and teenage. A word of warning: Juárez has more than 1.5 million people, so take the same personal safety precautions here that you would in any metropolitan area. Watch your billfolds and purses in crowds, and don't wander onto dark, deserted streets alone.

El Paso lays claim to the first real Thanksgiving and celebrates the event yearly the last weekend in April. The **Juan de Oñate First Thanksgiving Reenactment** commemorates the arrival in 1598 of Spanish explorer de Oñate on the banks of the Rio Grande, where his party feasted with the Indians and gave thanks for their safe journey across the desert. The event is sponsored by the El Paso Mission Trail Association, 800/351-6024.

From June through August, crowds gather for **Music Under the Stars**, 915/541-4481, free concerts each Sunday at 8 p.m. at the Chamizal National Memorial Amphitheater downtown by the Rio Grande. The Tigua Indians honor their patron saint with special celebrations yearly on **St. Anthony's Day**, June 13, at Ysleta del Sur Pueblo southeast of El Paso. For information, contact the tribe's administrative office, 915/859-7913.

From early June to late August, **Viva! El Paso**, 915/565-6900 and 800/915-VIVA, tells the area's 400-year history in song and dance against a spectacular outdoor backdrop at McKelligon Canyon Amphitheater in the Franklin Mountains. Performances are Wednesday through Saturday evenings. El Paso and Juárez share a number of two-nation multicultural festivals, one of the most colorful being the **Mexican Independence Celebration**, 915/533-3645, in mid-September. El Paso is also home to the **Sun Bowl**, 800/915-BOWL, which hosts numerous events, the best known being the traditional college football bowl game in December.

SHOPPING

All you real or wanna-be cowboys, this is the place to shop for boots and other Western apparel and accessories. Much of this gear is made in the El Paso area and available here at discounted prices. A number of stores are located around I-10 east of the airport exit. Check out the following: **Lucchese Boot Factory Outlet Store**, 6601 Montana Avenue, 915/778-8060; **Justin Retail Factory Outlet**, 7100 Gateway East (I-10 at Hawkins exit), 800/992-6687; and **Cowtown Boots**, 11451 Gateway West (I-10 at Zaragosa exit), 915/593-2929. There are also three **Tony Lama Factory Stores**: 5040 N. Desert Boulevard, 915/581-8192; 7156 Gateway East (I-10 at Hawkins exit), 915/772-4327; and 12151 Gateway West (I-10 at Zaragosa exit), 915/848-0124.

For everything Southwestern and Latin American, stop by the **El Paso Saddleblanket Co.**, 601 N. Oregon Street (downtown), 800/351-7847, a huge marketplace with rugs, pottery, leather, Indian jewelry, and imports from Mexico and Central America. It's like a Mexican market, U.S.-style. Also, spice up your life at **El Paso Chile Co.**, 909 Texas Avenue, 915/544-3434, maker of nationally popular salsas, which also sells Southwestern snacks at its downtown store. If you're a fancier of antiques and collectibles, check out **Placita Santa Fe**, 5024 Doniphan Drive (off I-10 West at Mesa Street), a collection of attractive shops and galleries along what was the old Spanish road, the Camino Real.

12
PANHANDLE/
HIGH PLAINS

Across the vast, open spaces of the Texas Panhandle, amber waves of grain stretch like a huge sea to the expansive blue sky, the flatness of the land randomly relieved by tall grain elevators. Ranging in elevation from around 3,000 to 4,000 feet, this northernmost region of the state is part of the High Plains.

Deep draws and canyons pierce the eastern edge of these plains. The Panhandle's dramatic, red-hued Palo Duro Canyon, an extensive 800-foot-deep chasm, is one of the state's best natural attractions. Long a center for cattle ranches, wheat farms, and oil fields, the Panhandle in recent years has added vineyards, its arid land and climate proving perfect for nurturing grapes. The Panhandle has the state's greatest extremes in weather—blinding blizzards in winter and sizzling heat in summer (though summer evenings do cool off nicely).

The Panhandle's two major cities are Amarillo and Lubbock. A crossroads of commerce on Old Route 66, Amarillo is a modern city that retains its ranching heritage. On the southern end of the region, Lubbock is an educational center, home of Texas Tech University, and hub of the area's wine production.

A PERFECT DAY IN THE PANHANDLE/
HIGH PLAINS

Starting from Amarillo, stoke up for a big day with the Cowboy Morning breakfast at the rim of Palo Duro Canyon. Learn the history of the area at

ANHANDLE/HIGH PLAINS

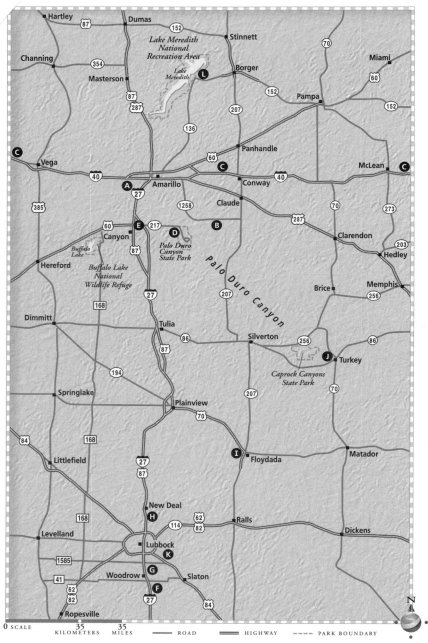

Hartley • 87 • Dumas • 152 • Stinnett • 70 • Miami

Lake Meredith National Recreation Area

Channing • 354 • Borger • 60

Masterson • Lake Meredith • L • 152

87 • 287 • 207 • Pampa • 152

136

Vega • C • 60 • Panhandle • McLean • C

40 • A • Amarillo • C • Conway • 40

27 • 1258 • Claude • 70 • 273

385 • 60 • E • 217 • D • B • 287 • Clarendon • 203

Canyon • 87 • Palo Duro Canyon State Park • Hedley

Buffalo Lake

Hereford • Buffalo Lake National Wildlife Refuge • Brice • Memphis

27 • 207 • 256

168 • Palo Duro Canyon

Dimmitt • Tulia • 86 • Silverton • 256 • 86

87 • J • Turkey

194 • Caprock Canyons State Park • 70

Springlake • 207 • Plainview • 70

84 • 168 • I • Matador

Littlefield • 27 • Floydada

87

New Deal

168 • H • 62 • Ralls • Dickens

Levelland • 114 • 82 • K • Lubbock

1585

41 • Woodrow • G • Slaton

62 • F

82 • 27 • 84

Ropesville

N

0 SCALE   35   35
KILOMETERS   MILES   ROAD   HIGHWAY   ---- PARK BOUNDARY

the Panhandle-Plains Historical Museum in the town of Canyon, then explore Palo Duro Canyon State Park. Return to Amarillo for a steak dinner or continue to Lubbock. There you can see the Buddy Holly Statue and Walk of Fame honoring West Texas musicians, and enjoy dinner and nightlife in the historic Depot district.

ORIENTATION

Palo Duro Canyon, the major attraction of the Panhandle, cuts through the landscape outside the small town of Canyon, just south of Amarillo; Lubbock is to the south about 120 miles from Amarillo, via I-27. While the destinations may be seen alone, it's also possible to combine all in a long weekend trip around the Panhandle. (See the High Plains Perspective scenic route at the end of this chapter.)

AMARILLO/CANYON AREA SIGHTSEEING HIGHLIGHTS

★★★★ PALO DURO CANYON STATE PARK
Hwy. 217, Canyon, 806/488-2227, www.tpwd.state.tx.us
The flat, flat plains of the Panhandle suddenly give way to a magnificent "Little Grand Canyon" south of Amarillo outside the town of Canyon. Paved roads twist down and through the 800-foot-deep Palo Duro Canyon, cut by a fork of the Red River over millions of years to expose varying geological strata in brilliant hues of red,

---

SIGHTS
- **Ⓐ** Cadillac Ranch
- **Ⓑ** Cowboy Morning
- **Ⓒ** Old Route 66
- **Ⓓ** Palo Duro Canyon State Park
- **Ⓔ** Panhandle-Plains Historical Museum

WINERIES
- **Ⓕ** Cap*Rock Winery
- **Ⓖ** Llano Estacado Winery
- **Ⓗ** Pheasant Ridge Winery

LODGING
- **Ⓘ** Historic Lamplighter Inn
- **Ⓙ** Hotel Turkey
- **Ⓔ** Hudspeth House

CAMPING
- **Ⓚ** Buffalo Springs Lake
- **Ⓛ** Lake Meredith National Recreation Area
- **Ⓓ** Palo Duro Canyon State Park

Note: Items with the same letter are located in the same area.

---

orange, and pink. Wind and water have carved spires, pinnacles, and hoodoos—oddly shaped rock formations similar to those seen in the canyons of Arizona and Utah. Inhabited by Native Americans for centuries, the area was settled by Anglos in the late 1870s. The park has nearly 23 miles of trails for horseback riding, mountain biking, and hiking. The **Goodnight Trading Post** has supplies, snack bar, and horse and bike rentals. On summer visits, don't miss the outdoor musical *Texas*, dramatically staged in the canyon (see Nightlife and Special Events).

Details: *12 miles east of Canyon on Rte. 217 (from Amarillo follow Route 1541 to Route 217). Daily 7 a.m.–10 p.m.; in winter, opens at 8 a.m. $3 ages 13 and older. (3 hours)*

★★★★ PANHANDLE–PLAINS HISTORICAL MUSEUM
2401 Fourth Ave., Canyon, 806/651-2244, museum@wtamu.edu, www.wtamu.edu/museum

From prehistoric Native American cultures to colorful cowboys, this gem of a museum tells the story of the Texas Panhandle. On the campus of West Texas State A&M University, the museum includes art works and exhibits on petroleum, Western heritage, paleontology, and transportation. Visitors see a reconstructed pioneer town and the headquarters of an old ranch.

Details: *On Route 217. Jun–Aug Mon–Sat 9–6 (rest of year until 5), Sun 1–6. $4 adults, $3 seniors, $1 ages 4–12; free Sundays. (1–2 hours)*

★★★ CADILLAC RANCH
Seven miles west of Amarillo on I-40

If you're traveling I-40 you won't miss this landmark, a tribute to Old Route 66 and the fin-tail cars revered by many Texans. Ten colorfully painted Cadillacs are planted nose-down in a field, at the same angle as Egypt's Cheops Pyramid. A project of Amarillo businessman Stanley Marsh, III, and a group of contemporary artists, the "bumper crop" has drawn worldwide attention.

Details: *(30 minutes–1 hour)*

★★★ COWBOY MORNING
Figure 3 Ranch, 800/658-2613

Ride to the rim of Palo Duro Canyon in an open wagon and chow down on sourdough biscuits and other Old West–style chuck wagon

AMARILLO

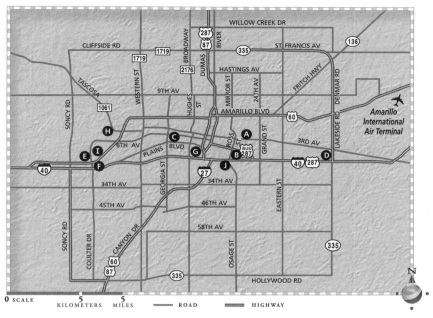

SIGHTS

- **A** Amarillo Livestock Auction
- **B** American Quarter Horse Heritage Center & Museum
- **C** Old Route 66/Sixth Avenue historic district

FOOD

- **D** Big Texan Steak Ranch & Opry
- **E** Cafe Roma
- **F** My Thai
- **G** Old Tascosa Steakhouse
- **A** Stockyards Cafe

LODGING

- **H** Adaberry Inn
- **I** Best Western Amarillo Inn
- **J** Hampton Inn

Note: Items with the same letter are located in the same area.

food cooked over an open fire. You'll also see ranch hands do some roping and branding.

Details: *Southeast of Amarillo on Route 1258. Apr–Oct with trips daily Jun–Aug and otherwise according to demand at 8:30 a.m. Reservations necessary. $19 adults, $14.50 ages 4–12. (2 hours)*

★★ AMERICAN QUARTER HORSE HERITAGE CENTER & MUSEUM
2601 I-40 East, Amarillo, 806/376-5181, www.aqha.com/hcm
International headquarters of the American Quarter Horse Association, this center traces the heritage of "America's breed." Interactive exhibits and videos will entertain even visitors who aren't part of the horsey set.

Details: Mon–Sat 9–5, Sun noon–5. $4 adults, $2.50 ages 6–18. (30 minutes–1 hour)

★★ OLD ROUTE 66/SIXTH AVENUE HISTORIC DISTRICT
Historical Route 66 Association, 806/372-US66, national66@earthlink.net, www.national66.com
Travelers will find remnants of the famous Chicago–to–Los Angeles highway in Amarillo and along the current I-40 running nearly straight across the Panhandle from the Oklahoma line to the New Mexico border. Within Amarillo, Route 66 runs along Sixth Avenue (often called Sixth Street, though), with an area generally between Georgia and Western Streets preserved as a historic district that has become popular for browsing. Also known as Old San Jacinto, it has more than 80 buildings on the National Register of Historic Places, many of them now antiques shops, specialty stores, and cafés.

Details: Old Route 66 Association of Texas, McLean, 806/267-2719. (1–3 hours)

WEST TEXAS CATTLEMEN VS. OPRAH WINFREY
It was High Noon, and all were gathered for the duel: West Texas cattlemen facing Oprah Winfrey. The cattlemen sued the TV talk-show host, claiming that comments about beef-eating made on one of her shows had caused the price of cattle to plummet. Oprah said "Let the trial begin," and it did—in Amarillo, where she not only went to court but also taped her talk show for several weeks. When the smoke from the duel had cleared, the jury of cattlemen's peers found in favor of Oprah.

HIKING IN PALO DURO CANYON STATE PARK

Texas Department of Transportation

★ **AMARILLO LIVESTOCK AUCTION**
100 S. Manhattan St., 806/373-7464
The largest auction in Texas offers the public an opportunity to see buying and selling of cattle. Sales are each Tuesday morning; check for times. Note: If you've never been to an auction, be still during the action—a slight movement could put you in the bidding.
Details: Free. (1–2 hours)

LUBBOCK AREA SIGHTSEEING HIGHLIGHTS

★★★★ **RANCHING HERITAGE CENTER**
Fourth and Indiana Sts., 806/742-0498
An old dugout shelter, log cabin, railroad depot, schoolhouse, and general store are among this collection of 33 historic buildings gathered from area towns and ranches to give visitors a glimpse into early Panhandle life. Part of the Museum of Texas Tech University, the center traces history of the cattle industry in Texas and the changing look of ranch homes.
Details: Tue–Sat 10–5, Sun 1–5. Free. (1–2 hours)

LUBBOCK

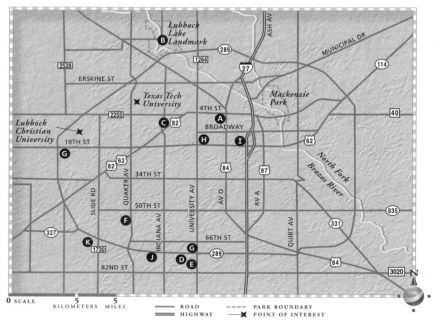

SIGHTS

- **A** Buddy Holly Statue and Walk of Fame
- **B** Lubbock Lake Landmark State Historical Park
- **C** Ranching Heritage Center
- **D** Science Spectrum and Omnimax Theater

FOOD

- **E** 50 Yard Line Steakhouse
- **F** Chez Suzette
- **G** Gordito's
- **H** Grapevine Cafe and Wine Bar
- **I** Hub City Brewery

LODGING

- **J** Ashmore Inn & Suites
- **K** Barcelona Court

★★★★ WINERIES

One of the state's major wine-producing regions, the Panhandle is home to three outstanding wineries around Lubbock. **Llano Estacado Winery**, about five miles from Lubbock (south on U.S. 87/I-27, then east on Route 1585), 806/745-2258, llanowine@

---

aol.com, www.llanoestacadowinery.com, is a consistent winner in national and international competitions, producing a wide range of wines from cabernets to Rieslings using both modern equipment and traditional oak barrels. **Cap*Rock Winery**, about seven miles from Lubbock (south on U.S. 87/I-27 and east on Woodrow Road), 806/863-2704, www.caprockwinery.com, a newer label, has won accolades for its premium wines, which visitors can sample in its eye-catching Southwest mission–style facility. **Pheasant Ridge Winery**, north of Lubbock on I-27 to Route 1729 at New Deal, then two miles east and one mile south, 806/746-6033, one of Texas' oldest vineyards, is known for its top-quality French-style wines.

Details: Llano Estacado: Mon–Sat 10–4:30, Sun noon–4:30. Cap*Rock: Mon–Sat 10–5, Sun noon–5. Pheasant Ridge: tours and tastings by appointment. (1 hour each)

★★★ BUDDY HOLLY STATUE AND WALK OF FAME
Eighth St. and Avenue Q
A larger-than-life statue pays tribute to Lubbock's favorite son, legendary musician Buddy Holly, and plaques honor other outstanding West Texas entertainers, including Waylon Jennings, Bob Wills, and Roy Orbison.

Details: (15–30 minutes)

★★ LUBBOCK LAKE LANDMARK STATE HISTORICAL PARK
2200 N. Landmark Dr., 806/741-0306, www.tpwd.state.tx.us
A site of ongoing scientific excavations, this land has yielded artifacts from 12,000 years of human habitation. Besides an exhibit center, the park has hiking trails around the excavation area and in summer offers tours to digs.

Details: Tue–Sat 9–5, Sun 1–5. $2 adults, $1 students. (1 hour)

★★ SCIENCE SPECTRUM AND OMNIMAX THEATER
2579 S. Loop 289, 806/745-2525
This hands-on museum entices all ages to discover the fun of science and technology. The theater's giant domed movie screen, 58 feet in diameter, envelopes the audience in sights and sounds.

Details: Mon–Fri 10–5:30, Sat 10–7, Sun 1–5:30. Theater has *extended hours; call for details. $5.50 adults, $4.50 seniors and ages 3–16 for Science Spectrum; $6 and $5, respectively, for Omnimax; or a combination ticket at $9 and $7, respectively. (2 hours)*

FITNESS AND RECREATION

In Amarillo, **Thompson Park**, Northeast 24th Street and U.S. 87/287, 806/381-7911, has a golf course and children's zoo. About 45 miles northeast of Amarillo, **Lake Meredith National Recreation Area**, 806/857-3151, spreads fingers of blue water beneath the buttes and cliffs of the Canadian River Valley, offering excellent fishing, boating, and off-road-vehicle trails. On the lakeshore off Route 136 about seven miles south of Fritch, **Alibates National Monument**, 806/857-3151, is the site of a major flint quarry dating back more than 10,000 years. Rangers lead small group tours daily at 10 a.m. and 2 p.m. Memorial Day through Labor Day and by appointment the rest of the year.

In Lubbock, **Mackenzie Park**, Fourth Street and I-27, 806/775-2687, is a popular sightseeing stop and recreational venue. It's home to **Prairie Dog Town**, one of the few remaining colonies of these little groundhog-like critters that once blanketed the plains. It also has a growing collection of old spinning windmills forming the **American Wind Power Center**, a museum of windmill history, 806/788-1499. The park also boasts equestrian trails; **Meadowbrook Golf Course**, 806/765-6679; and **Joyland Amusement Park**, 806/763-2719, which offers more than 20 rides, plus games and food, from mid-March through mid-September.

FOOD

This is beef country, so you will find a number of steak houses. But you won't go wanting for seafood and pasta, as well as Tex-Mex and a wide range of Asian foods.

In Amarillo, eat with real cowboys and ranchers at **Stockyards Café**, 100 S. Manhattan Street, 806/374-6024, which is particularly busy on Tuesdays when the adjacent Amarillo Livestock Auction attracts cattlemen for its weekly sales. While it has steaks of all sizes (and other foods), **Big Texan Steak Ranch & Opry**, 7701 I-40 East, 800/657-7177, gains the most attention for its 72-ounce steak and all the fixin's. The steak is free if you can eat the meal in one hour. (More than 3,600 guests, including a 95-pound grandmother, have earned the free meal.) There's music nightly, but Tuesday is the special foot-stompin' country-western opry night with top local talent. For less theatrics but excellent steaks, as well as barbecue and game, try the popular **Old Tascosa Steakhouse**, in a hacienda-like building at 1500 S. Madison Street, 806/372-3030. Upscale Italian **Cafe Roma**, 7312 Wallace Boulevard, 806/352-7721, serves pasta with creative flair in a romantic hilltop villa setting with alfresco dining. Most Texans like some chili powder in their food, so it's no wonder that Thai dishes are popular, even in the Panhandle. If you're seeking a fiery fix, or just yearn for an oriental stir fry, choose from a wide menu of dishes that range from delicate to biting at popular **My Thai**, 2029 Coulter, 806/352-9014. Most Amarillo dining is moderately priced, though for dinner some places may be slightly higher.

In Lubbock, **50 Yard Line Steakhouse**, 2549 S. Loop 289, 806/745-3991, was popular with local residents long before the current steak-house craze—not only for its custom-cut steaks but also for other grilled items, such as seafood. **Gordito's**, South Loop 289 and University Avenue, 806/745-5582, and at 19th Street and Frankford Avenue, 806/791-0888, has Mexican fare, ranging from traditional fajitas and enchiladas to specialties from interior Mexico. **Chez Suzette**, 4423 50th Street, 806/795-6796, serves French and Italian fare in a sidewalk-café setting; and the **Grapevine Cafe and Wine Bar**, 2407-B 19th Street, 806/744-8246, has New American cuisine with Southwestern and Asian touches and a selection of about 60 wines, most of them available by the glass. Beer fans will appreciate the wide selection at **Hub City Brewery**, 1807 Buddy Holly Avenue, 806/747-1535, where the menu pairs brews with your choice of food, including pizzas, burgers, other grilled items, and daily specials.

LODGING

In Amarillo, accommodations tend to be clustered on I-40 West around the medical center and I-40 East. On the west side, **Adaberry Inn**, 6818 Plum Creek Drive, 806/352-0022, is a small, new bed-and-breakfast with seven suites and two royal suites, each named for and decorated in the style of a popular city, such as Santa Fe, New Orleans and San Francisco. Rooms have TV/VCRs and there's a film library plus a theater. Rates start at $95 with full breakfast. Amarillo also has numerous chain motels, including **Hampton Inn**, 1700 I-40 East, 800/HAMPTON, where room rates start at $59 and include continental breakfast; and **Best Western Amarillo Inn**, 1610 Coulter (west side), 800/528-1234, with indoor pool, hot tub, and rooms from $69 including continental breakfast (ask about discounts). In nearby Canyon, the 1909 **Hudspeth House** with a wraparound porch, 1905 Fourth Avenue, 806/655-9800, is a country bed-and-breakfast retreat offering eight rooms with private baths. Rates begin at $55 and include full breakfast.

In Lubbock, **Barcelona Court**, 5215 S. Loop 289, 800/222-1122, has a Spanish flavor, with a Saltillo tile entrance and three-story atrium courtyard with fountains. Rates start at $80 and include full breakfast. **Ashmore Inn & Suites**, 4019 S. Loop 289, 800/785-0061, has a landscaped courtyard with pool. Rates start at about $70 and include continental breakfast and hospitality hour on weekday evenings.

Several smaller towns have bed-and-breakfast accommodations and historic hotels. In Turkey, southeast of Palo Duro Canyon on Route 86 about equidistant between Amarillo and Lubbock, the 1927 **Hotel Turkey**, 800/657-7110, is an Old West Victorian–style lodging with 15 rooms furnished in period decor. Rates start at $70 and include full breakfast. In Floydada, about 50 miles northeast of Lubbock, the 1912 **Historic Lamplighter Inn**, 102 South Fifth Street, 806/983-3035, has 20 rooms decorated in themes related to regional history. Pumpkins, a big crop here, slip into the decor and the breakfast menu. Rates begin at $50 and include full breakfast; note that not all rooms have private baths. Both hotels are members of Historic Accommodations of Texas.

CAMPING

The most scenic outdoor lodging is in **Palo Duro Canyon State Park**, 12 miles east of Canyon, 806/488-2227, or 512/389-8900 for reservations, which has about 150 campsites, both tent and full hookups, plus rest rooms and showers. Reservations are advised in summer. **Lake Meredith National Recreation Area**, about 40 miles north of Amarillo, 806/857-3151, also has camping.

On the edge of Lubbock, **Buffalo Springs Lake**, 806/747-3353, offers tent camping and full hookups, as well as fishing, hiking, a beach, and water sports. It's on East 50th Street, five miles outside Loop 289.

NIGHTLIFE AND SPECIAL EVENTS

In Amarillo, take to the dance floor for a fun country-western evening at **Midnight Rodeo**, 4400 S. Georgia Street, 806/358-7083; or stop by the **Brew Pub**, 3705-A Olsen Street, 806/353-2622, to sample some of the latest brews. Old Route 66 fans should definitely visit the **Golden Light Cafe**, 2908 W. Sixth Avenue, 806/374-9237, which dates back to the heyday of the Mother Road and serves burgers, of course, along with live music. **Ribs 'n' Blues**, 2917 W. Sixth Avenue, 806/372-7427, serves good barbecue—and pecan cobbler—in a cheery atmosphere augmented by some of the city's best live music. Weekends are the best time to catch the music scene.

In Lubbock, much of the night action centers around the **Depot District**, 19th Street and Avenue G, 806/747-6156, a historic area that's now home to a number of restaurants and nightclubs. The Depot itself is being turned into the Buddy Holly Center, a museum of memorabilia. Among popular spots in the Depot District are **Stubbs Bar-B-Q**, 19th Street and I-27, 806/747-4777, which offers rhythm and blues; **Hub City Brewery**, 1807 Buddy Holly Avenue, 806/747-1535, a microbrewery; and the **Liquid 2000 Nightclub**, 1812 Avenue G, 806/747-6156, the hot dance spot. Also in the district, the **Cactus Theatre**, 1812 Buddy Holly Avenue, 806/747-7047, presents community theater productions and live music shows; and **19th Street Warehouse**, 1824 Avenue G, 806/747-6156, often has live concerts and comedy acts. Close to the Texas Tech campus, **Jazz, A Louisiana Kitchen**, 3703C 19th Street, 806/799-2124, brings a touch of New Orleans food and music to the West Texas scene, drawing a younger audience.

Among crowd-pleasing annual events, the most outstanding is the outdoor musical extravaganza *Texas*, performed against the backdrop of a 600-foot cliff in scenic Palo Duro Canyon, 12 miles east of Canyon (about 25 miles southeast of Amarillo). Here, singers and dancers portray life in the early Panhandle days. Performances are every evening except Sunday from mid-June to mid-August, and reservations are advised. For information, call 806/655-2181.

Other noteworthy events in Amarillo are the **Annual Boys Ranch Rodeo** at Cal Farley's Boys Ranch on Labor Day weekend, 806/372-2341; the **Tri-State Fair**, which attracts about 200,000 people in mid-September, 806/376-7767; and the **World Championship Ranch Rodeo**, for working cowboys, in mid-November, 806/467-9722. In Lubbock, September is chock-full of events: the **Buddy Holly Music Festival**, 800/692-4035; the **Cowboy Symposium**, celebrating cowboy culture, 806/795-2455; and the **Panhandle South Plains Fair**, 806/763-2833.

High Plains Perspective

This route affords dramatic views of the High Plains tableland. From Lubbock, take U.S. 84 to Post. Go north on Route 651 to Crosbyton, then take U.S. 82 east to Route 70. Going north to Turkey, you will witness the beginning of the High Plains, at times a defined jagged edge of red-hued canyons. Follow Route 86 west by **Caprock Canyons State Park**, *806/455-1592, which offers scenic hiking. Go north on Route 207, which crosses the lower part of Palo Duro Canyon with its red-pink-orange rock strata. At Claude, take U.S. 287 to Amarillo. Head south on Routes 1541 and 217 into* **Palo Duro Canyon State Park**, *where the flat land suddenly plunges 800 feet, exposing vivid red earth and odd rock formations. Return on Route 217 to I-27 and follow it south to Lubbock or north to Amarillo.*

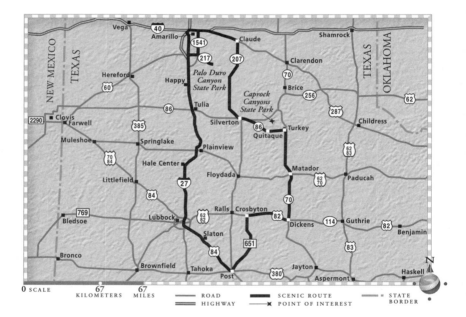

13
DALLAS

With a dramatic modern skyline, Dallas rises to prominence on the rolling prairies of north-central Texas. A major convention site and center for banking, transportation, insurance, and wholesale business, it's the ninth-largest city in the nation, home to 1.05 million residents. About 4.5 million people live in the Dallas–Fort Worth Metroplex.

Dallas is etched in the memory of millions of people around the world as the site of President John F. Kennedy's assassination in 1963. It also gained fame as the home of the fictional Ewing family of Southfork Ranch on the wildly popular 1980s TV show *Dallas*. The city today recognizes that history but promises—and delivers—so much more.

From its lively West End Historic District of renovated warehouses to its nationally acclaimed cultural attractions and its architecturally significant towers of commerce, the downtown is a vibrant social center. The city's restaurants often gain national spotlight, setting trends in cuisine. Its upscale hotels are hard to match for their luxury and service. And shopping—well, Dallas is home to the original Neiman Marcus. Need we say more?

A PERFECT DAY IN DALLAS

Start with a visit to the Dallas Museum of Art and the nearby Trammell Crow Sculpture Garden and Collection of Asian Art. Then stop by Pioneer Plaza to

DALLAS

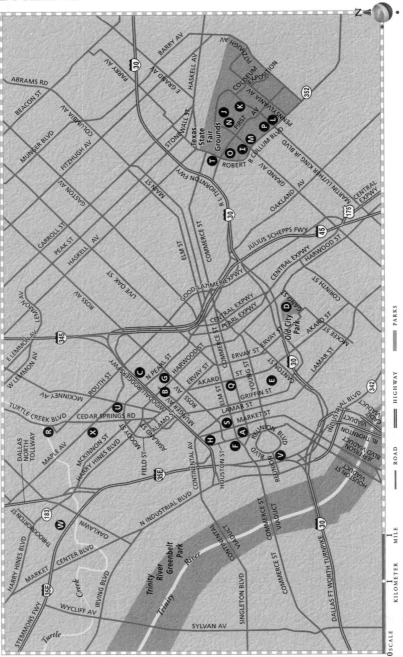

see the engaging statue of cowboys herding larger-than-life-size longhorns. Have lunch at one of the cafés in the West End Historic District, browse through the shops and tour the Sixth Floor Museum. Cap the day with a performance of the symphony, opera, or a summer musical. Or dine leisurely at one of the city's acclaimed restaurants.

ORIENTATION

Many of the city's sights, accommodations, restaurants, and nightlife venues are in and around downtown, loosely defined by a loop formed by I-30, I-45/U.S. 75, I-35 East, and the Woodall Rodgers Freeway. The Arts District, historical sights, and the West End are in the downtown area. Slightly east, Fair Park has a number of museums and other attractions; the Deep Ellum area has shops, restaurants, and clubs. North of the central business area, the McKinney Avenue–Oak Lawn–Turtle Creek area has upscale shops, restaurants, and hotels, and the Greenville Avenue area bustles with dining and entertainment spots. The area known as North Dallas—along Loop 635 (the LBJ Freeway) between U.S. 75 (Central Expressway) and the North Dallas Tollway—has upscale shopping, dining, and lodging.

SIGHTS

- Ⓐ Dallas County Historical Plaza
- Ⓑ Dallas Museum of Art
- Ⓒ Morton H. Meyerson Symphony Center
- Ⓓ Old City Park
- Ⓔ Pioneer Plaza
- Ⓕ Sixth Floor Museum
- Ⓖ Trammell Crow Center and Pavilion
- Ⓗ West End Marketplace

FAIR PARK

- Ⓘ African American Museum
- Ⓙ Age of Steam Museum
- Ⓚ Dallas Aquarium
- Ⓛ Dallas Horticulture Center
- Ⓜ Dallas Museum of Natural History
- Ⓝ Hall of State

FAIR PARK (continued)

- Ⓞ Music Hall
- Ⓟ Science Place and TI Founders IMAX Theater

FOOD

- Ⓠ French Room
- Ⓡ Mansion on Turtle Creek Dining Room
- Ⓢ Sonny Bryan's
- Ⓣ Tarantino's

LODGING

- Ⓠ Adolphus
- Ⓤ Hotel Crescent Court
- Ⓥ Hyatt Regency Dallas at Reunion
- Ⓡ Mansion on Turtle Creek
- Ⓦ Renaissance Dallas Hotel
- Ⓧ Stoneleigh Hotel

Note: Items with the same letter are located in the same area.

The easiest transportation between many sights is the developing Dallas Area Rapid Transit System, called DART, 214/979-1111, a light rail that is building lines within the city and a commuter line to Fort Worth and the airport. Currently, you can use DART between downtown sites and the West End, south to the zoo, and north to NorthPark Center and Greenville Avenue. Fares are $1 and 50¢, and tickets may be bought from vending machines at stations. From the downtown Arts District on St. Paul Street you can board the McKinney Avenue Trolley, 214/855-0006, which runs restored electric cars to "uptown Dallas," the McKinney Avenue district of shops, restaurants, and clubs. Round-trip fares are $1.50 adults, 50¢ seniors, $1 ages 12 and under.

THE DOWNTOWN TUNNEL SYSTEM

Downtown Dallas has an extensive underground tunnel system with shops and restaurants open during weekday business hours. On hot days you'll find more pedestrians down here than on the street level. Access the underground from major buildings or from Thanksgiving Square, which has waterfalls, a bell tower, and a striking circular chapel at Ervay and Pacific Streets.

DALLAS ARTS DISTRICT SIGHTSEEING HIGHLIGHTS

With the architecturally distinct Morton H. Meyerson Symphony Center and the Dallas Museum of Art, the north end of downtown has been transformed into a visual and cultural attraction known as the Dallas Arts District. With modern skyscrapers and sculptures, the area gives visitors a sense of the urban vibrance of the city.

★★★★ DALLAS MUSEUM OF ART
1717 N. Harwood St., 214/922-1200, www.dm-art.org

This large, modernistic building displays an extensive collection of works from Europe, Asia, and Africa, plus decorative arts and outdoor sculptures and fountains. The star attraction is its Museum of the Americas exhibit, focusing on the art and culture of the Western Hemisphere with one of the best pre-Columbian collections you'll find anywhere.

Details: Tue, Wed, Fri 11–4, Thu 11–9, Sat and Sun 11–5. *Free except for special exhibits, which also are free Thu 5–9. (2 hours)*

★★★★ **MORTON H. MEYERSON SYMPHONY CENTER**
2301 Flora St., 214/670-3600, www.dallassymphony.com
This I. M. Pei–designed performance hall is stunning to the eye on the outside, with its glass walls and angular lines, and to the ear on the inside, with its acoustics. It houses a $1.36 million organ with more than 4,500 pipes and is the venue for the symphony and other concerts.

The greater Dallas area requires 10-digit dialing—use the area code along with the seven digits for all phone numbers with area codes 214, 972, and the new 469.

Details: Open for scheduled performances; tours usually given Mon, Wed, Fri at 1 p.m. Free tour. (1–3 hours)

★★★★ **TRAMMELL CROW CENTER AND PAVILION**
2001 Ross Ave., 214/979-6100
Located between the museum and the Meyerson, the office tower adds to the arts scene with a **Sculpture Garden** of more than 20 classic French statues among cascading waters and gardens, and the new **Crow Collection of Asian Art**, 214/979-6430. On the pavilion ground floor, 300 works of art, including sculptures and architectural pieces, are displayed from a private collection of 7,000 pieces.

Details: Sculpture Garden open anytime. Art collection open Tue, Wed, Fri 11–6, Thu 11–9, Sat 10–6, and Sun 11–5. Free. (30 minutes–1 hour)

DOWNTOWN/WEST END SIGHTSEEING HIGHLIGHTS

★★★★ **DALLAS COUNTY HISTORICAL PLAZA/ SIXTH FLOOR MUSEUM**
A four-block area between Houston and Market Streets from Elm to Commerce Streets, known as the Dallas County Historical Plaza, has several notable old buildings in the shadow of newer

Texas Department of Transportation

glass-and-steel towers. The **John Neely Bryan Cabin** dates back to the early 1840s founding days of Dallas, and the Romanesque 1892 red sandstone courthouse is fondly called "**Old Red**." The plaza includes a **Kennedy Memorial**. Across from Houston Street is **Dealey Plaza**, where President John F. Kennedy was assassinated in 1963.

The focal point of the area is the **Sixth Floor Museum**, 411 Elm Street, 214/653-6666, jfk@jfk.org, www.jfk.org, occupying a building formerly known as the Texas School Book Depository, from which it was determined that the shots that killed Kennedy originated. For the older generation to remember and the younger generation to learn, the museum recounts Kennedy's visit to Texas, his assassination here on November 22, the events immediately following, and the impact of his death on the world. It's a powerful exhibit, including photographs, films, and interpretive displays.

Details: Open daily 9–6. $6 adults, $5 seniors and ages 6–18. (1 1/2–2 hours)

★★★★ **WEST END MARKETPLACE**
603 Munger Ave., 214/748-4801

The city's early business district—generally along Market Street from McKinney to Pacific—has numerous old red-brick warehouses that have been renovated into this trendy, day-and-night gathering spot. Sidewalk cafés, pushcart vendors and street entertainers augment shops, restaurants, and clubs. Much of the action centers around three adjoining buildings that have become the West End Marketplace, a festival market with a plaza for live music entertainment. The popular **Dallas Alley** nightspot is also here.

> **Details:** *Mon–Thu 11 a.m.–10 p.m., Fri and Sat 11 a.m.–midnight or later, Sun noon–6. Free. (2 hours)*

★★★ PIONEER PLAZA
Young and Griffin Sts.

A popular photo stop, this plaza pays tribute to the area's early cattle drive days with larger-than-life bronze statues of longhorns herded by three cowboys on horseback. With more than 40 animals now, the monument eventually will have 70 head of cattle, the largest such sculpture of its type in the world.

> **Details:** *By the convention center toward the south end of downtown. Free. (15–30 minutes)*

★★ OLD CITY PARK
1717 Gano St., 214/421-5141

This outdoor museum in the shadows of downtown skyscrapers reflects the cultural and architectural history of the area with its collection of 1840–1910 homes and businesses. The village includes a Victorian bandstand, bank, doctor's office, general store, log cabin, and Southern colonial mansions.

> **Details:** *Located on the south edge of downtown. Tue–Sat 10–4, Sun noon–4. $6 adults, $4 seniors, $3 ages 3–12. (1–1½ hours)*

GREATER DALLAS AREA SIGHTSEEING HIGHLIGHTS

★★★★ FAIR PARK
1300 Robert B. Cullum Blvd., 214/670-8400, pr@greatstatefair.com, www.texfair.com

Fair Park, a 277-acre National Historic Landmark, is home to the Cotton Bowl Stadium, the annual State Fair of Texas, a number of

DALLAS REGION

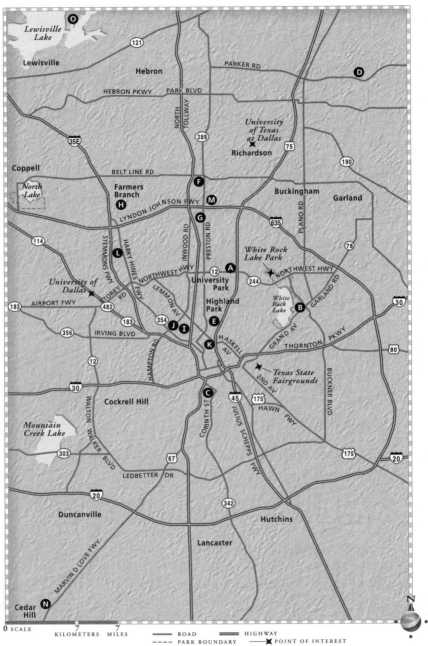

O SCALE

KILOMETERS   MILES

━━━ ROAD   ━━━ HIGHWAY
----- PARK BOUNDARY   ✦ POINT OF INTEREST

museums, and other cultural and educational attractions. Its art deco buildings, many from two international expositions in the 1930s, are considered one of the largest such architectural collections, all set among cobbled walkways and fountains.

The **State Fair**, a huge celebration in late September and early October, draws 3 million visitors to Fair Park for livestock exhibits, Broadway shows, football, and a huge midway of rides, in addition to the year-round sights in the park.

Any time of year, you can stroll through the area and choose from the following attractions according to your particular interests: The **African American Museum**, 3536 Grand Avenue, 214/565-9026, displays a large collection of historical artifacts, art, and folk art in a modern building with vaulted ceilings. Admission to the museum is free. The **Age of Steam Museum**, 1105 Washington Avenue, 214/428-0101, showcases vintage locomotives, Pullman sleepers, and lounge cars in a turn-of-the-century depot.

The **Dallas Aquarium**, First Street and Martin Luther King Jr. Boulevard, 214/670-8443, has both common and exotic freshwater and saltwater species, including fish in an Amazon River habitat. The **Dallas Horticulture Center**, 3601 Martin Luther King Jr. Boulevard, 214/428-7476, includes a variety of herbs and scented plants marked for the visually impaired in its seven-acre gardens. Admission is free. The **Dallas Museum of Natural History**, 3535 Grand Avenue, 214/421-3466, includes a prehistoric-Texas exhibit with fully reconstructed dinosaurs. The **Hall of State**, 3939 Grand

SIGHTS
Ⓐ Biblical Arts Center
Ⓑ Dallas Arboretum & Botanical Garden
Ⓒ Dallas Zoo
Ⓓ Southfork Ranch

FOOD
Ⓔ Adelmo's Ristorante
Ⓕ Chamberlain's Prime Chop House
Ⓖ Mainstream Fish House
Ⓗ Nuevo Leon
Ⓘ Ojeda's

FOOD (continued)
Ⓙ Sonny Bryan's
Ⓚ Star Canyon

LODGING
Ⓛ Hampton Inn-Dallas North
Ⓜ Terra Cotta Inn

CAMPING
Ⓝ Cedar Hill State Park
Ⓞ Lewisville Lake Park Campground

Avenue, 214/421-4500, built in 1936 for the Texas independence centennial, contains the Museum of Texas History with murals, statues, and artifacts telling the state's colorful past. Admission is free. The **Science Place and TI Founders IMAX Theater**, 1318 Second Avenue, 214/428-5555, boasts more than 250 hands-on exhibits, a planetarium, and a domed-screen theater. The **Music Hall**, 909 First Avenue, 214/565-1116, presents performances of the Dallas Opera and the Dallas Summer Musicals.

Details: The aquarium, natural history museum, and Science Place are open daily. The Age of Steam Museum is open Wed–Sun and others Tue–Sun. Hours and fees vary; call each for details. (2–4 hours)

★★★ DALLAS ARBORETUM & BOTANICAL GARDEN
8525 Garland Rd., 214/327-8263
Spread over 66 acres on the shore of White Rock Lake, only a few minutes from downtown, the garden and arboretum showcase seasonal blooms, permanent gardens (including a fog-shrouded fern dell), woodlands, and a historic Spanish colonial mansion filled with antiques and art.

Details: Mar–Oct daily 10–6, rest of year until 5. $6 adults, $5 seniors, $3 ages 6–12. (1½ hours)

★★★ DALLAS ZOO
650 S. R.L. Thornton Fwy. (I-35E), 214/670-5656, dallaszoo@airmail.net, www.dallas-zoo.org
With a 67-foot-tall giraffe sculpture at its entrance, the zoo is hard to miss. The top draw here is the 25-acre Wilds of Africa exhibit, with 90 species roaming in re-created natural habitats of bush, desert, forest, woodland, river, and mountains. Visitors can view the African exhibit via a nature trail or a mile-long monorail.

Details: Open daily 9–5. $6 adults, $4 seniors, $3 ages 3–11; $1.50 for monorail. (2 hours)

★★ BIBLICAL ARTS CENTER
7500 Park Ln., 214/691-4661, www.biblicalarts.org
From the fort-like exterior designed to resemble Paul's Gate in Damascus, to the permanent biblical art and visiting exhibitions inside, this museum is an unexpected highlight. The intent is to give people of all faiths an understanding of the people, places, and

events recounted in the Bible. The center's most striking element is the huge *Miracle at Pentecost* mural—124 feet wide by 20 feet tall with more than 200 biblical characters, the ones in front painted life-size. The mural is unveiled in a 30-minute light-and-sound presentation on the half hour, with the last show at 4:30 p.m. (or slightly earlier)

> **Details:** *Tue–Sat 10–5 (Thu until 9), Sun 1–5. Galleries: free; mural showing: $4 adults, $3.50 seniors, $2.50 ages 6–12. (1–1 ½ hours)*

★ **SOUTHFORK RANCH**
3700 Hogge Rd., Parker, 972/442-7800,
www.foreverresorts.com
Worldwide fans of the popular *Dallas* TV show always want to see Southfork, the ranch pictured as the home of the fictional Ewings. A major party site in a rural area northeast of Dallas, it's filled with memorabilia of the TV show and is open for tours and picture-taking.

> **Details:** *Off U.S. 75 (Central Expressway) on Parker Rd. to Route 2551, then south. Open daily 9–5. $6.95 adults, $5.50 seniors, $4.50 ages 4–12. (1 hour)*

FITNESS AND RECREATION

Bikers and hikers can head to close-in **White Rock Lake**, 8300 Garland, which has a nine-mile trail that connects with adjacent **White Rock Creek Park**'s seven-mile trail for scenic outings. To the southwest, near Joe Pool Lake, the **Dallas Nature Center**, 7171 Mountain Creek Parkway, 972/296-1955, has 360 acres of wilderness and mesquite prairie with six miles of hiking trails. It's open daily except Mondays.

Golfers will find a number of top courses in the area, including **Buffalo Creek Golf Club**, 624 Country Club Drive, Rockwall, 972/771-4003, located about 30 minutes east of Dallas; and **Timarron Country Club**, 1400 Byron Nelson Parkway, Southlake, 972/481-PLAY, to the northwest. For other options, see Arlington Mid-Cities and Fort Worth chapters.

Within easy access in the Metroplex area, visitors will find all kinds of professional sports, including **Texas Rangers** baseball at The Ballpark in Arlington, 817/273-5100; **Dallas Cowboys** football at Texas Stadium in Irving, 972/579-5000; **Dallas Mavericks** basketball and **Dallas Sidekicks** indoor soccer at Reunion Arena in Dallas, 972/988-3865; **Dallas Stars** hockey, 214/467-8277; and **Dallas Burn** outdoor soccer, 214/979-0303.

FOOD

Like Houston, Dallas presents a problem for diners—how to choose from among so many good . . . make that outstanding . . . restaurants. One of the top dining-out spots in the country, Dallas has everything from cutting-edge cuisine to down-home country cookin'.

At the top, chef Dean Fearing has achieved celebrity status with his innovative cooking at the **Mansion on Turtle Creek Dining Room**, 2821 Turtle Creek Boulevard, 214/559-2100, which matches the quality and elegance of its namesake hotel in a converted mansion. Some dishes definitely have the Southwestern flair, while others show Provençal touches, and some are even down-home but better than Mother ever cooked. Plan on spending more than $30 a person—for a memorable evening. Downtown, the **French Room** at the Adolphus, 1321 Commerce Street, 214/742-8200, has made a name for itself with lighter French cuisine in a romantic setting with prices usually topping $30. For Texan-influenced Southwestern fare, **Star Canyon**, 3102 Oak Lawn, 214/520-7827, earns high ratings with both the unusual and the mainstream, such as steaks expertly prepared. Meals will run $20 to $30.

In the avant-garde Deep Ellum/Fair Park area, **Tarantino's**, 3611 Parry Avenue, 214/821-2224, pleases crowds with its eclectic menu called "Euro-Latin," with mainly Mediterranean influences. It specializes in tapas-style small plates that allow tasting of different dishes, but hefty portions also are available. Prices are inexpensive to moderate.

For barbecue, the favorite for years has been **Sonny Bryan's**, which has a number of locations in the Metroplex, starting with the funky old site at 2202 Inwood, 214/357-7120, and including a café in trendy West End, 302 N. Market Street, 214/744-1610. Among the bounty of Mexican food restaurants: A longtime favorite for traditional Tex-Mex is the casual, inexpensive **Ojeda's**, 4617 Maple Street, 214/528-8383. **Nuevo Leon**, 2013 Greenville Avenue, 214/887-8148, and 12895 Josey Lane, (Farmers Branch area in North Dallas), 972/488-1984, tempts you with 18 varieties of salsa, Tex-Mex, and dishes from Mexico's Monterrey area. Prices are inexpensive to moderate.

Fresh seafood comes with flavorings from the Atlantic, Gulf, and Pacific coasts at **Mainstream Fish House**, 3858 Oak Lawn, 214/219-6246, and at Preston Forest Village shopping center, 11661 Preston Road, 214/739-3474, where moderately priced lobster specials are popular.

For Texas-style steaks, top choice is **Chamberlain's Prime Chop House**, 5330 Belt Line Road, Addison (North Dallas), 972/934-2467, where name chef Richard Chamberlain serves outstanding prime rib, steaks, lamb, and a mixed grill that includes game. The decor is cozy wood paneling and the prices are moderately expensive.

Adelmo's Ristorante, 4537 Cole Avenue, 214/559-0325, is a small bistro serving Mediterranean-Italian fare, including tasty *osso buco* and changing specials posted on the blackboard.

LODGING

From historic hotels to ultimate luxury accommodations, Dallas has an exceptionally good selection of upscale overnighting options, but families on budgets will also find traditional low-cost lodging in the metropolitan area. A number of hotels are located in the downtown area, around Market Center, and to the north along LBJ Freeway (Loop 635), which has numerous shops and restaurants.

Downtown, the landmark **Adolphus**, 1321 Commerce Street, 800/221-9083, built in 1912 and a gathering spot for the elite for years, remains a beautiful, highly rated property with an elegant lobby, outstanding dining, and nicely appointed rooms. Normal rates start around $300, but weekend rates often are from $160. An eye-catcher, the **Hyatt Regency Dallas at Reunion**, 300 Reunion Boulevard, 800/233-1234, has about 1,000 rooms and a revolving restaurant atop the 50-story Reunion Tower. It's close to all the West End action. Rates normally start at $275 but weekend rates are less than $200.

North of downtown, the elegant **Mansion on Turtle Creek**, 2821 Turtle Creek Boulevard, 800/527-5432, a converted 1926 home, provides a feeling of country quiet and charm within the busy city. Decorated with European antiques, it has about 140 spacious rooms, a top-rated restaurant, health club, and pool. Rates start around $300 but are often around $200 for weekends. Another posh place is **Hotel Crescent Court**, 400 Crescent Court, Maple and McKinney Avenues, 800/654-6541, modeled after the Royal Crescent in England and reminiscent of a manor house in its furnishings. It has a spa and about 200 rooms, starting around $300 weekdays and under $200 on weekends. Nearby, the boutique **Stoneleigh Hotel**, 2927 Maple Avenue, 800/255-9299, has 151 rooms in a restored brick building, a pool, and a fitness center. Some rooms have marble baths; its rates are about $195 weekdays, $130 weekends.

In the Market Center area, **Renaissance Dallas Hotel**, 2222 Stemmons Freeway, 800/468-3571, is a beautiful 30-story lodging with an elegant lobby and rooftop health club. Rates start about $140 weekdays, $70 weekends.

More economical accommodations include these two in the North Dallas area: **Terra Cotta Inn**, 6101 LBJ Freeway (Loop 635), is a Spanish-architecture lodging with balconies; rates start at $60 with continental breakfast. **Hampton**

GRAPEVINE

Northwest of Dallas, adjacent to DFW International Airport, the charming small town of Grapevine offers wine tastings, historical sites, family entertainment, and an old steam train.

Pick up a walking-tour map at the **Grapevine Convention & Visitors Bureau**, One Liberty Park Plaza, Main Street, 800/457-6338, or at the Visitor Information Center in the **Grapevine Depot**, 707 S. Main Street. Action centers along Main Street where most buildings are on the National Register of Historic Places. Several dozen restored nineteenth- and twentieth-century storefronts house a variety of shops and restaurants. On weekends, the **Grapevine Opry** plays country-western music at the **Palace Theatre**, 308 S. Main Street, 817/481-8733.

The Grapevine Depot also serves as the **Grapevine Historical Museum** and entrance to the **Grapevine Heritage Center**, where a blacksmith and other artisans demonstrate pioneer skills. From its home base at the depot, the **Tarantula Train**, 800/952-5717, makes round-trips to the **Fort Worth Stockyards**, with a steam engine pulling restored cars. It leaves Grapevine Wednesday through Saturday at 10 a.m., arriving at Stockyards at 11:15, leaving there at 2 p.m., and returning to Grapevine at 3:15; the Sunday run leaves Grapevine at 1, arrives at 2:15, leaves at 4:45, and returns at 6. Cost is $19.95 adults, $17.95 seniors, $9.95 ages 3–12 round-trip, or $12 adults, $7 children one-way.

La Buena Vida Vineyards, 416 E. College Street, 817/481-WINE, has a demonstration vineyard, gardens, fountains, tasting room, and retail shop. Outside town, **Delaney Vineyards & Winery**, Route 121 at Glade Road, 817/481-5668, has a showcase building housing its winery, including a Grand Barrel room with French oak casks and barrels, and a tasting room with retail shop.

Inn–Dallas North, 11069 Composite Drive in the Walnut Hill area off I-35 East, 800/HAMPTON, has rooms from $80, including continental breakfast. Economy and mid-priced chain motels, such as Best Western, Comfort Inn, Days Inn, and La Quinta Inn, have numerous locations in the greater Dallas area.

For bed-and-breakfast lodging, call the **Bed & Breakfast Texas Style** reservation service, 972/298-8586.

CAMPING

The Metroplex offers a number of campgrounds within easy driving distance of the city. To the north, not far from DFW International Airport, is **Lewisville Lake Park Campground**, 151 W. Church Street, Lewisville, 972/436-7445, with both tent sites and full hookups as well as numerous services. Adjacent to nearby Joe Pool Lake to the southwest, **Cedar Hill State Park**, 972/291-3900, has 355 spaces for tent and RV campers.

NIGHTLIFE AND SPECIAL EVENTS

The West End Historic District packs the crowds in at night, with live music in its clubs and restaurants, mimes and musicians on the street, horse-and-buggy rides through the area, and specialty shops for browsing. **West End Marketplace**, 603 Munger Avenue, is home to the lively **Planet Hollywood**, 214/749-STAR; adjacent is a complex of small nightclubs known as **Dallas Alley**, 2019 N. Lamar Street, 214/720-0170, set around a courtyard and offering live music.

Formerly an African American center that produced blues music and art, **Deep Ellum**, in the 3500 block of Elm Street east of downtown, 214/747-DEEP, offers an eclectic, avant-garde selection of galleries, restaurants, and clubs with all types of music from country to reggae. Two other popular areas with live music at night are **Greenville Avenue**, from Ross Avenue north of downtown, and **McKinney Avenue** to the north of the central business district. **Medieval Times**, 2021 Stemmons Freeway (I-35), 800/229-9900, delivers a rousing family night out with its jousting tournament and feast.

On the cultural side are numerous offerings, including the **Dallas Opera**, 214/443-1000; **Dallas Symphony Orchestra**, 214/692-0203; **Fort Worth–Dallas Ballet**, 800/654-9545; and **Dallas Theater Center**, 214/522-8499. Summer brings numerous outdoor festivals and concerts in parks and **Dallas Summer Musicals**, 214/565-1116 or 214/691-7200, at Fair Park Music Hall. The **Dallas Visitor Information Special Events Hotline**, 800/C-DALLAS or 214/746-6679, provides updated information.

Cotton Bowl festivities, 888/SWB-BOWL, at Fair Park on New Year's Day, lead off the year's special events. Others include **Art Fest**, 214/361-2011, at Fair Park in late May; **State Fair of Texas**, 214/565-9931, one of the largest in the country, at Fair Park from late September to late October; and the annual **University of Texas–University of Oklahoma** fall football classic, 214/565-9931, at the Cotton Bowl.

SHOPPING
Could the home of Neiman Marcus be anything but a great place to shop? Indeed, the city is a mecca for those who like to shop 'til they drop. The venerable **Neiman Marcus**, which opened here in the early 1900s as an exclusive women's ready-to-wear retailer, still has its original downtown store at 1618 Main Street, 214/741-6911, where a museum tells the history of this legendary retailer. N-M also has locations in two popular shopping centers: **NorthPark Center**, Northwest Highway (Loop 12) and Central Expressway (U.S. 75), 214/363-7441, with more than 160 stores; and **Prestonwood Mall**, North Dallas Tollway at Belt Line Road, 972/980-4275. The upscale **Galleria**, LBJ Freeway (Loop 635) at Dallas Parkway North, 972/702-7100, with a vaulted skylight and ice-skating rink, has 200 stores and more than two dozen restaurants. Close to the city is a little gem with Spanish architecture, **Highland Park Village**, Mockingbird Lane at Preston Road, 214/559-2740, one of the country's first shopping centers.

In the downtown area, **West End Marketplace**, 603 Munger Avenue, 214/748-4801, has more than 50 specialty shops. Antiquers should check out **McKinney Avenue** and around Love Field airport, along **Mockingbird Lane**, **Lovers Lane**, and **Cedar Springs Road**. For bargain-hunters, **Inwood Trade Center**, 1300 Inwood Road, 214/521-4777, has numerous outlet stores, and you can find many other discount stores through the *Hidden Values* guide from the **Dallas Convention & Visitors Bureau**, 214/571-1301.

14
FORT WORTH

A fun city unabashedly proud to be called Cowtown, Fort Worth has polished its cowboy past with an acclaimed cultural district. The combination makes Fort Worth a sophisticated yet casual, unpretentious destination.

The city was established in 1849 as a military fort to protect settlers moving west. It then became a stop on the Old Chisholm Trail between South Texas and Kansas, a route used by cattle drives in the mid-1800s. As the railroads pushed west, Fort Worth became a center for meat packing as well as cattle shipping—its stockyards growing to second-largest in the country, behind Chicago.

In its young years, Fort Worth was a wild, open frontier town. Cowboys drove their herds down the main street, then headed to saloons and brothels to spend their earnings. A portion of present-day downtown was tagged Hell's Half Acre, a favorite hangout for Butch Cassidy, the Sundance Kid, and other outlaws.

Dusting off its past, Fort Worth has renovated Hell's Half Acre, other parts of downtown, and the stockyards area, which is now a historic district.

The city has particularly strong art collections, which have won international attention and earned Fort Worth the title "Museum Capital of the Southwest." Besides its collection of museums, the city fields excellent programs in the performing arts and enhances the scene with top-quality restaurants. You'll still find plenty of cowboys here as well.

DOWNTOWN FORT WORTH (Cultural District)

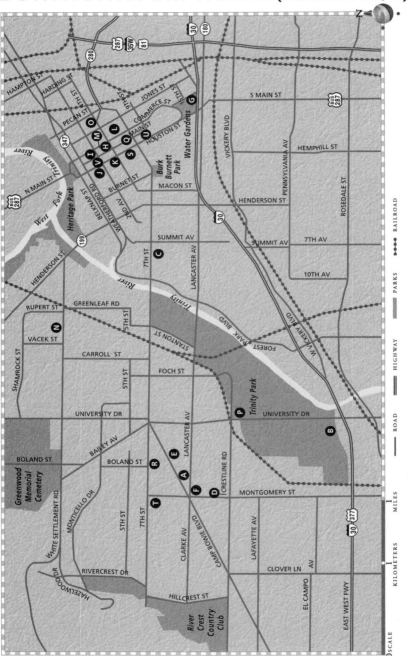

A PERFECT DAY IN FORT WORTH

In the cultural district, start museum-hopping at the Fort Worth Museum of Science and History, followed by the Kimbell Art Museum and the Amon Carter Museum. Wander through the Stockyards National Historic District, then head to Sundance Square, adding the Sid Richardson Collection of Western Art to your museum visits; then dine downtown.

Or go to Sundance Square first and end your day wandering in the Stockyards National Historic District where you will find shops, restaurants, and Old West entertainment. See a show at Cowtown Coliseum and dine out at one of the many fine restaurants.

ORIENTATION

An easy city to navigate, Fort Worth has three distinct areas for sightseeing: the historic Downtown/Sundance Square, the Cultural District/Zoo to the west, and the Stockyards National Historic District to the north. Within about two miles of each other, the three form a triangle, each offering sights and restaurants within walking distance of each other. While it's best to have a car if you're planning to see sights throughout the Metroplex, Fort Worth's attractions are close enough together that you could base yourself in one district and see the others by using cabs or the local bus system, known as the T, 817/215-8600. The T costs 75¢ and special routes for touring city attractions are available.

SIGHTS

- **A** Amon Carter Museum
- **B** Botanic Garden
- **C** Cattle Raisers Museum
- **D** Fort Worth Museum of Science and History
- **E** Kimbell Art Museum
- **F** Modern Art Museum of Fort Worth
- **G** Water Gardens

SIGHTS *(continued)*

Sundance Square Sights
- **H** Chisholm Trail Mural
- **I** Fire Station No. 1
- **J** Fort Worth Outlet Square
- **K** The Modern at Sundance
- **L** Nancy Lee and Perry R. Bass Performance Hall
- **M** Sid Richardson Collection of Western Art

FOOD

- **N** Angelo's Barbecue
- **O** Angeluna
- **P** Blue Mesa Grill
- **Q** Mi Cocina
- **R** Michaels
- **S** Reata
- **M** Riscky's Bar-B-Que
- **T** Saint Emilion

LODGING

- **Q** Blackstone Marriott Courtyard Hotel
- **U** Radisson Plaza
- **V** The Worthington

Note: Items with the same letter are located in the same area.

TRINITY RAILWAY EXPRESS

The Metroplex is building a commuter train, the Trinity Railway Express, that will connect downtown Fort Worth, downtown Dallas, Dallas–Fort Worth International Airport, and other communities. Progress has been slow, but check locally to see if segments are running when you visit.

CULTURAL DISTRICT/ZOO SIGHTSEEING HIGHLIGHTS

★★★★ AMON CARTER MUSEUM
3501 Camp Bowie Blvd., 817/738-1933, cartermuseum.org
The museum grew from the personal Western art collection of oil-man and newspaper publisher Amon Carter into a showcase of American art from the nineteenth and early twentieth centuries. Besides masterpieces by Frederic Remington and Charles Russell, the collection includes works by Georgia O'Keeffe and photographers Ansel Adams and Richard Avedon.

Details: Tue–Sat 10–5, Sun noon–5. Free. (1 hour)

★★★★ FORT WORTH ZOO
1989 Colonial Pkwy, 817/871-7050,
www.rwnet.com/FWZoo
Natural habitats give visitors a feel for animals in the wild in this out-standing zoo, considered one of the tops in the country. Among its 5,000 wild and exotic animals, you may see condors in Raptor Canyon and a white tiger at Asian Falls, with its grassy hills and wa-terfalls. A new Koala Outback exhibit has kangaroos, wallabies, and the cuddly koala from Australia. The World of Primates is a favorite for its apes, free-flying birds, and tropical rain forest for gorillas. There also are animals indigenous to the Lone Star State in a pioneer-town exhibit.

Details: Located in Forest Park, slightly south of the museums. Apr–Oct (Daylight Savings Time months) Mon–Fri 10–5, Sat and Sun 10–6; Nov–Mar daily 10–5. Hours may vary slightly; call for *information. $7 adults, $3 seniors, and $4.50 ages 3–12; half price Wed. (2–3 hours)*

★★★★ KIMBELL ART MUSEUM
3333 Camp Bowie Blvd., 817/332-8451, www.kimbellart.org
Considered one of the best small museums in the United States, the Kimbell is acclaimed for its collection of European works, comple-mented by Asian, Meso-American, and African art. Among the mas-ter artists represented are Rembrandt, Caravaggio, Gauguin, Picasso, and Matisse. The museum also hosts special exhibits, such as never-before-seen Monet paintings of the Mediterranean. The building itself is a work of art, with vaulted ceilings that allow exceptionally good natural lighting for the exhibits.

Details: Tue–Thu, Sat 10–5, Fri noon–8, Sun noon–5. Free; special exhibits may have fee. (1½–2 hours)

★★★ BOTANIC GARDEN
3220 N. Botanic Garden Dr. off University Dr., 817/871-7686
In a heavily wooded area of Trinity Park, south of the museums, the garden has 150,000 plants in formal and natural settings, a conserva-tory with a rain-forest environment to nurture more than 2,500 speci-mens from the tropics, and a Japanese Garden with a pagoda and teahouse.

Details: Garden: daily 8 a.m.–dark. Conservatory: Apr–Oct (Daylight Savings Time months) Mon–Fri 10–9, Sat 10–6, Sun 1–6; Nov–Mar same except until 4 weekends. Japanese Garden: Apr–Oct daily 9–6, Nov–Mar Tue–Sun 10–4. Garden: free; conservatory: $1 adults, 50¢ ages 4–12. Japanese Garden: $2 adults weekdays, $2.50 weekends, $1 ages 4–12. (1–2 hours)

★★★ FORT WORTH MUSEUM OF SCIENCE AND HISTORY
1501 Montgomery St., 888/255-9300, fwmshl@metronet.com, www.fwmuseum.org
Inside and outside, this place packs a lot of color and action for chil-dren and adults. Texas dinosaurs are a major part of the attraction here, starting with two giant ones in the exterior courtyard, where visitors of all ages can play like paleontologists. Children particularly love discovering "dinosaur bones"—molds of real ones found in the area and on exhibit in the museum. Inside are interactive exhibits

about such widely diverse subjects as your body and computers; the Omni Theater, with an 80-foot domed screen showing IMAX-format films; and a planetarium.

Details: Mon 9–5, Tue–Thu 9–8, Fri and Sat 9–9, Sun noon–8. *Planetarium and theater hours and programs vary; call for current schedules. $5 adults, $4 seniors, $3 ages 3–12 for museum, $3 for planetarium, $6 adults, $4 seniors and ages 3–12 for theater. (1 1/2–3 hours)*

★★★ MODERN ART MUSEUM OF FORT WORTH
1309 Montgomery St., 817/738-9215, mamfw.org

Soon to have a new home next to the Kimbell, this museum concentrates on twentieth-century works, with Pablo Picasso, Andy Warhol, and Mark Rothko among the artists featured.

Details: Tue–Fri 10–5, Sat 11–5 , Sun noon–5. Free. (1–1 1/2 hours)

★ LOG CABIN VILLAGE
University Dr. and Colonial Pkwy. in Forest Park (across from zoo), 817/926-5881

A collection of homes from the 1850s portrays early pioneer life in the area. Guides and interpreters in period dress demonstrate activities of the time.

Details: Tue–Fri 9–4:30, Sat 10–4:30, Sun 1–4:30. $1.50 adults, $1.25 ages 4–17. (1 hour)

DOWNTOWN/SUNDANCE SQUARE SIGHTSEEING HIGHLIGHTS

★★★★ SUNDANCE SQUARE ENTERTAINMENT DISTRICT
817/390-8711, info@sundancesquare.com, www.sundancesquare.com

Once a hangout for outlaws such as Butch Cassidy, the Sundance Kid, and other legendary characters of the Old West, the north end of downtown throbs with renewed life as Sundance Square. A prime example of urban revitalization that works, turn-of-the-century brick buildings have been renovated and dramatic new limestone, glass, and steel structures added along brick streets with brick sidewalks and intimate courtyards. Trendy restaurants, shops, galleries, theaters, and offices are augmented by apartments, offering true urban living, a rarity in Texas cities.

Between the convention center and the courthouse, the area known as Sundance Square encompasses about 16 blocks, generally between Throckmorton and Calhoun Streets from Second through Fifth Streets. A focal point of Sundance Square, the magnificent **Chisholm Trail Mural**, 400 Main Street, pays tribute to the city's cowtown heritage in a three-story trompe l'oeil depicting cattle drives in the mid to late 1800s. Glimpses into the city's cowboy/ranching heritage are offered at the landmark 1870s **Fire Station No. 1**, Second and Commerce Streets, 817/732-1631, which now houses "150 Years of Fort Worth," a timeline exhibit that is part of the Museum of Science and History.

Two small museums are located here. The **Sid Richardson Collection of Western Art**, 309 Main Street, 817/332-6554, is a don't-miss display of about 60 paintings of the American West by Frederic Remington and Charles Russell, plus some of their bronzes and some saddles. The city became a treasure trove of Western art as oilmen Richardson and Amon Carter engaged in a friendly rivalry of collecting. **The Modern at Sundance**, 410 Houston Street, 817/335-2915, has exhibits from the main Modern Art Museum in the Cultural District and an excellent gift shop.

Two 48-foot-high, three-dimensional angels with extended trumpets give a commanding appearance to the new $67 million **Nancy Lee and Perry R. Bass Performance Hall**, 555 Commerce Street, 817/212-4200. A classical building reminiscent of turn-of-the-century opera houses in Europe, it has three domes inside and seats about 2,000 for symphony, opera, ballet, and other live performances.

On the edge of Sundance Square, **Fort Worth Outlet Square**, Third and Throckmorton Streets, 817/414-2817, is a major retail center—with an ice-skating rink.

The city's colorful past comes to life on guided **walking tours** of historic downtown, which leave from the Radisson Plaza Hotel lobby, Eighth and Main Streets, Friday and Saturday at 9:30 a.m. They last about 2½ hours and cost $10 per person, and reservations aren't necessary. They're conducted by historian Bill Campbell, 817/327-1178.

Details: *Fire Station No. 1 open daily 9–7. Admission: Free. Sid Richardson museum open Tue and Wed 10–5, Thu and Fri 10–8, Sat 11–8, Sun 1–5. Admission: Free. The Modern at Sundance open Mon–Wed 11–6, Thu–Sat 11–10, Sun 1–5. Admission: Free. Check with the Bass Performance Hall about tours. (2–3 hours minimum)*

★★★★ WATER GARDENS
Commerce and 15th Sts., 817/871-7699

Adjacent to the large convention center at the south end of downtown, this striking plaza and terrace designed by noted architects Philip Johnson and John Burgee capture everyone's fancy with their sculptures, fountains, waterfalls, and cascading pools. You can admire the view from above or walk 38 feet down into a sunken garden, where you're surrounded by water rushing over a 710-foot wall.

Details: *(30 minutes)*

★★ CATTLE RAISERS MUSEUM
1301 W. Seventh St., 817/332-7064,
www.cattleraisersmuseum.org

The history of ranching in Texas comes to life in films, photos, and memorabilia in this museum, where Tex the Talking Longhorn welcomes visitors.

Details: *Located several blocks southwest of Sundance Square. Mon–Sat 10–5, Sun 1–5. $3 adults, $2 seniors and ages 12–18, $1 ages 4–12. (45 minutes)*

STOCKYARDS NATIONAL HISTORIC DISTRICT SIGHTSEEING HIGHLIGHTS

★★★★ STOCKYARDS NATIONAL HISTORIC DISTRICT
Exchange Ave., 817/624-4741,
www.fortworth.com/attrstock.htm

Just north of the modern skyscrapers defining downtown lies the heart of old Fort Worth, the stockyards area, where for years cowboys drove herds of cattle down Exchange Avenue to the pens and whooped it up in saloons. At one time the second-largest stockyard in the country, the area declined as oil replaced the cattle industry. Now on the National Register of Historic Places, the district has been restored and gives visitors a sense of the Old West in its brick streets and boardwalks. Besides historic sites, the district has about 30 stores, restaurants, saloons, and hotels. These tend to be quieter early in the week but busy Thursday through Sunday.

Most of the action is along or adjacent to Exchange Avenue. **Cowtown Coliseum**, 121 E. Exchange Avenue, 888/269-8696 or 817/625-1025, is the site of weekend rodeos, Wild West shows, and other entertainment. Old hog and sheep pens have been turned into **Stockyards Station**, 140 E. Exchange Avenue, 817/625-9715, a Western festival marketplace with restaurants, galleries, and shops. The Spanish-style **Livestock Exchange Building**, 131 E. Exchange Avenue, once bustled with cattle-buyers and -sellers. While the exchange still has auctions, it also now houses business offices and the **Stockyards Collection & Museum**, 817/625-5087, with memorabilia related to the stockyards, packing plants, and railroad.

Western-wear stores in this area still serve real cowboys and ranchers, as well as city slickers, seeking everything from hats to boots, both custom-fitted and custom-made. Even if you don't want a pair of boots, it's fun to go into some of the stores simply to see the many colors and designs offered.

Details: *Stockyards Visitor Information Center, 130 E. Exchange Ave., 817/624-4741. (1–2 hours minimum)*

★★★★ TARANTULA RAILROAD
140 E. Exchange Ave., 800/952-5717 or 817/625-RAIL, Ttrain@onramp.net, www.tarantulatrain.com

Daily excitement revs up at Stockyards Station with arrivals and departures of the Tarantula. Short rides in restored coaches pulled by a steam (sometimes diesel) locomotive give passengers an Old West experience. The train, named for the spiderlike rail lines that once extended from downtown Fort Worth, makes nine-mile round-trips across the city to the Eighth Avenue Train Yard and round-trips to the stockyards from nearby Grapevine. Short runs are one hour, longer ones five hours including about 2 1/2 hours to tour stockyards area.

FORT WORTH REGION

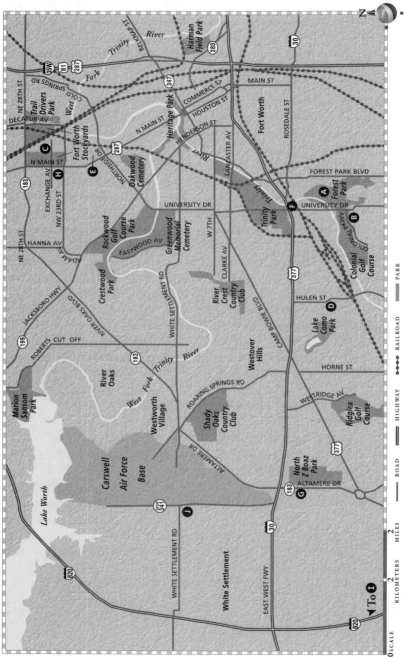

Details: *Stockyards–Eighth Ave. run: Mon–Sat at noon, Sun at 3. $10 adults, $9 seniors, $5.50 ages 3–12. Grapevine–Stockyards run: Wed–Sat leaves Grapevine at 10, returns at 3:15; Sun run leaves at 1 and returns at 6. $19.95 adults, $17.95 seniors, $9.95 ages 3–12 round-trip, $12 adults and $7 children one-way. Diesel trains run Mon and Tue and steam trains Wed–Sun. (1–5¼ hours)*

FITNESS AND RECREATION

Walkers and runners frequent the scenic trails in Trinity Park, which stretches for two miles along a fork of the Trinity River. Golfers have lots of options in the Metroplex, among the tops being two highly rated courses at **Hyatt Bear Creek Golf & Racquet Club**, West Airfield Drive by Dallas-Fort Worth International Airport, 972/453-8400; **Tour 18** at nearby Flower Mound, 817/430-2000; and **Four Seasons Resort and Club** PGA championship courses at Irving, 972/717-0700.

Sailing, boating, and fishing are popular on **Lake Worth** to the northwest and **Lake Arlington** bordering Fort Worth on the east. Within the Metroplex visitors will find professional sports, including **Texas Rangers** baseball at The Ballpark in Arlington, 817/273-5100; **Dallas Cowboys** football at Texas Stadium in Irving, 972/579-5000; and **Dallas Mavericks** basketball at Reunion Arena in Dallas, 214/748-1808.

The new **Texas Motor Speedway** in Fort Worth, north of Alliance Airport at I-35 West and Route 114, 817/215-8500, is the second-largest sports facility in the country, offering major-league auto racing, both stock car and Indy-style. It's also the site of major music events.

SIGHTS

A Fort Worth Zoo
B Log Cabin Village
C Stockyards National Historic District
C Tarantula Railroad

FOOD

D Bistro Louise
E Joe T. Garcia's
C Riscky's Bar-B-Que
C Sonny Bryan's

LODGING

F Days Inn
G Green Oaks Park Hotel
H Miss Molly's Hotel B&B
C Stockyards Hotel

CAMPING

I Cowtown RV Park
J Sunset RV Park

Note: Items with the same letter are located in the same area.

Nearby **Lone Star Park** at Grand Prairie, 972/263-RACE, has pari-mutuel horse racing.

FOOD

This may be beef country, but there's a lot more varied fare on the scene today as the downtown resurgence has fostered the growth of trendy new restaurants.

Downtown, **Reata**, 500 Throckmorton Street, (35th floor of Bank One Tower), 817/336-1009, has made a big splash with its upscale "cowboy" cuisine, which puts a Texas stamp on the popular Southwestern fare. You can bet no old-time cowboys who rode into Fort Worth ever had cilantro butter on grilled rib-eye steaks, or finished dinner with dessert tacos—all the while over-looking skyscrapers. Movie fans will remember that Reata was the name of the ranch in the classic 1950s movie *Giant*. Overlooking the new Bass Performance Hall with its angel sculptures, **Angeluna**, 215 E. Fourth Street, 817/334-0080, is the place to see and be seen eating imaginative continental–New American fare in a celestial setting with angels in the wall paintings. Both restaurants are moderate to moderately expensive.

Mi Cocina, 509 Main Street, 817/877-3600, serves its own brand of Tex-Mex favorites and dishes from interior Mexico, adding such specialties as chile garlic shrimp. It's moderately priced.

Barbecue is revered here, and a sure way to start a spirited discussion among local residents is to ask which eating spot has the best barbecue. Among longtime favorites: **Riscky's Bar-B-Que**, 300 Main Street, 817/877-3306, and Stockyards Station, 817/626-7777, has lip-licking-good pit-smoked beef brisket and pork ribs; its Stockyards site offers steak and fish also. **Angelo's Barbecue**, 2533 White Settlement Road, 817/332-0357, draws repeat crowds for its chicken as well as brisket and ribs. Hickory-smoked brisket is the favorite at **Sonny Bryan's**, 2621 N. Main Street (by the Stockyards), 817/626-7191, and two other locations. All are extremely casual and inexpensive.

The longtime favorite for Tex-Mex food in a laid-back atmosphere is **Joe T. Garcia's**, 2201 N. Commerce Street, 817/626-4356, which has an open-air garden. It's next to the Stockyards area and serves from a menu at lunch but has only enchiladas and fajitas for dinner. Joe T.'s is inexpensive.

In the Cultural District, **Michaels**, 3413 W. Seventh Street, 817/877-3413, serves excellent "contemporary ranch" fare with Southwestern flavors and yummy desserts amid minimalist black-and-white decor. **Saint Emilion**, 3617 W. Seventh Street, 817/737-2781, is a small country-French restaurant that's consistently rated high for more-classic French cuisine, including its specialty tuna tartare. In the nearby university area, **Blue Mesa Grill**, 1600 S. University Drive, Suite 609, 817/332-6372, debuted in 1997 serving Santa Fe–style cuisine. Near the Cultural District, **Bistro Louise**, 2900 S. Hulen Street, 817/922-9244, draws from the Mediterranean with Spanish/French/Italian influences on its dishes, including pastas and fresh seafood. Meals are moderate to moderately expensive in these restaurants.

LODGING

Downtown, the premier hotel is **The Worthington**, 200 Main Street, 800/433-5677, offering about 500 luxury rooms by all the action around Sundance Square. The hotel has exercise facilities, golf privileges, a pool, and private patios and balconies. Rates run around $150. **Radisson Plaza**, 815 Main Street, 800/333-3333, also has about 500 rooms, a pool, sauna, exercise equipment, and golf privileges; rooms run around $120. The 1929 art deco Blackstone Hotel has been renovated into the **Blackstone Marriott Courtyard Hotel**, 601 Main Street, 800/321-2211, with 203 rooms, starting at about $60.

In the historic Stockyards area, the restored, turn-of-the-century **Stockyards Hotel**, 109 E. Exchange Avenue, 800/423-8471, is a step back into cattle-baron days with its ranch-like decor in the lobby and Old West theme rooms. Rates run about $120, higher on weekends.

Also in the district, the early 1900s **Miss Molly's Hotel B&B**, 109½ W. Exchange Avenue, 800/99-MOLLY, once a boarding house and then a bordello, now sits atop the Star Café. The livingroom–style lobby is surrounded by eight bedrooms with country/Victorian furnishings, including quilts on all beds. Most rooms share baths—bathrobes are provided—with rates from $95, including continental breakfast with homemade muffins and fresh fruit.

Green Oaks Park Hotel, 6901 W. Freeway, 800/772-2341 or 817/738-7311, has two pools, restaurant, lounge, and exercise equipment. Its rooms and suites start at $75. **Days Inn**, 1551 S. University Drive, 800/DAYS INN, has rooms from $39.

For other nearby accommodations in the Metroplex, see the Dallas and Arlington/Mid-Cities chapters.

CAMPING

Cowtown RV Park, 7000 I-20 West, Aledo (just west of Fort Worth), 800/781-4678, is a Good Sam park with more than 100 hookups, laundry

GRANBURY AND GLEN ROSE

Less than an hour from Fort Worth, the Granbury–Glen Rose area provides an excellent change-of-pace side trip for visitors or weekend escape for Metroplex residents.

About 35 miles from Fort Worth on U.S. 377, Granbury is a charming country town with more than 50 antiques and specialty shops surrounding its 1870s town square and limestone Victorian courthouse. The restored 1886 **Granbury Opera House**, 116 E. Pearl Street, 817/573-9191, stages a variety of musicals, plays, and melodramas throughout the year. Other attractions include scenic cruises on Lake Granbury April through December; the **Brazos Old-Fashioned Drive-In Theater**, 1800 W. Pearl Street, 817/573-1311, a 1950s-era outdoor theater open on weekends spring through fall; and walking, driving, and carriage tours of the historic areas. The town has a number of motels and romantic bed-and-breakfasts. For information, contact the **Granbury Convention & Visitors Bureau**, 800/950-2212, www.granbury.org.

About 20 miles south of Granbury on Route 144 and U.S. 67, **Glen Rose** serves as the gateway to two attractions. At **Dinosaur Valley State Park**, four miles west on Route 205, 254/897-4588, the solid-rock bed of the Paluxy River has yielded a number of dinosaur tracks, including the first sauropod tracks ever discovered. There are interpretive exhibits about the tracks, the dinosaurs that roamed the area, and the environment of the time. The park also has hiking and biking trails, camping, and a state park store.

Fossil Rim Wildlife Center, three miles southwest of Glen Rose off U.S. 67, 254/897-2960, has giraffes, ostriches, zebras, antelope, and more exotic wildlife and endangered species roaming its scenic hills and canyons.

A conservation project and game ranch, the center allows visitors to see the animals on a drive-yourself 9.5-mile route or by touring with a naturalist guide. Visitors can stay overnight in a lodge or indulge in a wildlife safari, spending the night in tents (air-conditioned, heated, and with private bath). For information on lodging call, 254/897-4933 or 888/775-6742.

facilities, a pool, and other amenities. **Sunset RV Park**, 4921 White Settlement Road, 800/238-0567, has 70 hookups among trees. For other camping options, see the chapters on Dallas and Arlington/Mid-Cities.

NIGHTLIFE AND SPECIAL EVENTS

From live theater, opera, ballet, and symphony performances to Wild West saloons and fine dining, nighttime fun takes many different tacks here. For a schedule of cultural events, contact the **Fort Worth Symphony**, 817/926-8831; the **Fort Worth Opera**, 817/731-0833; the **Fort Worth–Dallas Ballet**, 800/654-9545; live theater venues, 817/792-9800; and the **Convention and Visitors Bureau Events Line**, 817/332-2000. The city has a magnificent new forum for the cultural arts in Sundance Square, the $67 million **Bass Performance Hall**, Fourth and Commerce Streets, 817/212-4200, a 2,000-seat theater built in the manner of grand opera houses. In the Cultural District, **Casa Mañana Theatre**, 3101 W. Lancaster Avenue, 817/332-2272, presents popular Broadway musicals and other shows in a large playhouse in the round.

Downtown, much of the nighttime action centers around Sundance Square, a 16-block area of upscale restaurants, shops, clubs, and theaters. In the area, **Caravan of Dreams**, 312 Houston Street, 817/877-3000, is a performing arts center with a popular live-music club drawing major entertainers and a fun rooftop Grotto Bar. **USA Cafe**, 425 Commerce Street, 817/335-5400, hops late into the night.

For country-western, head to the historic Stockyards district. Don't miss **Billy Bob's Texas**, 2520 Rodeo Plaza, 817/624-7117, a huge saloon with entertainment and dancing nightly and live bull-riding (yep, they're real) on weekends. Billy Bob's claims to be the world's largest honky-tonk, able to accommodate several thousand revelers. Along nearby Exchange Avenue, drop into the historic **White Elephant Saloon**, 106 E. Exchange Avenue, 817/624-1887, where the rustic setting makes you feel as if Matt Dillon, Doc, and Miss Kitty will arrive any minute. The saloon became legendary after a street gunfight in which the bar owner was killed by a Fort Worth marshal. Today there's live music and dancing.

Across the street, in the Stockyards Hotel, **Booger Red's Saloon & Restaurant**, 109 E. Exchange Avenue, 817/625-6427, has saddles for bar stools. Wild West shows, rodeos, and concerts are frequent entertainment options at the **Cowtown Coliseum**, 121 E. Exchange Avenue, 817/625-1025.

Among special events are the **Southwestern Exposition and Livestock Show**, 817/877-2400, starting the third Friday in January and running 17 days;

Main Street Fort Worth Arts Festival, 817/336-ARTS, in mid-April; **Mayfest**, 817/332-1055, a family festival along the Trinity River in early May; and the **Chisholm Trail Roundup/Chief Quanah Parker Comanche Pow-Wow**, 817/625-7005, in mid-June.

SHOPPING

From name-brand outlet stores to art galleries and custom Western wear, Fort Worth has a surprising array of shopping opportunities. **Fort Worth Outlet Square**, Third and Throckmorton Streets, 800/414-2817, one of the few such discount malls in a downtown area, has major names in clothing, electronics, and housewares. Stores in the historic **Stockyards district** have been outfitting cowboys and ranchers with hats, boots, saddles, jeans, and everything else Western for years. City slickers are welcome, too. Stores here include **M. L. Leddy's Boot and Saddlery**, 2455 N. Main Street, 817/624-3149, and **Maverick Fine Western Wear**, 100 E. Exchange Avenue, 817/626-1129. Shopaholics should check out **Grapevine Mills**, 972/724-4900, a megamall of outlets with more than 200 stores, restaurants, and entertainment. It's about two miles north of Dallas–Fort Worth International Airport on Route 121 north and Route 2499.

15
ARLINGTON/MID-CITIES

Within sight of the skyscrapers of Dallas and Fort Worth, the towns of Arlington, Grand Prairie, and Irving literally meld into each other, becoming what's commonly called the mid-cities. Like kid sisters, these communities have all the fun—from the roar of the crowd at major-league baseball and football games to the chills and thrills of roller coaster rides.

The family playground of the Metroplex, Arlington is home to the Texas Rangers and their field, The Ballpark, with its Legends of the Game Baseball Museum, and to Six Flags Over Texas, one of the country's major theme parks. Neighboring Grand Prairie augments the entertainment with several family-oriented attractions, and Irving has a major movie studio with tours and the Dallas Cowboys at Texas Stadium.

First settled by Caddo Indians, the area was the site of trading posts as pioneers came west in the mid-1830s. With the arrival of the railroad in 1876, the town of Arlington was born and remained a center of agriculture through the first half of the twentieth century.

Part flat and part rolling hills, the three towns are next to the giant Dallas–Fort Worth International Airport, the world's largest airport in acreage and one of the busiest. Since the airport opened in 1974, neighboring communities have mushroomed with homes, office complexes, and hotels. Even so, with all the strip shopping centers, fast-food restaurants, and freeways crisscrossing the area, visitors will still see fields where cattle and horses graze.

A PERFECT DAY IN ARLINGTON/MID-CITIES

Try to time your visit between spring and early fall when you can enjoy both Six Flags Over Texas and The Ballpark in Arlington. Even if the Texas Rangers are not playing, start the day with a visit to The Ballpark in Arlington, the Legends of the Game Baseball Museum, and the Children's Learning Center, then do Six Flags Over Texas until you drop. If the team is in town, adjust your schedule to take in a game.

ORIENTATION

Irving borders the Dallas–Fort Worth International Airport, and Arlington and Grand Prairie lie just south of it. Arlington joins the east side of Fort Worth, while Grand Prairie and Irving touch the west side of Dallas. The area is laced with freeways. I-30 and I-20 connect Dallas, Grand Prairie, Arlington, and Fort Worth, and most of the mid-cities attractions are near I-30. Texas Routes 183 and 114 connect Dallas, Irving, and the DFW Airport, and there are many accommodations and restaurants along Route 114 in particular.

Most visitors go sightseeing and dining throughout the Metroplex. Since the commuter rail system is still under construction in the Metroplex, it's essential to have a car when visiting this area. From the attractions in Arlington, it's about 30 minutes into downtown Dallas and slightly less into downtown Fort Worth. There are, however, more than a dozen hotels in Arlington that offer guests free trolley shuttles to the major attractions, such as Six Flags Over Texas, Six Flags Hurricane Harbor, and The Ballpark. Ask about the service when booking.

ARLINGTON SIGHTSEEING HIGHLIGHTS

★★★★ THE BALLPARK
I-30 at Hwy. 157, 817/273-5098 (recorded information)
Home to the popular Texas Rangers baseball team, this striking pink-granite ballpark is worth seeing even if it's not the season for batters-up. Opened in spring of 1994, the park has a classic look reminiscent of older ballparks with an open-air playing field. The Legends of the Game Baseball Museum showcases the history of the game, including 100 pieces of memorabilia from the National Baseball Hall of Fame and Museum. At the one-of-a-kind Children's Learning Center, put your hand in a glove and catch a pitch by Nolan Ryan in one of many interactive exhibits using baseball to teach math, science, and history. Tours of The Ballpark take visitors behind the scenes, sometimes into

ARLINGTON

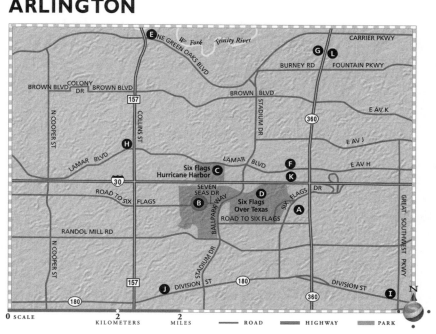

SIGHTS

- **Ⓐ** Air Combat School
- **Ⓑ** The Ballpark in Arlington
- **Ⓒ** Six Flags Hurricane Harbor
- **Ⓓ** Six Flags Over Texas

FOOD

- **Ⓔ** Al's Hamburger's
- **Ⓕ** Cacherel
- **Ⓖ** Friday's Front Row Sports Grill
- **Ⓖ** Marsala Ristorante
- **Ⓗ** Piccolo Mondo

LODGING

- **Ⓘ** Best Western Great Southwest Inn
- **Ⓙ** Comfort Inn
- **Ⓚ** Fairfield Inn by Marriott
- **Ⓛ** Hampton Inn/ Arlington–DFW Airport

Note: Items with the same letter are located in the same place.

the Rangers clubhouse and dugout. The stadium is the centerpiece of a developing entertainment complex, which already has two small lakes stocked with catfish (no fee, just have a fishing license).

Details: *Texas Rangers: 817/273-5100. Ballpark tours and museum: 817/273-5600, tours year-round, Mon–Sat on the hour 9–4,*

Sun noon–4 when team is away, varying hours in season; call for details.
Tours: $5 adults, $4 seniors, $3 age 13 and younger; those under 36
inches tall free. Museum and learning center: Mar–Oct Mon–Sat
9–7:30 and Sun noon–5, Nov–Feb Tue–Sat 9–5 and Sun noon–5. $6
adults, $5 ages 62 and older, $4 ages 6–13. Combination tour/museum: $10 adults, $8 seniors, $6 ages 6–13. (3 hours)

★★★★ SIX FLAGS OVER TEXAS
I-30 at Hwy. 360, 817/640-8900, www.sixflags.com
The granddaddy of amusement parks, this 205-acre playground consistently sets new records for innovative rides—from the world's first
flume ride to the first total free-fall ride and first back-to-back looping
roller coaster. With the Texas Giant (repeatedly named the best
wooden roller coaster), the 218-foot-tall Mr. Freeze, and the new
Batman The Ride, this park delivers the ultimate in spine-tingling thrills.
A $14 million expansion includes a new Escape from Dino Island 3D
TurboRide that brings visitors face to face with flying pteranodons. Not
every attraction is hair-raising. Young children will find rides just their
size in Looney Tunes Land, and top entertainers perform in shows, including six new offerings.

Details: *Weekends Mar–mid-May (daily for two weeks at spring
break in mid-Mar), daily mid-May–late Aug, weekends and special events
Sep–Dec. Summer hours are usually 10–10 but otherwise vary so call for
specifics. $35.50 adults, $29 seniors and children under 48 inches tall;
two-day tickets at reduced prices. (5 hours minimum)*

★★★ SIX FLAGS HURRICANE HARBOR
I-30 at Ballpark Way North, 817/265-3356,
www.sixflags.com
Whether you like to raft through raging rapids, shoot down a water
slide, or float lazily along a stream, this 47-acre water park provides
cool entertainment for all ages. Previously called Wet 'n' Wild, this
family recreation center puts you into the tropics, where the adventurous can disappear on their inner tubes into the Black Hole or
plummet 830 feet down the tallest water raft slide in the country.
Take plenty of sunscreen.

Details: *Located across from Six Flags Over Texas. Mid-May–mid-Aug 10–6 or later, to mid-Sep weekends 10–6. Verify hours and days of
operation. $22.97 adults, $15.95 seniors and children under 48 inches.
(4 hours minimum)*

★★ AIR COMBAT SCHOOL
921 Six Flags Dr., #117 (across from Six Flags Over Texas), 817/640-1886

Ever fantasized about being a top-gun fighter pilot? Well, you can suit up, strap into a real jet cockpit, and take off to do battle in the skies in the simulator here, after a short ground-school course and mission briefing. Minimum height: 4 feet, 8 inches.

Details: Mon–Sat 10–3 and also Sun in summer; reservations recommended. $39.95. (1½ hours)

GRAND PRAIRIE SIGHTSEEING HIGHLIGHTS

★★★ PALACE OF WAX AND RIPLEY'S BELIEVE IT OR NOT!
601 E. Safari Pkwy., 972/263-2391

David Letterman himself welcomes you as a guest in the Palace of Wax, where about 200 life-like wax figures include names from TV, Hollywood, and history. You'll see Forrest Gump with his box of chocolates, the Star Trek crew, Whoopi Goldberg, Mother Teresa, and many others. You may end up spending more time in Ripley's Believe It or Not! laughing at the collection of weird curiosities spawned by Robert Ripley's newspaper cartoon. The building itself qualifies for Believe It or Not!—it's a Moorish-style castle with onion-shaped domes.

All numbers with area codes 972, 214, and the new 469 require 10-digit dialing, even when calling within the same area code.

Details: Memorial Day–Labor Day daily 10–9; rest of year Mon–Fri 10–5, Sat and Sun 10–6, with ticket sales stopping one hour before closing, or two hours earlier for combination tickets. $9.95 adults for each attraction or $13.95 combination; $6.95 and $9.95, respectively, for ages 4–12. (1½–2 hours)

★★ LONE STAR PARK AT GRAND PRAIRIE
1001 Meyers Rd., 972/263-RACE, www.lonestarpark.com

With a striking Spanish colonial, 8,000-seat grandstand, this new racetrack is off and running as a full entertainment complex for more than just race fans. A Family Fun Park offers pony rides, petting

ARLINGTON/MID-CITIES

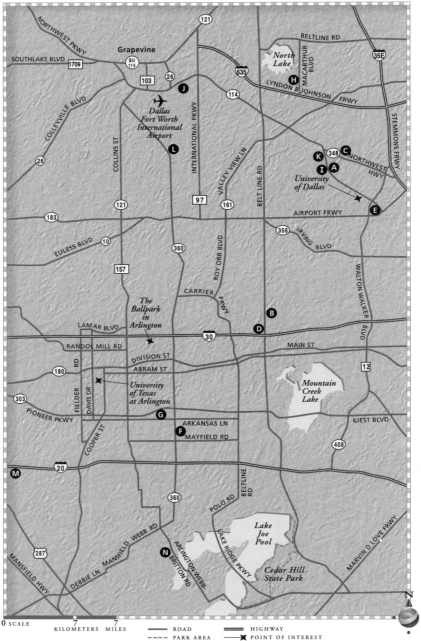

NORTHWEST PKWY

121

BELTLINE RD

SOUTHLAKE BLVD 1709

Grapevine

North Lake

35E

BU 114

103 26

635

LYNDON B JOHNSON FRWY

H

MACARTHUR BLVD

COLLEYVILLE BLVD

114

STEMMONS FRWY

26

J

COLLINS ST

Dallas Fort Worth International Airport

L

INTERNATIONAL PKWY

VALLEY VIEW LN

BELT LINE RD

K 348 C NORTHWEST HWY

I A

University of Dallas

E

183

121

97

161

AIRPORT FRWY

EULESS BLVD 10

157

360

ROY ORR BLVD

356 IRVING BLVD

WALTON WALKER BLVD

The Ballpark in Arlington

CARRIER PKWY

B

LAMAR BLVD

30

D

RANDOL MILL RD

MAIN ST

180

FIELDER RD

DAVIS DR

DIVISION ST

ABRAM ST

12

303

University of Texas at Arlington

Mountain Creek Lake

PIONEER PKWY

COOPER ST

G

ARKANSAS LN

F MAYFIELD RD

KIEST BLVD

M 20

408

360

BELTLINE RD

POLO RD

287

MANSFIELD HWY

DEBBIE LN

MANSFIELD WEBB RD

N

ARLINGTON-WEBB-BRITTON RD

LAKE RIDGE PKWY

Lake Joe Pool

Cedar Hill State Park

MARVIN D LOVE FRWY

N

0 SCALE

7

7

KILOMETERS MILES

ROAD

HIGHWAY

PARK AREA

POINT OF INTEREST

zoos, and other attractions, while the pavilion has racing via simul-cast year-round. Food service is available. Numerous community events are held here, too.

Details: Pavilion: open year-round Wed–Mon usually 10:30–10:30, live-racing season mid-Apr–mid-Jul Wed–Sun and Oct–Nov Wed–Sat; check for post times. $1 pavilion, $2 grandstand, parking $2. (2–3 hours)

★★ TRADERS VILLAGE
2602 Mayfield Rd., 972/647-2331

For the flea-market fan, this 106-acre marketplace has more than 1,600 vendors selling everything imaginable. With numerous food and entertainment concessions and crowds of 50,000 or more, it's like a big fair.

Details: Sat and Sun 8 a.m.–dusk. Free, parking $2. (1 hour minimum)

IRVING SIGHTSEEING HIGHLIGHTS

★★★ MOVIE STUDIOS AT LAS COLINAS
6301 N. O'Connor Rd., 972/869-FILM,
tours@studios.gte.net, www.studiosatlascolinas.com

Don't be surprised if you run into a movie star or other celebrities

SIGHTS
- **A** Las Colinas Mandalay Canal and Mustangs
- **B** Lone Star Park at Grand Prairie
- **C** Movie Studios at Las Colinas
- **D** Palace of Wax and Ripley's Believe It or Not!
- **E** Texas Stadium
- **F** Traders Village

FOOD
- **G** Arc-en-Ciel
- **H** Cowboys Sports Café
- **I** Via Real

LODGING
- **J** Country Suites by Carlson
- **K** Four Seasons Resort and Club
- **L** Hyatt Regency-DFW
- **A** Omni Mandalay at Las Colinas

CAMPING
- **M** Arlington Forest Acres
- **N** Loyd Park
- **F** Traders Village RV Park

Note: Items with the same letter are located in the same area.

here. The only working movie studio between the two coasts, this site sees reel action daily—from movies, TV shows, and commercials, to recording artists' rehearsals and video productions. Behind-the-scenes tours teach you the technical secrets of filming—step up and see if you can punch all the right sound-effects buttons to dub in an *Addams Family* segment.

You'll also see costumes and other movie memorabilia and tour the National Museum of Communications, where early radios, telephones, phonographs, and TVs will surely evoke many memories—and laughter.

Details: *Tours daily at 12:30, 2:30, and 4, plus 10:30 Sat and most holidays; mid-Jun–mid-Aug tours hourly 12:30–5:30 plus 10:30 Sat and most holidays. Confirm times by phone. Reservations not necessary, but arrive half-hour early. $12.95 adults, $10.95 seniors, $7.95 ages 4–12. (2 hours)*

★★ LAS COLINAS MANDALAY CANAL AND MUSTANGS
Off Hwy. 114 northwest of Hwy. 183, 972/556-0625
For a romantic outing, take a stroll on the cobbled path around the European-style village of shops and cafés by Mandalay Canal. Ride a Venetian water taxi and dine at one of the restaurants. At Williams Square Plaza visit the *Mustangs of Las Colinas*—nine larger-than-life bronze horses splashing through a stream. Believed to be the largest equestrian sculpture in the world, the mustangs are a great photo shoot. Learn the interesting story behind the making of these horses in the Mustang Sculpture Exhibit. Las Colinas is a planned urban business–commercial–residential development.

Details: *Complex accessible all hours. Mustang Sculpture Exhibit, 972/869-9047, Tue–Sun 10–6. Free (1–2 hours)*

★★ TEXAS STADIUM
Loop 12 and Carpenter Fwy., 972/438-7676
The Dallas Cowboys play here and practice in nearby Valley Ranch subdivision. If you can't catch a game in this arena, you can still see where the action is on a tour, which will take you to the playing field and into private boxes.

Details: *Tours Mon–Sat on the hour 10–3 and Sun 11–3 except day before and day of a game or during special events. $5 adults, $3 seniors and ages 5–12. (1 hour)*

FITNESS AND RECREATION

An urban greenbelt along the Trinity River, **River Legacy Parks**, 817/860-6752, encompass more than 600 acres of unspoiled natural wilderness laced with hike-and-bike trails. The parks are home to 400 species of wildlife, 193 species of birds, and 28 species of trees. Free, guided nature hikes leave at 10 a.m. Saturday from the new Living Science Center, a bird-shaped, environmentally sensitive building that houses interactive exhibits and classrooms.

Joe Pool Lake, 817/467-2104, at the southern tip of Grand Prairie, is a favorite recreational spot, offering parks with hiking, biking, and equestrian trails; a marina; fishing; water sports; and sandy beaches.

Called a country-club experience at a public facility, **Grand Prairie's Tangle Ridge Golf Club**, 972/299-6837, has a 6,836-yard, par-72, 18-hole championship course on rolling terrain with a beautiful flagstone-and-pine clubhouse. Arlington's new public **Tierra Verde Golf Club**, 7005 Golf Club Drive (Eden Road off U.S. 287 South), 817/572-1300, has 18 holes, each with five tee locations. Planned in cooperation with Audubon International, it's designed to preserve the natural environment. For other golf options, see the Dallas and Fort Worth chapters.

For information on **Texas Rangers** baseball, call 817/273-5100, and for **Dallas Cowboys** football, call 972/579-5000.

FOOD

Despite having big-name neighbors, the mid-cities area attracts Metroplex residents and visitors with some outstanding restaurants. For upscale dining, **Cacherel**, 2221 E. Lamar Boulevard, Arlington, 817/640-9981, wins accolades for its French and American cuisine served in an elegant country-French decor overlooking the Metroplex from the ninth floor of the Brookhollow II Building. Menu choices change daily; you may find ostrich, duck, and salmon entrées, as well as always-popular escargot and soufflés. **Arc-en-Ciel**, 2208 New York Avenue, Arlington, 817/469-9999, has an extensive Chinese-Vietnamese menu, and offers dumplings and other tasty tidbits at dim sum for lunch.

Piccolo Mondo, 829 E. Lamar Boulevard, Arlington, 817/265-9174, does the traditional pasta dishes with flair and presents a wide-ranging off-the-menu selection. **Marsala Ristorante**, 1618 N. Highway 360, Grand Prairie, 972/988-1101, blends French and Italian, with a nice selection of veal and fish dishes. Both are moderately priced.

Via Real, 4020 N. MacArthur Boulevard, Irving, 972/255-0064, combines

innovative Southwestern cuisine in an upscale setting overlooking a golf
course. It's near the Four Seasons Resort.

For reasonably priced all-American fare and the latest in sports on big-
screen TVs, fans can try **Friday's Front Row Sports Grill at The
Ballpark** at Arlington, 1000 Ballpark Way, 817/265-5191; and **Cowboys
Sports Café**, 9454 N. MacArthur Boulevard, Irving, 972/401-3939, the latter owned by several former Dallas Cowboys. Also in Arlington, **Al's
Hamburgers**, 1001 N.E. Green Oaks Boulevard, 817/275-8918, serves
great burgers and fries in a casual spot, but expect to wait in line at lunch.

LODGING

Because of their proximity to DFW Airport, Arlington and nearby cities have
the lion's share of accommodations in the Metroplex. Lodging ranges from
top luxury resorts to budget motels.

On the upscale end, **Four Seasons Resort and Club**, 4150 N.
MacArthur Boulevard, Irving, 800/332-3442 or 972/717-0700, combines elegant lodging with a full spa, health center, two 18-hole championship golf
courses, 12 tennis courts, and four pools. The resort is home to the PGA-tour
GTE Byron Nelson Classic. Rates start around $300, but ask about specials. On
five landscaped acres, **Omni Mandalay at Las Colinas**, 221 E. Las Colinas
Boulevard, Irving, 800 THE-OMNI or 972/556-0800, overlooks Mandalay Canal
and adjacent Lake Carolyn, offering some rooms with balconies and patios.
Among amenities are a pool, exercise room, and saunas. Rates start around
$250, but $109 weekend specials are often available. **Hyatt Regency–DFW**
at DFW Airport, 972/453-1234, has more than 1,300 rooms, a pool, tennis
courts, 36 holes of golf, and an exercise room. Rates run around $200 but spe-
cials at $79 to $99 are often available on weekends.

More than a dozen hotels are clustered around Six Flags Over Texas, The Ballpark in Arlington, and adjacent attractions. Choices include **Fairfield Inn by Marriott**, 2500 E. Lamar Boulevard, Arlington, 800/228-2800, with a pool and rooms from $59; **Best Western Great Southwest Inn**, 3501 E. Division, Arlington, 800/346-BEST, with a pool, restaurant, and rooms from $59; and **Comfort Inn**, 1601 E. Division, Arlington, 800/221-2222, with a pool, lounge, and health club, and rooms from $39. All include continental breakfasts in their rates, which are likely to be higher in summer.

Other options convenient for attractions in this area include **Country Suites by Carlson**, 4100 W. John Carpenter Freeway (Route 114), Irving, 972/929-4008 or 800/456-4000, with studios and one- and two-bedroom suites from $59; and **Hampton Inn/Arlington–DFW Airport**, 2050 N. Highway 360, Grand Prairie, 800/HAMPTON, with 140 rooms starting at $75 with free continental breakfast.

Rates may vary seasonally. For more options, see the Dallas and Fort Worth chapters.

CAMPING

Even in this urban area, campers will find nice spots. Largest in the area is **Traders Village RV Park**, 2602 Mayfield Road, Grand Prairie, 972/647-8205, a Good Sam park rated among the best in the country. Located at the flea market and with 200 full hookups, the park is tree-shaded and has numerous amenities including a pool and recreation hall. **Joe Pool Lake**, Loyd Park, 3401 Ragland Road, Grand Prairie, 817/467-2104, has 221 wooded sites with water, electricity, concrete pads, and hiking, biking, and equestrian trails. Among several campgrounds and RV parks in Arlington, **Arlington Forest Acres**, 4800 Kelly Elliott Road, 817/478-5805, has 30 full hookup sites with patios, a pool, and more.

NIGHTLIFE AND SPECIAL EVENTS

In Arlington, for a toe-tapping good time on the weekend, head to **Johnnie High's Country Music Revue**, 224 N. Center Street, 800/540-5127, which presents fun family shows in the restored Arlington Music Hall. Veteran entertainers take the stage Saturdays at 7:30 p.m., new singers are presented the first Friday, and a gospel group performs the third Friday of each month. There also are special theme shows during holiday periods. Tickets are $12.

Elsewhere in Arlington, check out **Cowboy's**, 2540 E. Abram Street, 817/265-1535, where the 3,500-square-foot dance floor is, appropriately,

Texas-size; **Humperdink's Bar and Grill**, 700 Six Flags Drive, 817/640-8553, which has the Big Horn microbrewery and a live DJ; **Friday's Front Row Sports Grill at The Ballpark**, 1000 Ballpark Way, 817/265-5192; and **Trail Dust Steak House**, 2300 E. Lamar Boulevard, 817/640-6411, with live country-western music to accompany dinner.

On the cultural side, **Irving Arts Center**, 3333 N. MacArthur Boulevard, 972/252-7558, has art shows, live stage productions, musicals, and many other family-friendly events throughout the year.

The **Dallas Cowboys**, 972/579-5000, **Texas Rangers**, 817/273-5100, and **Lone Star Park**, 971/263-RACE, provide seasonal action; and the **Texas Motor Speedway**, north of Alliance Airport at I-35 West and Route 114, 817/215-8500, has auto racing, concerts, and other events. Other special events include the **Texas Scottish Festival and Highland Games**, 817/654-2293, celebrating the Scot and Celtic culture with games, music, dancing, and food in Arlington in June, and the **Championship Indian Pow Wow**, 972/647-2331, at Traders Village in Grand Prairie in September.

16
EAST TEXAS
PINEY WOODS

Most visitors are surprised by East Texas—it doesn't fit the normal image of the state. The terrain is rolling, not flat, and lush green, not arid. Highways undulate through forests, where pine trees tower so high they block all but a sliver of sunlight. Numerous lakes dot the land, some sprawling for thousands of acres and others intimately small, yet all are prize fishing territory. Magnolia trees and moss-draped swamps conjure images of the Deep South.

Known as the Piney Woods, East Texas is laid back. It's a place to escape urban woes, enjoy the outdoors, and explore the early history of the state—from its Indian heritage through explorations by the Spanish and its frontier days during the pioneer movement west.

The prime tourist destination lies in the northeast section of this region, a little jewel called Jefferson, at one time the state's largest city. It was a major inland port, visited by dozens of steamboats from New Orleans during the mid- to late 1800s. Today its riches lie in beautiful homes dating back to the 1850s and a pride in preserving its historic downtown. Nearby Caddo Lake is swampy and mystical.

Farther south are more lakes, several national forests and preserves, and the Texas State Railroad, a popular steam train that chugs through the woods between Rusk and Palestine. Anglers share big—and often true—tales of catches in the East Texas lakes. There is a wide range of fish inhabiting these parts, so you never know what you might reel in.

EAST TEXAS PINEY WOODS

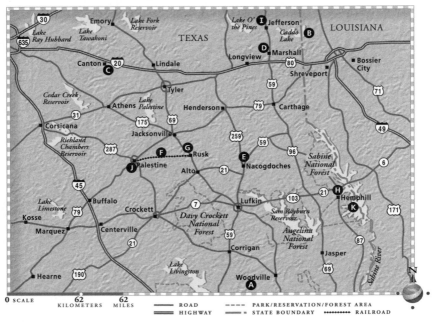

0 SCALE   62   62
       KILOMETERS   MILES   ▬▬▬ ROAD   ----- PARK/RESERVATION/FOREST AREA
                            ▬▬▬ HIGHWAY   ▬▬ STATE BOUNDARY   ••••••••• RAILROAD

SIGHTS

🅐 Alabama-Coushatta Indian
   Reservation
🅑 Caddo Lake
🅒 Canton Trade Days
🅓 Marshall Pottery & Museum
🅔 Nacogdoches
🅕 Texas State Railroad

FOOD

🅔 The Californian

LODGING

🅔 Fredonia
🅖 Gables on Main

CAMPING

🅗 Alpine Marina
🅘 Bullfrog Marina
🅑 Caddo Lake State Park
🅗 Frontier Park
🅘 Lake O' the Pines
🅖 Rusk/Palestine State Park
🅙 Rusk/Palestine State Park
🅚 Toledo Bend Reservoir

Note: Items with the same letter are located in the same area.

A PERFECT DAY IN EAST TEXAS PINEY WOODS

Pamper yourself by staying in one of the historic bed-and-breakfasts in Jefferson, indulging in the large Southern-style breakfast traditionally served by most of these accommodations. Browse through the town, visit some of the historic homes and buildings, and take a bayou tour. End the day with a sunset cruise on nearby Caddo Lake and dinner at Stillwater Inn in Jefferson.

SIGHTSEEING HIGHLIGHTS

★★★★ CADDO LAKE/CADDO LAKE STEAMBOAT CO.
Off Rte. 2198 outside the town of Uncertain, 888/325-5459
A maze of sloughs and bayous with Spanish moss dripping off old cypress trees, this natural lake has a captivating beauty that makes it appeal to everyone, not just fishing enthusiasts. Located east of Jefferson and sprawling into Louisiana, this watery wilderness is steeped in lore of the Caddo Indians who lived on its shores. During the mid to late 1800s, numerous steamboats plied the water on their route from New Orleans to Jefferson. Boat and canoe rentals are available around the lake.

Visitors today can sample the steamboat era on a replica of the 1890s paddle-wheel riverboat *Graceful Ghost*, piloted by two licensed captains who share legends of the lake. Their sunset tours are particularly popular.

Details: *Boat: operates mid-May–Aug weeknights at 7; Sat at 1, 3, 5, and 7; and Sun at 3 and 5. Hours vary rest of year; check for specifics. $15 adults, $12 seniors, $6 ages 12 and under on weekends; reduced rates weekdays. Call ahead to confirm schedule; boat doesn't operate in unfavorable weather. (1 1/2 hours)*

★★★★ JEFFERSON
About two hours east of Dallas, near the Louisiana border, info@jeffersontexas.org, www.jeffersontexas.org or www.jeffersontx.com
A favorite getaway for those in the know, this little town could easily be missed by the average tourist not realizing its treasures. Jefferson exudes Southern charm, its rolling, tree-shaded streets graced with antebellum, Greek Revival, and Victorian homes. Looking at this small town on a little bayou today, it's hard to imagine that Jefferson was a

JEFFERSON

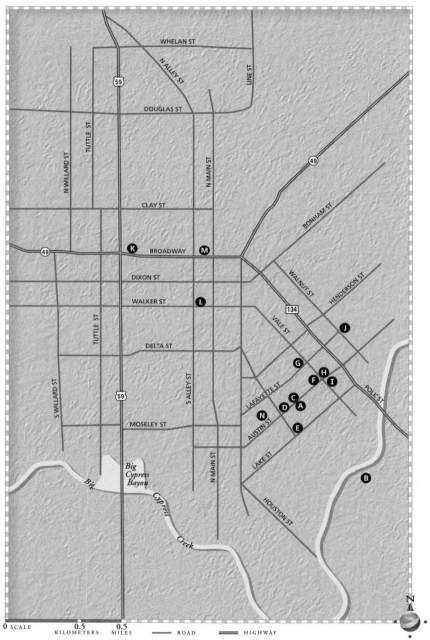

major river port in the 1800s, its streets bustling with passengers leaving steamboats from New Orleans and gearing up from this gateway to head west by wagon.

Historic downtown: Visitors can get a sense of the town's heyday as a port on a one-hour cruise on the little *Bayou Queen*, run by Jefferson Riverboat Tours, from the landing across from downtown; tours daily at 10 a.m., noon, and 2 and 4 p.m., but tours may be reduced in winter and added on weekends and holidays. Tours cost $6 for adults and $3.50 for children ages 3 to 12. Call 903/665-2222 for more information. From the bayou, stroll around downtown, which extends for several blocks generally from Walnut to Marshall Streets and from Lake to Lafayette Streets. Many of the buildings dating back to the 1800s have been restored, some still serving their original purposes and others now housing shops and restaurants. Since the 1850s, the **Excelsior House**, 211 W. Austin Street, 903/665-2513, has been the lodging choice of presidents (and former First Lady Lady Bird Johnson, who is from the area) and the social center of town. It's open for tours and has numerous artifacts, along with pictures of celebrity visitors. Across the street is an 1890 private railcar of financier Jay Gould, the **Atalanta**, 903/665-2513, which is open daily from 9:30 a.m. to noon and from 2:30 to 4:30 p.m. Gould wanted to bring the railroad through the town, but residents staked their future on steamboats instead. When the railroad bypassed Jefferson, the town slowly died—as Gould predicted—but awoke in the 1900s to a wealth of historic buildings.

Also downtown, the **Jefferson Historical Society & Museum**, 223 W. Austin Street, 903/665-2775, showcases memorabilia dating back to the Caddo Indians in a red brick 1880s federal building. The society and museum are open daily from 9:30 to 5. The **Texas**

SIGHTS
- **A** Atalanta
- **B** Bayou Queen
- **C** Excelsior House
- **D** Jefferson Historical Society & Museum
- **E** Texas Heritage Archives & Library

FOOD
- **F** The Bakery
- **G** City Drug Co.
- **H** Galley Restaurant
- **I** Lamache's Pasta Depot
- **J** Old Store and Jefferson Fudge Co.
- **K** Stillwater Inn

LODGING
- **L** Captain's Castle
- **C** Excelsior House
- **I** Jefferson Hotel
- **M** Pride House
- **N** Steamboat Inn

Note: Items with the same letter are located in the same area.

Heritage Archives & Library, 202 S. Market Street, 903/665-1101, has more than 600 rare maps of the New World, dating from 1513, and old Texas national banknotes. Housed in an 1865 building, the archives and library are open Monday through Saturday from 9:30 to 5:30 and Sunday from noon to 5.

Home tours: Jefferson's historic homes range from small cottages to two-story mansions filled with antiques; while gracious, they're not opulent in the manner of some antebellum homes elsewhere. A number of historic homes may be toured year-round and others open their doors during spring and Christmas pilgrimages.

Downtown and the homes can be seen on a do-it-yourself walking or driving tour, or you can tour by horse-drawn carriage, mule-drawn wagon, or motorized trolley, all of which depart from downtown on Austin Street.

Details: The Historic Jefferson Tour Headquarters, 115-B E. Austin St., 903/665-1665, can provide maps for walking tours and book tours. (full day minimum)

★★★★ **TEXAS STATE RAILROAD**
Rusk/Palestine, 800/442-8951 in Texas or 903/683-2561, www.tpwd.state.tx.us
Everyone from kids to grandparents feels the excitement as the mighty locomotive hisses, belches, and starts chugging its way through the Piney Woods on a 50-mile round trip between Rusk and Palestine in the central part of East Texas. One of the state's favorite attractions, and a designated state historical park, the steam train lets today's jet-set tourists experience a journey in wooden railcars with windows that open. Trains operate from both Rusk and Palestine, passing over 30 bridges and through dense forests inhabited by wildlife. Trips take 90 minutes each way, and an hour is allowed at each station for lunch and exploring.

Details: Rusk depot is three miles from downtown on U.S. 84 West, Palestine depot two miles from Loop 256 on U.S. 84 East; train operates mid-Mar–Jun weekends and sometimes Fri; Jun–early Aug Thu–Sun; mid-Aug–Oct weekends; Sat only until late Nov. Trains leave both Rusk and Palestine at 11 a.m. $10 one way, $15 round-trip adults; $6 and $9, respectively for ages 3–12. Reservations advised. (1½–4 hours)

★★★ **ALABAMA-COUSHATTA INDIAN RESERVATION**
17 miles east of Livingston on U.S. 190, 800/444-3507,

rap44342@livingston.net,
www.livingston.net/chamber/actribe
Located outside Livingston, this reservation has dioramas that portray the history of these two forest tribes and a Living Indian Village, where tribe members perform ceremonial dances in costumes and demonstrate traditional skills such as making baskets, jewelry, and leather goods. Visitors can take short tours into the adjacent Big Thicket National Preserve via open-air swamp buggies and a miniature train, and sample Indian food at the Inn of 12 Clans Restaurant.

Details: Jun–Aug Mon–Sat 9–6, Sun 12:30–6; Mar–May and Sep–Nov Fri and Sat 10–5, Sun 12:30–5; closed rest of year. $12 adults, $10 ages 4–12. (2–3 hours)

★★★ NACOGDOCHES
**U.S. 59, info@visitnacogdoches.org,
www.visitnacogdoches.org**
One of the oldest settlements in the state and home to Indians before the arrival of the Spanish, this tree-shaded college town combines its historic setting with proximity to recreational pursuits at Toledo Bend Reservoir and Lake Sam Rayburn. It's on El Camino Real, the King's Highway, forged across the southern half of the country by the Spanish, who built a mission here in 1716. North Street (named La Calle del Norte by the Spanish) is considered the oldest thoroughfare in the country, used by Indians before the Spanish. The cemetery at North Lanana and Hospital Streets has graves of four men who signed the Texas Declaration of Independence in 1836.

On the **Stephen F. Austin University** campus, the reconstructed 1779 **Stone Fort Museum**, Clark and Griffith Boulevards, 409/468-2408, tells the history of Indians, Spanish, and early American settlers.

Early life in the area is displayed at **Millard's Crossing**, 6020 North Street, 409/564-6631, a collection of nineteenth-century buildings ranging from a log cabin to a schoolhouse, church, and farmhouse—all furnished in period pieces. Visitors may walk around the grounds on their own or take 90-minute guided tours into the homes.

Details: Museum: open Tue–Sat 9–5 and Sun 1–5; free. Millard's Crossing: Mon–Sat 9–4, Sun 1–4. $3 adults, $2 ages 5–12. (3–4 hours total)

★★ CANTON TRADE DAYS
At Kaufman and Capitol Sts, Canton, 903/567-6556, city-hall@vzinet.com, www.firstmondaycanton.com
Flea-market fanatics come from across the country to this legendary monthly shopping bonanza that offers more than 4,000 vendors and 150 food concessions. Items include antiques, collectibles, arts and crafts, and new and used merchandise. The market has grown from the traditional 1800s farmer trading days still observed in many small Texas towns.

Details: Fri–Sun before the first Mon of each month, usually about 8 a.m.–sunset. (Some vendors start selling on Thu, but most of the action is Sat and Sun.) Free. (2–3 hours minimum)

★★ MARSHALL POTTERY & MUSEUM
4901 Elysian Fields Rd., Marshall, 903/938-9201
Odds are strong that you, your parents, or your grandparents had some Marshall Pottery country-style stoneware with two blue stripes (all sizes of pitchers for water and tea are popular). In business in the town of Marshall for slightly more than 100 years, the company is one of the country's largest pottery manufacturers, turning out glazed ware and terracotta pots. Its 100,000-square-foot store has a museum showing the development of pottery as art, demonstrations by artists and potters, and a huge inventory of stoneware and pots, glassware and gifts of all types.

Marshall calls itself the pottery capital of the world—and might well be, with about a dozen potteries and outlets in the area.

Details: Mon–Sat 9–6, Sun 10–6. Free. (1 hour)

FITNESS AND RECREATION
The lakes of East Texas lure fishing enthusiasts from all across the country with their bounty of varying species of bass and catfish, plus crappie, bream, and more. **Toledo Bend Reservoir**, **Lake Sam Rayburn**, and **Caddo Lake** are excellent fishing territories, but some of the area's smaller lakes also yield good catches. Fishing guide services are available at most marinas to help visitors find the hot spots. Among the options are **Mossy Brake Lodge**, 800/607-6002, and **Johnson's Ranch**, 903/789-3213, at Uncertain on Caddo Lake.

The Piney Woods is home to four national forests with primitive camping and some recreational venues. **Sabine National Forest** borders Toledo Bend Reservoir on the eastern edge of the state, and just to the west is **Angelina National Forest** around Lake Sam Rayburn. A bit farther west, **Davy Crockett National Forest**, outside Lufkin, offers **Big Slough Canoe Trail and Wilderness Area** on the Neches River and a 19-mile hiking trail. To the south, **Sam Houston National Forest** outside Huntsville includes the 27-mile **Lone Star Hiking Trail**, part of the **National Recreation Trail**. For information on these East Texas forests and recreation sites, contact the USDA Forest Service office in Lufkin, 409/639-8501.

Big Thicket National Preserve, encompassing 84,000 acres of wilderness, woods, and swamps north of Beaumont, has hiking trails and canoeing on the Neches River. The information center, 409/246-2337, is located north of Kountze on Farm Road 420.

FOOD

Though it's small, Jefferson has a good selection of restaurants. There's upscale dining with such options as rack of lamb and grilled seafood served in a restored Victorian home at **Stillwater Inn**, 203 E. Broadway, 903/665-8415. **Lamache's Pasta Depot**, 124 W. Austin Street, 903/665-6177, next to the historic Jefferson Hotel, provides a warm setting for Italian cooking, which ranges beyond the usual pasta to include such specialties as lobster in wine sauce. In an 1860s brick building with ironwork, the **Galley Restaurant**, 121 W. Austin Street, 903/665-3641, evokes a feeling of New Orleans. Its eclectic menu has home cookin' at lunch and great steaks for dinner.

It's hard to pass up the **Old Store and Jefferson Fudge Co.**, 123 Walnut Street, 800/227-1030, which has chocolates, fudge, hard candies, and jellies. Then you can drop by the old-fashioned soda fountain at the **City Drug Co.**, 109 W. Lafayette Street, 800/287-0378, known for its cherry limeades made with fresh-squeezed limes. **The Bakery**, 201 W. Austin Street, 903/665-2253, serves breakfast and lunch featuring home-baked goods.

In Nacogdoches, **The Californian**, 342 University Drive, 409/560-1985, specializes in fresh seafood and steaks served in a cozy setting.

At most eateries, meals will run $10 to $15, often less, but you can expect to pay around $20 at the more upscale spots, such as Stillwater Inn and The Californian. Note that a number of these small-town restaurants are open for set hours rather than continuously all day, so check schedules locally, particularly for lunch hours.

LODGING

Jefferson brims with historic lodging, offering restored frontier hotels and more than 60 bed-and-breakfasts. A number of accommodations specialize in scrumptious Southern-style breakfasts with hot dishes, fresh fruit, and home-baked breads and muffins.

Excelsior House, 211 W. Austin Street, 903/665-2513, an 1850s two-story hotel in the historic downtown, offers a gracious Southern setting amid Victorian antiques; rooms with private baths start at $65. The hotel is known for its breakfasts of orange-blossom muffins, biscuits, and ham and eggs, priced at $6.50 and available to guests and those who make reservations the night before. The recently restored 1860s **Jefferson Hotel**, 124 W. Austin Street, 903/665-2631, has 24 guest rooms, some with fireplaces and whirlpools. All rooms have private baths. Rates start at $65. Beware: Sightings of friendly ghosts have been reported.

Pride House, 409 Broadway, 800/894-3526, has antiques-furnished rooms with stained-glass windows and private baths in an ornate two-story Victorian mansion and separate cottage. Rates start at $65, including gourmet breakfast with such specialties as praline pears, banana parfait, and several styles of egg dishes. The **Captain's Castle**, 403 E. Walker Street, 800/650-2330, a two-story plantation-style home with columns, has three guest rooms in the main house, three in the carriage house, and a suite in a separate cottage, all overlooking a shaded lawn. All rooms have private baths and some have fireplaces. Breakfast is served in the main house and a glassed-in gazebo. Rates start at $95, including full breakfast.

A lovely Greek Revival cottage with porches overlooking tree-shaded gardens, the **Steamboat Inn**, 114 N. Marshall Street, 903/665-8946, carries its name into the decor, with pictures of old steamboats and each of the four guest rooms named for a riverboat that docked here. All guest rooms have private baths and fireplaces; rates start at $95, including full breakfast.

To find the right bed-and-breakfast for you, work with one of the booking services: **Book-a-Bed-Ahead**, 800/468-2627 for reservations, 903/665-3956 for information; **AAA Reservation Service**, 800/299-1593; **Sunset Reservations**, 800/533-0532; and **Jefferson's Concierge**, 903/665-9776, which handles bookings and arranges romantic packages and special events. Lodging also is available around Caddo Lake.

In Nacogdoches, the **Fredonia**, 200 N. Fredonia Street, 800/594-5323, in the historic area, is a renovated 1950s hotel with 113 rooms and rates starting at $52. Rusk has a number of bed-and-breakfasts, including the **Gables on Main**, 212 Main Street, 903/683-5641, an 1884 Victorian home with eight fireplaces and three guest rooms, which are suites with private baths. Rooms start at $75, including full breakfast.

CAMPING

Caddo Lake State Park, 903/679-3351, is 17 miles from Marshall and Jefferson, on Route 2198 off Route 134 from Jefferson and Route 43 from Marshall. It offers all types of campsites, rest rooms and showers, picnic areas, a fishing dock, boat launch, and hiking trails.

Just west of Jefferson, scenic **Lake O' the Pines**, a favorite recreational area, has campsites, including RV and tent camping at **Bullfrog Marina**, 903/755-2712.

Rusk/Palestine State Park, 903/683-5126, site of the Texas State Railroad steam-train excursions, has full hookups at the Rusk site, which has a lake, and water hookup sites at Palestine.

Toledo Bend Reservoir, which straddles the Texas-Louisiana line, has numerous campsites along its shores. Around the Hemphill area, options include **Alpine Marina**, 800/432-1506, with 28 full-hookup sites, and **Frontier Park**, 409/625-4712 with about 50 full-hookup sites.

NIGHTLIFE AND SPECIAL EVENTS

For nighttime action, there are country-western music venues such as **Diamond Bessie's Saloon and Dance Hall**, 124 E. Austin Street, Jefferson, 903/665-7454. Some towns have community theaters, so check locally for scheduled events. And if you like casinos, there's plenty of action only a short distance across the state line in Louisiana on Mississippi River gambling boats at Bossier City and Shreveport. Shreveport is also home to the Louisiana Downs thoroughbred racetrack.

Numerous historic homes open for tours during the **Jefferson Historical Pilgrimage**, 903/665-2413, in early May. March and April bring azalea and dogwood festivals throughout the area, and the **Tyler Rose Festival**, 903/597-3130, showcases the town's beautiful Rose Garden in mid-October. Fall brings a feast of arts-and-crafts festivals, and many towns light up for the Thanksgiving-Christmas holidays, offering parades and other celebrations of the season. The **Jefferson Christmas Candlelight Tour**, 800/299-1593, takes visitors into historic homes decorated in nineteenth-century finery for the holidays; and **Marshall's Wonderland of Lights**, 903/935-7868, extends from Thanksgiving to New Year's, bringing in crowds to see millions of tiny white lights on everything from the courthouse to businesses and homes throughout the town.

For fishing enthusiasts, there are numerous tournaments on area lakes; check locally or with the **East Texas Tourism Association**, 903/757-4444, for details.

APPENDIX

Consider this appendix your travel tool box. Use it along with the material in the Planning Your Trip chapter to craft the trip you want. Here are the tools you'll find inside:

1. **Planning Map.** Make copies of this map and plot out various trip possibilities. Once you've decided on your route, you can write it on the original map and refer to it as you're traveling.

2. **Mileage Chart.** This chart shows the driving distances (in miles) between various destinations throughout the state/region. Use it in conjunction with the Planning Map.

3. **Special Interest Tours.** If you'd like to plan a trip around a certain theme—such as nature, music, or art—one of these tours may work for you.

4. **Calendar of Events.** Here you'll find a month-by-month listing of major area events.

5. **Resources.** This guide lists various regional chambers of commerce and visitors bureaus, state offices, bed-and-breakfast registries, and other useful sources of information.

PLANNING MAP: Texas

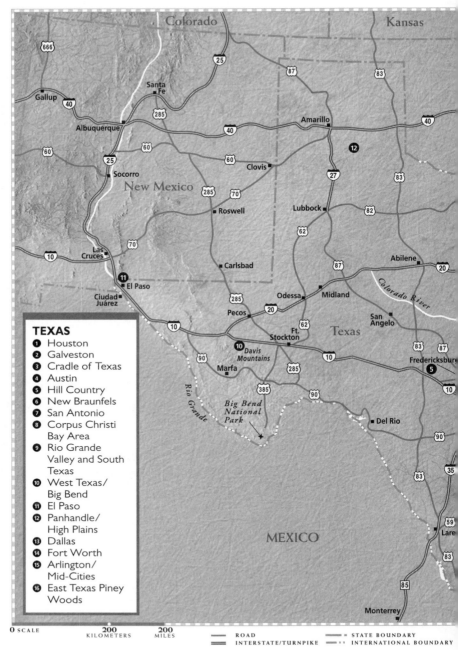

TEXAS

1. Houston
2. Galveston
3. Cradle of Texas
4. Austin
5. Hill Country
6. New Braunfels
7. San Antonio
8. Corpus Christi Bay Area
9. Rio Grande Valley and South Texas
10. West Texas/ Big Bend
11. El Paso
12. Panhandle/ High Plains
13. Dallas
14. Fort Worth
15. Arlington/ Mid-Cities
16. East Texas Piney Woods

0 SCALE | 200 KILOMETERS | 200 MILES

ROAD ——— ——— STATE BOUNDARY
INTERSTATE/TURNPIKE ━━━ ━••━ INTERNATIONAL BOUNDARY

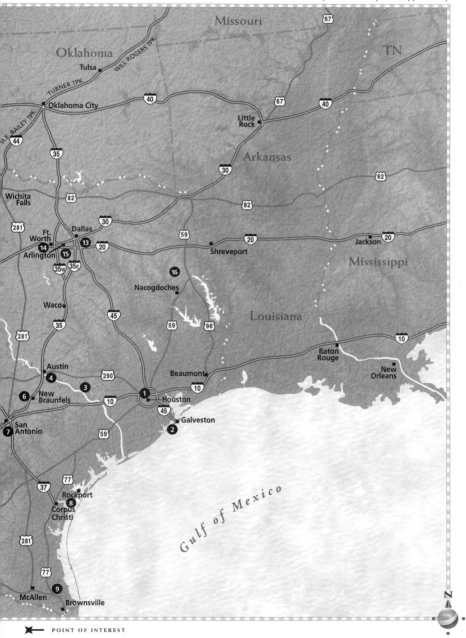

POINT OF INTEREST

TEXAS MILEAGE CHART

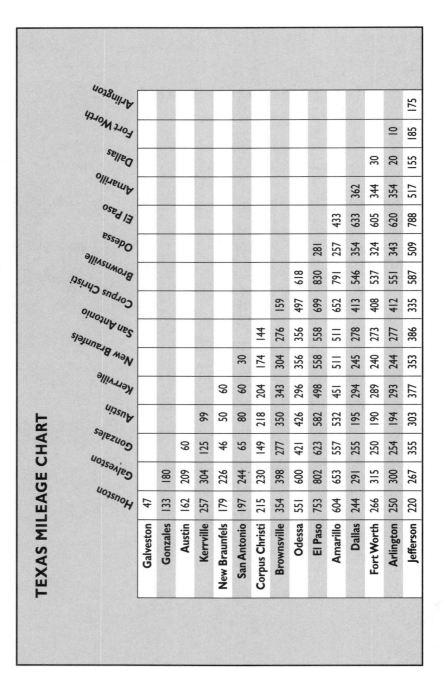

	Houston	Galveston	Gonzales	Austin	Kerrville	New Braunfels	San Antonio	Corpus Christi	Brownsville	Odessa	El Paso	Amarillo	Dallas	Fort Worth	Arlington
Galveston	47														
Gonzales	133	180													
Austin	162	209	60												
Kerrville	257	304	125	99											
New Braunfels	179	226	46	50	60										
San Antonio	197	244	65	80	60	30									
Corpus Christi	215	230	149	218	204	174	144								
Brownsville	354	398	277	350	343	304	276	159							
Odessa	551	600	421	426	296	356	356	497	618						
El Paso	753	802	623	582	498	558	558	699	830	281					
Amarillo	604	653	557	532	451	511	511	652	791	257	433				
Dallas	244	291	255	195	294	245	278	413	546	354	633	362			
Fort Worth	266	315	250	190	289	240	273	408	537	324	605	344	30		
Arlington	250	300	254	194	293	244	277	412	551	343	620	354	20	10	
Jefferson	220	267	355	303	377	353	386	335	587	509	788	517	155	185	175

SPECIAL INTEREST TOURS

With *Texas Travel•Smart,* you can plan a trip of any length—a one-day excursion, a getaway weekend, or a three-week vacation—around any special interest. To get you started, the following pages contain six tours geared toward a variety of interests. For more information, refer to the chapters listed—chapter names are bolded and chapter numbers appear inside black bullets. You can follow a special interest tour in its entirety or shorten, lengthen, or combine parts of each, depending on your starting and ending points.

Discuss alternative routes and schedules with your travel companions— it's a great way to have fun, even before you leave home. And remember: Don't hesitate to change your itinerary once you're on the road. Careful study and planning ahead of time will help you make informed decisions as you go, but spontaneity is the extra ingredient that will make your trip memorable.

BEST OF TEXAS TOUR

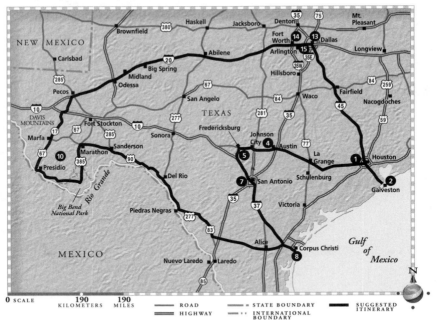

This itinerary shows off the multifacted destinations within Texas, from sophisticated cities with world-acclaimed cultural attractions to historic sites, pristine beaches, and remote wilderness areas.

- ❶ **Houston** (Space Center Houston, cultural attractions, shopping, dining)
- ❷ **Galveston** (historic districts, beaches)
- ❹ **Austin** (Texas Capitol, LBJ Library and Museum)
- ❺ **Hill Country** (river sports, guest ranches, German heritage sites, wineries)
- ❼ **San Antonio** (River Walk, historic sites, museums, amusement parks)
- ❽ **Corpus Christi Bay Area** (Texas State Aquarium, wildlife, beaches)
- ❿ **West Texas/Big Bend** (wilderness, pioneer history, mountains)
- ⓮ **Fort Worth** (art museums, cowboy history, Fort Worth Zoo)
- ⓯ **Arlington/Mid-Cities** (baseball, family attractions)
- ⓭ **Dallas** (cultural attractions, museums, dining, shopping)

Time needed: 3 weeks

NATURE LOVERS' TOUR

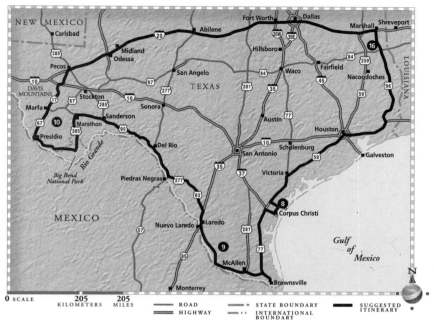

Stretching across the southern half of Texas, this route shows the diversity of the state's natural beauty, from dense woods to coastal swamps and desert.

⑯ East Texas Piney Woods (lakes, national forests and preserves, fishing, hiking, Texas State Railroad)

⑧ Corpus Christi Bay Area (Padre Island National Seashore, Aransas National Wildlife Refuge, birding)

⑨ Rio Grande Valley and South Texas (birding, wildlife refuges, South Padre Island, beaches)

⑩ West Texas/Big Bend (desert, canyons, mountains, Big Bend National Park, Davis Mountains State Park, McDonald Observatory)

Time needed: 10 days to 2 weeks

ARTS AND CULTURE TOUR

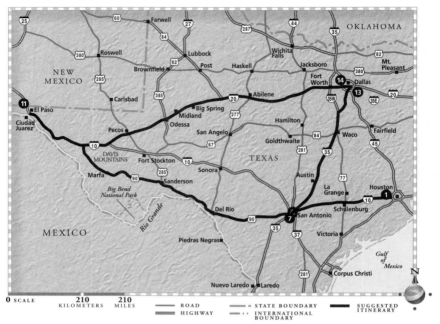

This itinerary takes in the cultural attractions of the state's major cities.

● **Houston** (Museum of Fine Arts, Contemporary Arts Museum, Houston Museum of Natural Science, Children's Museum, Menil Collection, Bayou Bend Collection, Alley Theatre, Jones Hall for Performing Arts, Wortham Theater)

● **San Antonio** (Witte Museum, McNay Art Museum, San Antonio Museum of Art, Institute of Texan Cultures, missions)

● **Dallas** (Dallas Museum of Art, Morton H. Meyerson Symphony Center, Fair Park, African American Museum, Museum of Natural History, Science Place, Hall of State, Music Hall, Dallas Theater Center)

● **Fort Worth** (Kimbell Art Museum, Amon Carter Museum, Modern Art Museum, Museum of Science and History, Sid Richardson Collection of Western Art, opera, ballet)

● **El Paso** (El Paso Museum of Art, mission trail, Juárez)

Time needed: 2 weeks

FAMILY FUN TOUR

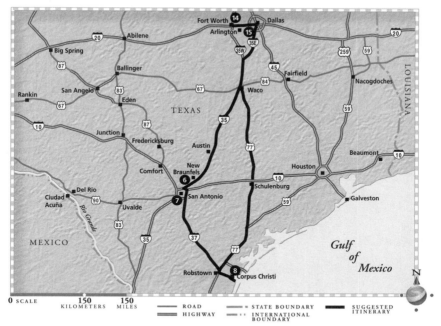

Focusing on family activities, this tour moves from cities to beaches, taking in both commercial and natural attractions that please all ages.

- ⑭ **Fort Worth** (Fort Worth Zoo, Fort Worth Museum of Science and History, Tarantula Railroad)
- ⑮ **Arlington/Mid-Cities** (Six Flags Over Texas, The Ballpark, Legends of the Game Baseball Museum, Six Flags Hurricane Harbor)
- ⑥ **New Braunfels** (Comal and Guadalupe Rivers, Schlitterbahn)
- ⑦ **San Antonio** (Mission Trail, The Alamo, Sea World of Texas, Six Flags Fiesta Texas, Brackenridge Park)
- ⑧ **Corpus Christi Bay Area** (Texas State Aquarium, Columbus fleet, Corpus Christi Museum of Science & History, USS *Lexington* Museum on the Bay, beaches)

Time needed: 10 days to 2 weeks

FOOD, WINE, AND MUSIC LOVERS' TOUR

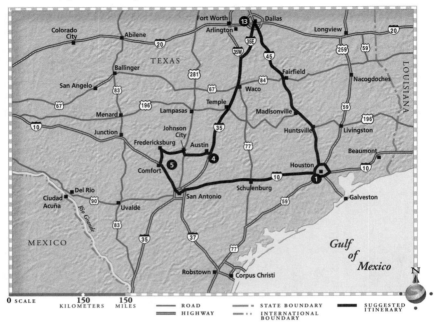

This itinerary allows visitors to sample some of the nation's top-ranked restaurants and music venues in Houston and Dallas, enjoy Austin's outstanding live music scene, and explore wineries in the Hill Country, Austin, and Dallas areas.

⓭ Dallas (fine dining, Grapevine-area wineries, symphony, other concerts)
❹ Austin (live music clubs, wineries)
❺ Hill Country (wineries, ethnic food)
❶ Houston (fine dining, ethnic restaurants, symphony, other concerts)

Time needed: 8 to 10 days

LORE OF THE WEST TOUR

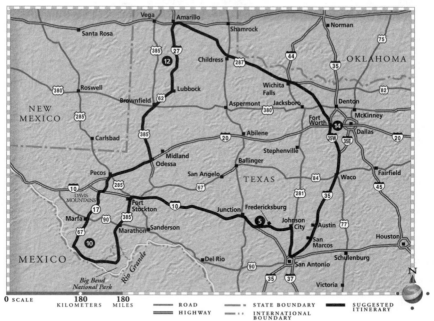

The state's cowboy heritage comes to life in this itinerary, which takes in cities as well as beautiful open stretches of West Texas and the Plains.

- **⑭ Fort Worth** (Stockyards National Historic District, Tarantula Railroad, Western art museums)
- **⑫ Panhandle/High Plains** (Cowboy Morning, Panhandle-Plains Historical Museum, Palo Duro Canyon State Park, *Texas* outdoor musical)
- **⑩ West Texas/Big Bend** (Big Bend National Park, Big Bend Ranch State Park, Lajitas, Fort Davis National Historic Site)
- **⑤ Hill Country** (guest ranches, Cowboy Artists of America Museum, Y.O. Ranch)

Time needed: 10 days

CALENDAR OF EVENTS

January
Cotton Bowl, Dallas, 800/SWB-BOWL
Houston International Boat, Sport and Travel Show, Houston,
    800/4-HOUSTON
Southwestern Exposition and Livestock Show & Rodeo, Fort Worth,
    817/877-2400
Texas Citrus Fiesta, Mission in Rio Grande Valley, 956/585-9724

February
Charro Days, Brownsville, 956/542-4245
George Washington's Birthday Celebration, Laredo, 800/292-2122
Houston Livestock Show & Rodeo, Houston, 713/791-9000
Mardi Gras, Galveston, 888/GAL-ISLE
San Antonio Livestock Show & Rodeo, San Antonio, 210/225-5851
Texas Square Dance Jamboree, McAllen in Rio Grande Valley, 956/
    682-2871

March
Cowboy Poetry Gathering, Alpine in West Texas, 800/561-3735
Dogwood Trails Festival, communities throughout East Texas
Easter Fires Pageant, Fredericksburg, 830/997-6523
Jerry Jeff Walker's Birthday Celebration, Austin, 512/477-0036
Oysterfest, Fulton, 800/826-6441
South by Southwest Music & Media Conference, Austin, 512/467-7979
Spring Break, Galveston, Corpus Christi Bay Area, South Padre Island, and
    Rio Grande Valley and South Texas
Texas Independence Day, Washington-on-the-Brazos State Historical Park,
    409/878-2214

April
Buccaneer Days, Corpus Christi, 361/882-3242
Fiesta San Antonio, San Antonio, 210/227-5191
Houston International Festival, Houston, 713/654-8808
Juan de Oñate First Thanksgiving Reenactment, El Paso, 800/351-6024
Main Street Fort Worth Arts Festival, Fort Worth, 817/336-ARTS
Round Top Antiques Fair, Round Top, 281/493-5501
Spamarama, Austin, 512/416-9307

Texas Hill Country Wine & Food Fest, Austin, 512/329-0770
Wildflower Festivals, South and Central Texas and Hill Country
Worldfest: Houston International Film Festival, Houston, 713/965-9955

May
Art Fest, Dallas, 214/361-2011
Jefferson Historical Pilgrimage, Jefferson, 903/665-2413
Kerrville Folk Festival, Kerrville, 830/257-3600
Mayfest, Fort Worth, 817/332-1055
Texas State Arts & Crafts Fair, Kerrville, 830/896-5711
U.S. Open Windsurfing Regatta, Corpus Christi, 361/985-1555

June
Chisholm Trail Roundup/Chief Quanah Parker Comanche Pow-Wow, Fort
    Worth, 817/625-7005
St. Anthony's Day, El Paso, 915/859-7913
Texas (outdoor drama runs until mid-August), Canyon, 806/655-2181
Texas Scottish Festival/Highland Games, Arlington, 817/654-2293
Viva! El Paso (outdoor drama runs until late August), El Paso,
    800/915-VIVA

July
Austin Aqua Fest, Austin, 512/472-5664
Borderfest, Laredo, 800/361-3360
Rockport Art Festival, Rockport, 361/729-6445
Shakespeare at Winedale (performances until mid-August), outside Round
    Top, 409/278-3530

August
Kerrville Wine & Music Festival, Kerrville, 800/435-8429
Texas Folklife Festival, San Antonio, 210/458-2300

September
Bayfest & Folklife Celebration, Corpus Christi, 361/887-0868
Boys Ranch Rodeo, outside Amarillo, 806/372-2341
Buddy Holly Music Festival, Lubbock, 800/692-4035
Diez y Seis de Septiembre, Mexican holiday celebrated in many Texas cities
    with strong Spanish/Mexican heritage, particularly San Antonio, El Paso,
    and South Texas
Fiestas Patrias, Laredo, 800/361-3360

Hummer/Bird Celebration, Rockport-Fulton, 800/826-6441
National Championship Indian Pow-Wow, Grand Prairie, 972/647-2331
Panhandle/South Plains Fair, Lubbock, 806/763-2833
Shrimporee, Aransas Pass, 800/633-3028
State Fair of Texas, (continues into October), Dallas, 214/565-9931
Tri-State Fair, Amarillo, 806/376-7767

October
Pirate Days, South Padre Island, 800/SOPADRE
Round Top Antiques Fair, Round Top, 281/493-5501
Tyler Rose Festival, Tyler, 903/665-2413
Wurstfest (could start in late October or November), New Braunfels,
    800/221-4369

November
World Championship Chili Cookoffs, Terlingua in Big Bend area,
    800/359-4138
World Championship Ranch Rodeo, Amarillo, 806/467-9722

December
Christmas Candlelight Tour, Jefferson, 800/299-1593
Dickens on the Strand, Galveston, 409/765-7834
Fiesta de las Luminarias, San Antonio, 210/227-4262
Fiestas Navidenas in El Mercado, San Antonio, 210/207-8600
Las Posadas, San Antonio, 210/224-6163
Sun Bowl, El Paso, 800/915-BOWL
Weihnachten in Fredericksburg, Fredericksburg, 830/997-6523
Wonderland of Lights, Marshall, 903/935-7868

RESURCES

Alpine Chamber of Commerce/Big Bend Area Travel Association, 800/561-3735, chamber@alpinetexas.com, www.alpinetexas.com

Amarillo Convention & Visitor Council, 800/692-1338, amarcvb@arn.net, www.amarillo-cvb.org

Arlington Convention & Visitors Bureau, 800/342-4305, visitinfo@acvb.org, www.arlington.org

Austin Convention & Visitors Bureau, 800/926-2282, gspain@austintexas.org, www.austintexas.org

Bandera Convention & Visitors Bureau, 800/364-3833, bandera@hctc.net, www.tourtexas.com/bandera

Brownsville Convention & Visitors Bureau, 800/626-2639, visitinfo@brownsville.org, www.brownsville.org

Corpus Christi Area Convention & Visitors Department, 800/678-OCEAN, rgoonan@cctexas.org, www.cctexas.org

Dallas Convention & Visitors Bureau, 800/C-DALLAS or 214/571-1301, info@dallascvb.com, www.cityview.com/dallas

Dallas–Fort Worth Area Tourism Council, 817/329-2438

East Texas Tourism Association, 903/757-4444, www.easttexasguide.com

El Paso Convention & Visitors Bureau, 800/351-6024, elpaso@huntleigh.net, www.elpasocvb.com

Fort Worth Convention & Visitors Bureau, 800/433-5747, linda@fortworth.com, www.fortworth.com

Fredericksburg Convention & Visitor Bureau, 830/997-6523, asstdir@fbg.net, www.fredericksburg-texas.com

Galveston Island Convention & Visitors Bureau, 888/GAL-ISLE, cvb@galvestontourism.com, www.galvestontourism.com

Grand Prairie Convention & Visitors Bureau, 800/288-8386, rsisson@flash.net, www.gptexas.com

Greater Houston Convention & Visitors Bureau, 800/4-HOUSTON, houstongde@aol.com, www.houston-guide.com

Greater New Braunfels Chamber of Commerce, 800/572-2626, nbcc@nbcham.org, www.nbcham.org

Harlingen Area Chamber of Commerce, 800/531-7346, www.harlingen.com

Historic Accommodations of Texas, 800/HAT-0368, innroute@worldnet.att.net, www.hat.org

Irving Convention & Visitors Bureau, 800/2-IRVING,
   icvb@airmail.net, www.irvingtexas.com
Kerrville Convention & Visitors Bureau, 800/221-7958,
   kerrcvb@ktc.com, www.ktc.net/kerrcvb
Laredo Convention and Visitors Bureau, 800/361-3360,
   lcvb@icsi.net, www.visitlaredo.com
Lubbock Convention & Tourism Bureau, 800/692-4035,
   lubbock@nts-online.net, www.lubbocklegends.com
Marion County Chamber of Commerce, Jefferson, 903/665-2672, info@jef-
   fersontexas.org, www.jeffersontexas.org or www.jeffersontx.com
McAllen Convention & Visitors Bureau, 800/250-2591,
   chamber@mcallen.org, www.mcallen.org
Midland Chamber Convention & Visitors Bureau, 800/624-6435
Odessa Convention & Visitors Bureau, 800/780-HOST,
   info@odessacvb.com, www.odessacvb.com
Port Aransas–Mustang Island Convention & Visitors Bureau, 800/45-COAST,
   www.portaransas.org
Rockport-Fulton Area Chamber of Commerce, 800/826-6441,
   chamber@dbstech.com, www.rockport-fulton.org
San Antonio Convention & Visitors Bureau, 800/447-3372,
   SACVB@ci.sat.tx.us, www.sanantoniocvb.com
South Padre Island Convention & Visitors Bureau, 800/SO-PADRE,
   info@sopadre.com, www.sopadre.com
Texas Department of Economic Development Tourism Division/Texas State
   Travel Guide, 800/8888-TEX, www.traveltex.com
Texas Parks & Wildlife Department, 800/792-1112 or 512/389-4800,
   512/389-8900 for reservations, www.tpwd.state.tx.us
Texas Travel Industry Association, 512/476-4472, info@tourtexas.com,
   www.tourtexas.com
Wimberley Chamber of Commerce, 512/847-2201,
   www.wimberley-tx.com

INDEX

Admiral Nimitz Museum and Historical Center, 77

Air Combat School, 223

Alabama-Coushatta Indian Reservation, 236–237

Alamo, The, 104–105

Amarillo, 175–179

Amarillo Livestock Auction, 179

American Airpower Heritage Museum and Confederate Air Force, 155

American Quarter Horse Heritage Center & Museum, 178

Amon Carter Museum, 206

Antique Rose Emporium, 51

Aransas National Wildlife Refuge, 127–129

Arlington/Mid-Cities, 219–230

Ashton Villa, 34

Astrodome Complex, 25–26

Austin, 57–72

Austin & Texas Central Railroad, 65

auto racing, 213

Bastrop, 46–47

bat watching, 61

Bayfront Arts and Science Park, 125

Bayfront/Harbor, 124–125

Bayou Bend Collection and Gardens, 20

beaches, 35, 125–126

Bentsen-Rio Grande Valley State Park, 141

Biblical Arts Center, 196–197

bicycling, 53, 67, 81, 130, 168, 196–197, 227

Big Bend National Park, 149–150

Big Bend Ranch State Park, 151

bird-watching, 126–127, 130

Bishop's Palace, 34

Blue Bell Creameries, 52

boating, 67, 96–97, 142, 213

Bolivar Ferry, 38

Botanic Garden, 207

Brackenridge Park/San Antonio Zoological Gardens and Aquarium, 109

Buckhorn Saloon & Museums, 108

Buddy Holly Statue and Walk of Fame, 181

Cadillac Ranch, 176

Caddo Lake/Caddo Lake Steamboat Co., 233

camping, 29; 41–42; 55–56; 69; 84–85; 99; 116; 133; 145; 158, 170; 184; 200; 215; 229; 241

Canton Trade Days, 238

Canyon Area, 175–179

Children's Museum of Houston, 20

Chinati Foundation, 155

Civic Center/Theater District, 18–19

Columbus, 48

Comal and Guadalupe Rivers, 91–92

Confederate Air Force/Rio Grande Valley Wing, 138–139

Conservation Plaza, 96–97

Contemporary Arts Museum, 22

Corpus Christi Bay Area, 121–134

Cowboy Artists of America Museum, 79

Cowboy Morning, 176–177

Cradle of Texas, 45–56

Dallas, 187–202

Dallas Arboretum & Botanical Garden, 196

Dallas County Historical Plaza/Sixth Floor Museum, 191–192

Dallas Cowboys, 197, 213

Dallas Mavericks, 197, 213

Dallas Museum of Art, 190–191

Dallas Sidekicks, 197

Dallas Stars, 197

Dallas Zoo, 196

Davis Mountains, 152–155, 160

Davis Mountains State Park, 152

De Menil Museums, 20–21

East Texas Piney Woods, 231–242

El Paso Museum of Art, 162–163

El Paso, 161–172

Elisabet Ney Museum, 66
Enchanted Rock State Natural Area, 77–78

Fair Park, 193–196
fishing, 39, 53, 96–97, 127, 142, 213, 238–239
Floating the Guadalupe and Medina Rivers, 80–81
Fort Bliss Museums, 167
Fort Davis, 152–154
Fort Davis National Historic Site, 152–154
Fort Worth, 203–218
Fort Worth Museum of Science and History, 207–208
Fort Worth Zoo, 206–207
Fredericksburg, 75–79
Fulton, 127–130
Fulton Mansion State Historical Park, 129

Galleria, 23
Galveston, 31–44
Galveston Beaches, 35–36
Galveston County Historical Museum, 39
Galveston Island Trolley, 37
Gladys Porter Zoo, 137–138
Glen Rose, 216
golf, 26, 67, 113–114, 142–143, 168, 181–182, 213, 227
Goliad, 48–49
Gonzales, 51–52
Governor's Mansion, 61
Granbury, 216
Grand 1894 Opera House, 36–37
Grand Prairie, 223–225
Grapevine, 200
Greater Houston, 23–26

Hertzberg Circus Museum, 108–109
High Plains Perspective, 186
Highland Lakes, 70
hiking, 67, 81, 113, 168, 196–197, 239
Hill Country, 73–87, 119
Hill Country Back Roads, 87
Hill Country Loop, 119
Hill Country Museum, 80
Historic Gruene, 92
Historic New Braunfels, 92–93
history, 2–3, 33–35
Holocaust Museum Houston, 22
horseback riding, 81–82, 182, 227
Houston, 15–30

Houston Aeros, 26–27
Houston Astros, 27
Houston Museum of Natural Science, 21
Houston Rockets, 27
Houston Zoo, 22–23
Hummel Museum, 95–96

Institute of Texan Cultures, 105
Irving, 225–226
Iwo Jima Memorial and Museum, 139

Jefferson, 233–236
jogging, 67, 130
Johnson City, 75–79
Joyland Amusement Park, 182
Juárez, 163–165

Kerrville, 79–80
Kimbell Art Museum, 207
King William District, 108

La Villita, 107
Lady Bird Johnson Wildflower Center, 65–66
Laguna Atascosa National Wildlife Refuge, 140
Laguna Madre Nature Trail, 141
Las Colinas Mandalay Canal and Mustangs, 226
lodging, 28–29; 40–41; 54–55; 68–69; 83–84; 98–99; 115–116; 131–133; 144; 157–158; 169–170; 183–184; 199–200; 215; 228–229; 240–241
Log Cabin Village, 208
Lone Star Flight Museum, 39
Lone Star Park at Grand Prairie, 223–225
Lubbock, 179–182
Lubbock Lake Landmark State Historical Park, 181
Luckenbach, 81
Lyndon B. Johnson Library and Museum, 58–59
Lyndon B. Johnson State and National Historical Parks, 75

Magoffin Home State Historical Park, 167
Mardi Gras Museum, 39
Market Square, 107–108
Marshall Pottery & Museum, 238
McDonald Observatory, 154–155
McNay Art Museum, 109
Mexico's Border Towns, 141–142
Mission Trail, 111, 165–166

Modern Art Museum of Fort Worth, 208
Moody Gardens, 39–40
Moody Mansion and Museum, 34–35
Morton H. Meyerson Symphony Center, 191
Movie Studios at Las Colinas, 225–226
Museum District, 20–23
Museum of Fine Arts, 21–22
Museum of Handmade Furniture, 96
Museum of Health & Medical Science, 22

Nacogdoches, 237
Natural Bridge Caverns, 96
New Braunfels, 89–102
nightlife, 29–30; 42–43; 56; 69; 71; 85; 99–100;
    116–117; 134; 145–146; 158–159, 170–171;
    184–185; 200–201; 217; 229–230; 241–242

O. Henry Home and Museum, 63
Offshore Energy Center, 37
Old City Park, 193
Old Route 66/Sixth Avenue Historic District,
    178

Palace of Wax and Ripley's Believe It or Not!,
    223
Palo Duro Canyon State Park, 175–176
Panhandle-Plains Historical Museum, 176
Panhandle/High Plains, 173–186
Permian Basin Petroleum Museum, 155–156
Pioneer Museum Complex, 78
Pioneer Plaza, 193
Port Isabel Lighthouse State Historic Site, 139
Prairie Dog Town, 182
professional sports, 26–27, 113, 197

Railroad Museum, 36
Ranching Heritage Center, 179
recommended reading, 13–14
restaurants, 27–28; 39–40; 53–54; 67–68;
    82–83; 97–98; 114–115; 130–131; 143;
    156–157; 168–169; 182–183; 197–199;
    214–215; 227–228; 239–240
Rim Road, 166
Rio Grande Valley and South Texas, 135–146
River Road, 102
River Road/Lajitas/Terlingua, 150–151
River Walk, 105–107
rock climbing, 168
Rockport, 127–130
Round Top, 49–51

Sabal Palm Audubon Center and Sanctuary,
    141
Sam Houston Historical Park, 19–20
San Antonio, 103–119
San Antonio Botanical Gardens and Lucile
    Halsell Conservatory, 112
San Antonio Museum of Art, 112
San Augustin Plaza, 139
San Jacinto Battleground State Historical Park,
    26
Santa Ana/Lower Rio Grande National
    Wildlife Refuge, 140–141
Schlitterbahn, 93–95
Science Spectrum and Omnimax Theater,
    181–182
Sea Turtle, Inc., 140
Sea World of Texas, 112
Six Flags Fiesta Texas, 113
Six Flags Hurricane Harbor, 222
Six Flags Over Texas, 222
Sophienburg Museum & Archives, 97
Southfork Ranch, 197
Space Center Houston, 23–25
Spanish Governor's Palace, 108
Stockyards National Historic District, 210–211
Sundance Square, 208–210
Sundance Square Entertainment District,
    208–210

Tarantula Railroad, 211–213
Texas Air Museum, 139
Texas Capitol, 59
Texas Maritime Museum, 130
Texas Rangers, 197, 213, 227
Texas Seaport Museum and Elissa, 37–39
Texas Stadium, 226
Texas State Aquarium, 123
Texas State Railroad, 236
The Ballpark, 220–222
The Great Storm, 37
The Strand/Harborfront Area, 35–39
Tigua Cultural Center, 166
Traders Village, 225
Trammell Crow Center and Pavilion, 191
Transmountain Road/Museums, 166–167
transportation, 10–11, 228

University of Texas at Austin, 62
USS Lexington Museum on the Bay, 123–124

Washington-On-The-Brazos State Historical
     Park, 51
Water Gardens, 210
West End Marketplace, 192–193
West Texas/Big Bend, 147–160
Whooping Crane Tours, 129
Wildseed Farms Market Center, 78–79
Wimberley, 80
wind surfing, 130
wineries, 70, 78, 200
Witte Museum, 111–112
World of Discovery:Christopher Columbus
     Ships/Corpus Christi Museum of Science &
     History, 124

Y.O. Ranch, 79

Zilker Park, 63–65

Map Index

Amarillo: Sights/Food/Lodging, 177
Arlington: Sights/Food/Lodging, 221
Arlington/Mid-Cities: Sights/Food/
     Lodging/Camping, 224
Arts and Culture Tour: 250
Austin: Sights/Food/Lodging, 60

Bastrop: Sights/Food/Lodging, 50
Best of Texas Tour: 248

Corpus Christi: Sights/Food/Lodging, 122
Corpus Christi Bay Area: Sights/Food/
     Lodging/Camping, 128
Cradle of Texas: Sights/Food/Lodging/
     Camping, 47

Dallas: Sights/Fair Park/Food/Lodging, 188
Dallas Region: Sights/Food/Lodging/Camping,
     194
Davis Mountains: 160
Downtown New Braunfels: Sights/Food/
     Lodging/Camping, 90

East Texas Piney Woods: Sights/Food/
     Lodging/Camping, 232

Family Fun Tour: 251
Food, Wine, and Music Lovers' Tour: 252

Fort Davis: Sights/Food/Lodging, 153
Fort Worth Cultural District/Downtown:
     Sights/Sundance Square/Food/Lodging, 204
Fort Worth Region: Sights/Food/Lodging/
     Camping, 212
Fredericksburg: Sights/Wineries/Food/
     Lodging, 74

Galveston: Sights/Food/Lodging/Camping, 32
Greater Austin: Sights/Food/Lodging/
     Camping, 64
Greater El Paso: Sights/Food/Lodging/
     Camping, 164
Greater San Antonio: Sights/Food/Lodging/
     Camping, 110

High Plains Perspective: 186
Hill Country: Sights/Wineries/Food/
     Lodging/Camping, 76
Hill Country Back Road: 87
Hill Country Loop: 119
Houston: Sights/Food/Lodging, 16
Houston Region: Sights/Food/Lodging/
     Camping, 24

Jefferson: Sights/Food/Lodging, 234

Lore of the West Tour: 253
Lubbock: Sights/Food/Lodging, 180

Nature Lovers' Tour: 249
New Braunfels: Sights/Food/Lodging/
     Camping, 94

Panhandle/High Plains: Sights/Wineries/
     Lodging/Camping, 174
Planning Map: 244–245

Rio Grande Valley/South Texas: Sights/
     Food/Lodging/Camping, 136
River Road: 102

San Antonio: Sights/Food/Lodging, 106
Scenic Routes: 87, 102, 119, 160, 186
Special Interest Tours: 247–253

West Texas/Big Bend: Sights/Food/Lodging/
     Camping, 148

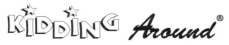